Implications of Race and Racism in Student Evaluations of Teaching

Race and Education in the Twenty-First Century

Series Editors: Kenneth J. Fasching-Varner, Louisiana State University; Roland Mitchell, Louisiana State University; and Lori Latrice Martin, Louisiana State University

This series asks authors and editors to consider the role of race and education, addressing questions such as "how do communities and educators alike take on issues of race in meaningful and authentic ways?" and "how can education work to disrupt, resolve, and otherwise transform current racial realities?" The series pays close attention to the intersections of difference, recognizing that isolated conversations about race eclipse the dynamic nature of identity development that play out for race as it intersects with gender, sexuality, socioeconomic class, and ability. It welcomes perspectives from across the entire spectrum of education from Pre-K through advanced graduate studies, and it invites work from a variety of disciplines, including counseling, psychology, higher education, curriculum theory, curriculum and instruction, and special education.

Recent Titles in Series

Implications of Race and Racism in Student Evaluations of Teaching: The Hate U Give, edited by LaVada Taylor

Technology Segregation: Disrupting Racist Frameworks in Early Childhood Education, by Miriam B. Tager

Surviving Becky(s): Pedagogies for Deconstructing Whiteness and Gender, edited by Cheryl E. Matias

Latinx Curriculum Theorizing, edited by Theodorea Regina Berry

Intersectional Care for Black Boys in an Alternative School: They Really Care About Us, by Julia C. Ransom

Culture, Community, and Educational Success: Reimagining the Invisible Knapsack, edited by Toby S. Jenkins, Stephanie Troutman, and Crystal Polite Glover

Whiteness at the Table: Antiracism, Racism, and Identity in Education, edited by Shannon K. McManimon, Zachary A. Casey, and Christina Berchini

The Classroom as Privileged Space: Psychoanalytic Paradigms for Social Justice in Pedagogy, by Tapo Chimbganda

Curriculum and Students in Classrooms: Everyday Urban Education in an Era of Standardization, by Walter S. Gershon

Race, Population Studies, and America's Public Schools: A Critical Demography Perspective, edited by Hayward Derrick Horton, Lori Latrice Martin, and Kenneth Vasching-Varner

Implications of Race and Racism in Student Evaluations of Teaching

The Hate U Give

Edited by
LaVada U. Taylor

LEXINGTON BOOKS
Lanham • Boulder • New York • London

Published by Lexington Books
An imprint of The Rowman & Littlefield Publishing Group, Inc.
4501 Forbes Boulevard, Suite 200, Lanham, Maryland 20706
www.rowman.com

6 Tinworth Street, London SE11 5AL, United Kingdom

Copyright © 2021 The Rowman & Littlefield Publishing Group, Inc.

All rights reserved. No part of this book may be reproduced in any form or by any electronic or mechanical means, including information storage and retrieval systems, without written permission from the publisher, except by a reviewer who may quote passages in a review.

British Library Cataloguing in Publication Information Available

Library of Congress Cataloging-in-Publication Data

Names: Taylor, LaVada U., 1969- editor.
Title: Implications of race and racism in student evaluations of teaching : the hate u give / edited by LaVada U. Taylor.
Description: Lanham : Lexington Books, [2021] | Series: Race and education in the twenty-first century | Includes bibliographical references and index.
Identifiers: LCCN 2021009333 (print) | LCCN 2021009334 (ebook) | ISBN 9781793643032 (cloth) | ISBN 9781793643049 (epub) | ISBN 9781793643056 (pbk)
Subjects: LCSH: Minority college teachers—Rating of—United States. | Student evaluation of teachers—United States. | Minority college teachers—United States—Social conditions. | Racism in higher education—United States.
Classification: LCC LB2333 .I44 2021 (print) | LCC LB2333 (ebook) | DDC 371.14/4—dc23
LC record available at https://lccn.loc.gov/2021009333
LC ebook record available at https://lccn.loc.gov/2021009334

This work is dedicated to:
The late Dr. Reavis L. Mitchell, Fisk University Professor of History,
Civil Rights Activist, and Chair of the Tennessee Historical Commission
and
Dr. Joyce E. King, Benjamin E. Mays Endowed Chair for Urban Teaching,
Learning and Leadership, Professor of Education Policy Studies in the
College of Education & Human Development at Georgia State University

Contents

Epigraph	ix
Foreword H. Richard Milner IV	xi
Acknowledgments	xiii
Introduction: Implications of Race and Racism in Student Evaluations of Teaching: The Hate U Give LaVada U. Taylor	1
1 Their Voices Must be Heard LaVada U. Taylor	17
2 Dismantling the Architecture of "Good" Teaching Donyell L. Roseboro	43
3 Be(Rate) My Professors Dot Com: Cautionary Tales from the Curious World of Student Evaluations Hilton Kelly, Eleanor Branch, and Stacey Coleman	67
4 Wonderful Evaluations in the Face of Teaching Anti-Racism and Multicultural Education Ramon Vasquez	89
5 Journey to Critical Whiteness in Higher Education Yvette Freter	113
6 Keeping It 100: Speaking Black Truth to White Power Jonathan Lightfoot	139

| 7 | Desuperhumanizing Whiteness
Björn Freter | 159 |

Index 179

About the Editor and Contributors 187

We who believe in freedom cannot rest until it comes.

—Sweet Honey in the Rocks—Ella's Song

Foreword
H. Richard Milner IV

In the book, *Implications of Race and Racism in Student Evaluations of Teaching: The Hate U Give*, LaVada Taylor has assembled a diverse group of voices to illustrate and illuminate the ways in which faculty, particularly Black, Indigenous, People of Color (BIPOC), must navigate and negotiate "hate" in institutions of higher education. As teaching evaluations and other forms of evaluation structures can have detrimental influence on faculty promotion, awards, and retention, it is necessary for us to critically examine how whiteness, privilege, and an ethos of hate can perpetuate an inequitable status quo in higher education. Faculty, administrators, and students interested in more deeply understanding how student feedback, in particular, can serve as a tool to harm BIPOC should read this book.

It is well known that when faculty—particularly faculty of color—engage in what might be considered "tough" and "controversial" topics in their courses such as white privilege, inequity, racism, sexism, and other forms of discrimination that white students' feedback on course evaluations may be negative. Although negative feedback can certainly be constructive, negative feedback can be a result of deep cognitive dissonance where white students are challenged to face ingrained beliefs that challenge their own notions of merit and upward mobility, for instance. Too many white students in higher education and beyond have come to believe that they have rightfully earned their positions and status inside and outside of higher education without critical examinations of the structures and systems designed to advantage and privilege them through their whiteness and white supremacy.

This book fills an important void in the literature by unapologetically centering teaching evaluations as a site of potential "hate" and harm for BIPOC faculty who deliberately strive to disrupt an inequitable status quo. But the book also discusses how faculty of color navigate and negotiate these negative, unfortunate situations that attempt to push them out of teaching positions at colleges and universities. The individual and broader units of analyses that the authors in this book examine provide an intellectually stimulating collection of insights.

Indeed, the book not only builds knowledge about individual faculty members' experiences but also addresses the ways in which systems need to be studied. In short, in what ways do teaching evaluations privilege white students and disadvantage faculty of color? Addressing and critically analyzing institutional structures, particularly as inequities are intensified in and across institutions of high education, allow us to reimagine what it means to provide punitive and constructive feedback to faculty as they work to design courses and teach content that humanizes all their students and simultaneously push them to confront oppression.

To be clear, white students deserve to be humanized and experience informative and transformative learning opportunities just as other students. However, when structures and systems are in place to maintain white people's privilege and whiteness, we must carefully probe why teaching evaluations can actually do more harm than good in the overall cycle of feedback to faculty to improve their practices. Or perhaps, more importantly, are teaching evaluations actually designed to help faculty of color improve their teaching or are they designed as mechanisms to intentionally push out particular faculty in order to maintain a white-centric, male majority university?

In short, this is a necessary book that has the potential to shed light on challenges and struggles among BIPOC faculty in higher education. The book also outlines ways in which faculty name, address, counter, and disrupt pervasive systems of oppression—particularly related to student feedback.

Acknowledgments

My heart drops each semester when I receive the alert that it is now time for student course evaluations (SETs). Yes, it remains true that I have had many positive student evaluations of my teaching. However, it remains equally valid that I have had more than my fair share of negative student evaluations. During my graduate school experience, I recall being traumatized by student evaluations of my teaching in my first diversity and education class. This was the first course I ever taught on a college or university campus.

One of my favorite graduate professors attempted to provide comfort by sharing with me that student course evaluations were no big deal. Specifically, he stated, "You will have some semesters where students will love you, and you will have some semesters when they will frankly not like you at all." I remember his words as if they were just spoken yesterday. His decree, though satisfying at the time, failed to prepare me for the ways student evaluations of teaching mirrored understandings of racism, sexism, and classism.

His words did not inform me of the way students weaponize evaluations of teaching against BIPOC faculty. Nor did he tell me how SET results influence promotion and tenure considerations, merit pay increases, and contract renewals. His words did lend credence to my subsequent findings that SETs lack validity and reliability. However, he failed to share with me that because SET results are often subjective and inconsistent they are inept instruments when measuring teaching effectiveness. As I reflect on yesterday, my new awareness only makes me more puzzled today.

I now find myself wondering: if student evaluations of teaching do not measure teaching effectiveness, then what do student evaluations of teaching measure? Additionally, why are student evaluations of teaching so intimately tied to high stakes rewards and punishments?

For me, these questions laid the foundation of a problem. As a researcher, this problem was one that needed exploring. After first providing a narrative supported by research for why my more recent course evaluations were so whimsical during my annual review, I decided to submit a conference prospectus on the implications of race and racism in student evaluation of teaching. The 2019 American Educational Studies Association (AESA) conference, in Baltimore, Maryland, would be the space where my ideas and postulate would further develop and take form. Over nightcaps, coffee-talks, crab boils, and a very engaging interactive session entitled: *Experiences of Oppression, Pain, and Privilege in Higher Education*, I learned that I was not alone in my experience with student evaluations of teaching. I also learned that others shared my query over the importance of SETs and the role of race and racism played in students' assessment of instruction. As a result of these conversations in AESA space, our book project, *Implications of Race and Racism in Student Evaluations of Teaching: The Hate U Give* took form.

I am so very thankful for the opportunity to lead and serve as editor for this book project. I am incredibly grateful to my life partner, Mr. J. W. Jones, III. Without his gentle nudge, support, and encouragement for me to go back to my true north, the inception of this book would not have been possible. I would like to thank Mr. Jose Reed for reading my works and providing feedback while honoring my voice. I thank Drs. Jonathan Lightfoot and Björn Freter for seeing the possibilities of an AERA symposium in this piece and pulling us together to submit a successful proposal. I thank Dr. Björn Freter for converting two of the manuscripts in this volume from *APA* to *Chicago Manual Style*. I am also eternally grateful for the courage of each contributor to this volume. Thank you for theorizing, your willingness to tell your story, your courage to speak truth to power, and your activism. Thank you for daring to envision a more just and humane society starting with ourselves, the students we teach, and in the spaces where we work. Thank you! Thank you! Thank you!

Introduction

Implications of Race and Racism in Student Evaluations of Teaching: The Hate U Give

LaVada U. Taylor

T-H-U-G L-I-F-E (The hate you give little Infants F-U-C-K-S everyone) meaning: what you feed us as seeds grows and blows up in your face.[1] In 1994, *From the Cradle to the Grave* was released. The ninth song on the only album entitled: *Thug Life Volume 1*[2] produced by 2Pac and his group: Thug Life. Created from the acronym: The Hate U Give Little Infants Fucks Everyone, *Thug Life Volume 1* in lyrics and experiences portrayed through image and video representation an interrogation of systemic oppression, that is, institutional racism, sexism, police brutality, the prison industrial complex, policing, social class exploitation, de jure segregation, eugenics, and political/economical disenfranchisement. A multigenerational beat *Thug Life Volume 1* spoke to the experiences of America's youth in the 1990s while forecasting how the hate given to our children would one day inform who they would one day inform who they would become as adult human beings divorced from humanity.[3]

Later the movie *The Hate U Give*,[4] a spinoff of 2Pac's notion of thug life, touched on racism, hinted at social class exploitation and de jure segregation, while focusing specifically on police brutality, a fragment of 2Pac's larger reflection on systemic racism, sexism, the prison industrial complex, social class exploitation, de jure segregation, eugenics, economic, and political disenfranchisement. Social practices that create ism's in today's society that are so powerfully shaping the experiences of our children while molding their emerging adulthood to be divorced from human compassion.[5]

Practical applications are witnessed as our children watch the kind of hate that allows a man to put his knee on the neck of another man and choke him to death while he cries for and loses his life in 8:46 seconds on every news syndicate both nationally and internationally. Learned behavior garnered as the Attorney General of the United States, William Barr tells them—our children—that their reactions to what they saw, their riots, their outcry, their pain, and their humanity experienced in connection with a loss of human life was too extreme. Those who protested were thugs. Their deviant behavior represents a thug's life.

Played out in mainstream culture thug life of the June 2020 riots mirrored 2Pac's imagery of defiant urban street culture spitting, fighting back while talking Black to white dominant culture and systemic oppression. However, to date, what has not been captured is the effect of the hate given to U.S. young adults who were or were not in the streets with their peers mourning and fighting against the abomination that made the deaths of George Floyd, Breonna Taylor, Ahmad Aubrey, and countless others Black and Brown bodies both probable and possible.[6] To date few have explored the impact on this type of hate on students[7] situated in classrooms and enrolled at college and university campuses nor how this hate informs their interactions and learning experiences with faculty of color. Young adults who are equally products of dominate U.S. culture unfortunately emulating a society shaped by institutional racism, sexism, police brutality, the prison industrial complex, social class exploitation, de jure segregation, eugenics, as well as political and economic disenfranchisement. Here, I am referring to youths, largely due to re-segregation (Tatum, 2007), whose experience with difference and oppression are often illuminated through schooling and by media representations of otherness: the poor/working poor, women/LGBT/Queer, and/or people of color: African Americans, Latino American, Native American, South East Asian Americans, Blackness (hook, 2015). And, perhaps more intriguing is the ways these colonizing images, memories, and teachings (Ahmad-Noors, 2020) influence the hate students give Black, Indigenous, People of Color (BIPOC) faculty through their evaluations of teaching.

REVIEW OF LITERATURE

Documented as the single most researched topic in higher education, literature on student course evaluations is vast and considered a hot topic in academia.[8] Proponents of student evaluations of teaching (SETs) argue that SETs are necessary for accreditation purposes and are a prudent measure of teaching effectiveness.[9] Other researchers argue that SETs are not reliant measures of teaching effectiveness at all, but rather are mirrors informing university administrators that class size, anticipated grades, discipline of study, and teacher-directed individual assignments,[10] as well as few to no courses focusing on diversity and/or multiculturalism are the keys to students' happiness. In these conversations research on class size posits a direct relationship between class size and positive evaluations. Specifically, this body of work argues that the smaller the class size (based on number of students), the better are students' evaluations of teaching.[11] Other researchers note that grades are a truer indication of student's perceptions of experience. Here, they hold that when students are doing well in both elective and required courses, faculty receives more positive course evaluations.[12] A student's discipline of study has also been cited as a determining factor of positive and/or negative course responses. To this end, researchers maintain that professors who teach in the humanities receive better student evaluations than those teaching in the science and social science fields.[13] Moreover, a direct correlation between individual student course assignments and positive responses on students' evaluation of teaching is also found in current bodies of literature on SETs. Specifically, Mohr & Mohr note that digital age generation Xers fear working in groups and hold that requiring little to no group work assignments will yield better student course evaluations.[14] While other researchers reveal the tendency for faculty who teach courses on or related to diversity or multiculturalism to receive more negative course evaluations.[15]

Additional studies in this vast body of literature on SETs highlight the influence of likeability,[16] social class positionality,[17] gender,[18] political views,[19] perceived attractiveness,[20] as well as allure[21] on students' perceptions of experience gleaned in students' evaluations of teaching.[22] Yet, when disaggregated by race in each of the variables and nuances named above, faculty of color overwhelmingly receive poorer SETs when compared to their white counterparts—irrespective of class size, grades, discipline of study, course assignment, likeability, social class, gender, political views, perceived attractiveness, and allure.[23]

STATEMENT OF THE PROBLEM

Students' evaluations of teaching are more than objective measures of teaching effectiveness. Rather, SETs are a subjective kaleidoscope infused with implicit bias and reflections of racial hate. Given to students to evaluate faculty of color, these evaluations often demonized BIPOC faculty whose intended presence in the academy is to broaden students' experiences with diversity while preparing them to interact with and participate in a global society. A vision stunted by what 2Pac named, a hate given to little infants that "F's" us all.

To date, research on race and racism[24] is limited in discussions on students' evaluation of teaching.[25] Actually, research that addresses the experiences of faculty of color in academic spaces is scarce.[26] However, those that do this work note faculty of color feelings of isolation, alienation, and invisibility.[27] Others reference the promotion and tenure hazing process with its lack of consideration given to scholarship on marginalized populations. This dearth experience in funding focuses on limited resources given to and/or a lack of appreciation for research that specifically focuses on ethnic and minority/majority populations.[28] While other studies highlight the expectations of faculty of color to mentor students with a moral conscience and philanthropic zeal to fulfill multiple service obligations at their respective institutions.[29] More research is beginning to focus on the experiences of faculty of color in classroom spaces, here the multi-layered shades of race are explored to discuss inclass interactions between faculty of color and the students they teach.[30] The outcomes of this research note that often faculty of color's authority and expertise are challenged, students exhibit negative behavior, and have poor attitudes toward faculty of color.[31] This behavior is in consequence of sociopolitical institutions (re-segregated schools, the prison industrial complex, policing, media, and political/economical disenfranchisement) informed by "isms" (race, class, and gender) shaping lived situations of racism, classism, and sexism. As a result, students regardless of race are raised in a society where they are taught to loathe Blackness. This is probably most easily recognized through reproduction of media images. Rarely if ever do you find more positive Black characterization as learned and intellectual. Rather, Blacks are imaged through media as foolish, hateful, sexual exploits, and/or buffoons. When stories and memories are shared in textbooks the dominant narrative most often rehearsed is that Blacks were slaves. Now you have a foolish, hyper-sexualized servant designated to impart knowledge to you . . . under the guise of systemic racism why should students respect a Black(en) teacher? Thus, more bastardized representations of Blackness[32] and intellectual inferiority make permissible if not expected for faculty of color to receive poor teaching evaluations.[33]

In their article, "Perceptions of European American and African American Instructors Teaching Race Focused Courses," Littleford et al. bring light to these perceptions as they note that the person teaching a course can directly influence how students make meaning of the information being taught.[34] For example, when teaching about inequitable distribution of resources, based on race and social class positionality, if the teacher is a working-class member of a minority group then students presume that the information being presented is both questionable and sincere. These notions are derived because the teacher is assumed by students to be speaking from her or his direct experiences. However, students also believe that the information being presented is biased and as such lacks the ability to be either impartial or scholarly. In practice these sentiments are reflected below in students' evaluation of my teaching in course entitled: Multiculturalism and Diversity. They write:

> Student A: I did feel that this was more of a one-sided politics class rather than looking at education. Instead we talked about how history informs education and not how we should be teaching in diverse classroom.

Student B: The instructor is very well educated and certainly knows what she is talking about in terms of the course content [multiculturalism and education].

Noting these phenomena in their work Perry et al. concluded the following:

> Students' first impression of their professors, even when they are based solely on their instructors' race, do influence their judgments of their professors' perceived bias and consequently, their perceptions of professors' subjectivity and expertise; thus, a professor's race/ethnicity can directly influence student evaluations.[35]

Referring to these phenomena as the "source effects," further, Littleford et al. highlight that source effects also apply to European American instructors. However, unlike their African American counterparts who likewise teach similar subject matter, European American teachers were more often deemed credible and legitimate because they shared the racial positionality of those conceptually recognized as professors.[36] Addressing my teaching in relation to and with my European American junior faculty counterpart, students share the following responses in their evaluation of our two distinct courses that shared the same students. One course is entitled: Literacy and Middle Childhood. The other course is entitled: Social Studies in Elementary Schools. Students reflect:

Student C: This course was interdisciplinary with [literacy]. Without ----, I wouldn't have done as well in this semester. My professor did not promote my learning and did not help me further my teaching career in this course. It is very poorly set up and needs a lot of improvement.

Student D: It was frustrating when our professor would say one thing and ---- would contradict her, and the course tie together. There needs to be communication between her and --- because their lack of communication makes important parts of the course very confusing.

Student E: Very open minded and understanding when having discussions. She made everyone feel safe.

Student F: I requested feedback on all my lessons and received quality responses from Dr. T. each time. She gives great feedback that I believe is beneficial to my students now and in the future. I admire this about her. She is very supportive and willing to meet individually and provides unyielding support to her students.

African American women's stereotyped perceptions as being Black (not legitimate nor deserving of your position as well as difficult/aggressive and incompetent) and woman (communal, mothering, gentle, and amicable) often provide complicated contradictions in their social construct as raced illegitimate, difficult/aggressive while gendered kind, servile, yet ultimately less academic than their white peers.[37] Continuing their perception of the course, one student evaluator notes the following in a lengthy reflection:

> Student G: One of my least favorite courses I've ever taken. The professor is inconsistent with instruction and what she expects for students; different groups of students receive different information/directions from her about assignments (and not in a "differentiation of learning" type of way-it just confuses everyone in the class). She has also made snide comments when we express confusion about her directions. There is clear favoritism taking place, which is reflected in the scores on our lessons. She has made several students cry throughout the semester because of the way she has ripped apart their lessons in front of the entire class. In my opinion, she has been unprofessional and inappropriate, and I wouldn't be surprised if students weren't asked to come back to our current field site next semester. I feel like I have gotten absolutely nothing out of this semester in her class. I urge someone to find a new professor to take her place so that future students can actually benefit from this class. Students have been unhappy with her as a professor for a long time.

In their research entitled "The Effect of Professor Ethnicity and Gender on Student Evaluations: Judged before Met," Bavishi et al. note that female African American professors were rated the lowest on competence, interpersonal skills, and legitimacy scales compared to all other groups.[38] They found that the complexities of being woman, Black, and professor often created dichotomies through which women of color faced multiple stigmas as less qualified, callous, rude and were often denigrated for being both a woman and a minority.

What is significant in the research findings above juxtaposed to students' evaluations of teaching are the following positions:

1. The person teaching the course can directly influence how students make meaning of the information being taught.
2. If the teacher is a member of a minority group then students presume that the information being presented is both questionable and sincere.
3. European American teachers were more often deemed credible and legitimate because he or she shared the racial positionality of those conceptually recognized as professor.
4. African American women's stereotyped perceptions as being "Black" and woman often provide complicated contradictions in their social

construct as raced illegitimate, difficult/aggressive while gendered kind, servile, and less academic.
5. Female African American professors were rated the lowest on competence, interpersonal skills, and legitimacy scales.
6. The complexities of being woman, Black, and professor often creates dichotomies through which women of color face multiple stigmas as less qualified, callous, rude and were often denigrated for being both woman and minority.

Research outcomes positing what is without giving consideration to students' behavior and subsequent appraisal of faculty of color teaching as reflections of systemic racism.[39] Ism's learned as early as childhood that have now blown up in society's face as children become adults who dehumanize their actions towards and reactions to faculty of color.

Nonetheless, over and over colleges and universities rely on students' evaluation of teaching to provide critical feedback on teaching and learning experiences. Institutional practices that use course evaluations—in very punitive ways—further marginalize faculty of color by relying on a very subjective measure of teaching effectiveness based on student perception of experiences.[40] In so doing, systemic racism is perpetuated on college and university campuses as administrators ignore the influence of race and racism in students' evaluative feedback.[41]

Weaponized against faculty of color and left unquestioned or unchallenged by research, SETs then become a tool in the name of college and university accreditation used to deny promotion and tenure, merit increases, and contract renewals—rewards intimately tied to positive student evaluations of teaching.[42] Practices used to deny opportunities to faculty of color based on ideals couched in a historicity of racism helpful in our understanding of both how and why race and dysconscious[43] notions of racism influence and inform students' course evaluations? How colonial memory in a moment of post-racial politics is used as a conduit to shape college students' perception of themselves in relation to their professors of color racialized as "other"? A contextualization employed to help us better understand: why are student course evaluations typically biased against faculty of color? Why do students challenge the authority of faculty of color? Why do students question the expertise of faculty of color? Why do students display negative and or disrespectful behavior toward faculty of color? Why do students evaluate faculty of color poorly?

Though student evaluations of teaching are not a reliable instrument for determining quality of instruction or teacher effectiveness,[44] course evaluations are however very useful in revealing the influence of race and racism in classroom dynamics. SETs are also useful in examining the ways in which students make meaning of teaching and learning situations in relationship with faculty of color.

Contextualizing the aforementioned questions also helps to establish a feasible and viable data-driven platform exploring classroom dynamics in an effort to uncover: why are student course evaluations typically biased against faculty of color? Why do students challenge the authority of faculty of color? Why do students question the expertise of faculty of color? Why do students display negative and/or disrespectful behavior toward faculty of color? And, why do students evaluate faculty of color poorly?

To this end, this book, comprised of seven chapters, is written to grapple with implications of race and racism in student evaluations of teaching—hate given to students that inevitably "F" us all. The work opens with chapter 1 entitled "Their Voices Must be Heard" written by LaVada U. Taylor. In this opening argument, critical race theory is used to interrogate race-neutral discourse illuminating the experiences of faculty of color as members of historically marginalized groups teaching in the academy. The paper contributes to broader conversations regarding the experiences of Black faculty teaching in the academy and explores how race(ism) influences college students' perception of self in relation to faculty of color as historically marginalized others. Chapter 2 is entitled "Dismantling the Architecture of 'Good' Teaching"[45] in this piece, author Donyell L. Roseboro explores the presence and epistemology of faculty of color teaching at predominately white institutions (PWI) as a mechanism to disrupt notions of an "other" in relation to a self, power, authority, knowing, and being. Her work teases out how Black faculty members enter evaluative spaces when white students disassociate Black racial identity with intellectualism thereby promulgating questioning of their collegiate teaching competence. In chapter 3, "Be (Rate) My Professors Dot Com: Cautionary Tales from the Curious World of Student Evaluations," authors Hilton Kelly, Eleanor Branch, and Stacy Coleman illuminate the role of self-interest in student evaluations of teaching. Specifically, drawing upon interpretative autoethnography,[46] Kelly, Branch, and Coleman draw on three autobiographical accounts to outline three cautionary tales for educators and administrators to inform the ways good/bad student evaluation of teaching impact the professional experiences of those teaching in the academy. Chapter 4 is entitled "Wonderful Evaluations in the Face of Teaching Anti-Racism and Multicultural Education." In this work, author Ramon Vasquez examines opportunities and risks for BIPOC faculty in teacher education programs (TEPs). Specifically drawing on the concept of epistemic disobedience, Vasquez confronts white supremacy and how to resist "Othering" by white students, while supporting abolitionist education.[47] In chapter 5, "Journey to Critical Whiteness in Higher Education," author Yvette Freter unpacks cultural dissonance and the constant negotiation of privilege and marginalization experienced by her as white South African doctoral students at a U.S. southwestern university as she interact with her Black faculty supervisor. Through the use of narrative, Freter wrestles with knowing and growing through their relationship couched in Black/white subjectivity navigating through a process of being and becoming anti-racist. Chapter 6 is entitled "Keeping It 100: Speaking Truth to White Power"; here, author Jonathan Lightfoot forefronts cognitive dissonances that students encounter when naming their experiences with faculty of color on students' evaluation of teaching (SETs). He offers strategic alternatives to SETs that include peer observation, creation of small student focus groups, and requiring student to self-evaluate their learning; strategies empirically found as better indicators of competent teaching among historically marginalized faculty of color. Finally, highlighting recent and past epistemologies of ignorance enabling anti-Black epistemicide,[48] in chapter 7, "Desuperhumanizing Whiteness," philosopher Björn Freter concludes our works with a critique on pseudo-colorblind racism. Specifically deconstructing the superhumanization of whiteness, Freter draws attention to fake nonracial practices whose created façade of racial inclusion serves only to intentionally invalidate the experiences of all those suffering from systemic racism.

SIGNIFICANCE OF THE STUDY

Colleges and universities rely heavily on student evaluations of teaching to inform promotion and tenure decisions, merit increases, and contract renewals (Diggs, 2009; Flaherty 2015; Seldin, 1993). However, in comparison to their white counterparts, faculty of color score lower on SETs?[49] Weaponized against faculty of color and left both unquestioned and unchallenged by vast research on SETs,[50] student course evaluations are often used in very punitive ways to marginalize faculty of color in the spaces of the academy. This is accomplished in the name of college and university accreditation and by administrative reliance on a very subjective instrument used by the academy weaponizing SETs against faculty of color in an attempt to measure teaching effectiveness while ignoring the role of race and racism play in shaping students' perception of classroom experiences.

Drawing on Tupac Shakur's notion of thug life meaning: the hate you give little infants "f" us all,[51] this work examines the influence of race and racism in students' evaluation of teaching. The work problematizes systemic practices in the academy that rely on student evaluation of teaching couched in a historicity of racism. This is useful in understanding both how and why race and dysconscious notions of racism[52] influence and inform students' evaluation of teaching—a mere reflection of the hate given to students from our society that "F" us all. To this end, the work taps the past to grapple with historical and colonizing influences of race and racism in teaching and learning situations today and adds to a very limited body of research focusing on the interplay between race and racism and students' evaluation of teaching.[53]

NOTES

1. Shakur 2007.
2. Shakur 1994.
3. To be divorced from humanity here I refer to being separated by difference and void of spirit in connection with another human being.
4. See Tilman Jr. 2018.
5. See Shukur 2007.
6. See Peters 2020. National Association for the Advancement of Colored People 2020.
7. By student I am referring to all U.S. students regardless of racial identity.
8. See Berk 2013, Feldman, 2007.
9. See Chapman & Jones 2017, Erikson et al. 2016, Linse 2017, To & Tang 2019, Volkwein, 2010.
10. See Reid & Garson 2017.
11. See Miles & House 2015.
12. See Gorry 2017, Miles & House 2015, Reid 2010, Stroebe 2016.
13. See Feldman 2017.
14. See Mohr & Mohr 2016.
15. See Bernal & Villapando 2002, Larke & Larke 2009, Littleford et al. 2010, Ludwig & Meacham 1997.
16. See Clayson & Sheffet 2006, Delucci 2000, Gurung & Vespia 2007, Marks 2000.
17. See Uttl et al. 2017.
18. See Han 2017, Larke & Larke 2009, Pittman 2010, Aruguete et al. 2017, Borting 2017, Clayson 2020, Martin 2016, Martin & Chamberlin 2000, Subbaye & Vithal 2017, Templeton 2016, Valencia 2020.
19. See Clayson 2000, Woessner & Woossner 2006.
20. See Arguete et al. 2017, Felton et al. 2004.
21. See Felton et al. 2008.
22. See Linse 2017.
23. See Basow et al. 2013, Boatright-Horowitz & Soeung 2009, Huston 2006, Merritt 2008, Reid 2010, Smith & Hawkins 2011.
24. It is important to note that research on the interplay between gender and student evaluations of teaching is plentiful in scholarship on SETs. However, there is little discussion that focus on race and/or social class. It is no secret in U.S. society that African Americans, Latino Americans, and Native Americans are disproportionately casted in lower- and working-class positions (see Wilkerson 2020. Stated simply, disproportionately non-Asian people of color are also poor in the United States.

For this reason, particularly in addressing the experiences of people of color race is intimately tied to social class stratification. Understanding this embedded relationship, for the purpose of this work race and racism are the focus of this book.

25. See Mengel et al. 2017, Perry 2015, Reid 2010, Smith & Hawkins 2011, Turner 2002, Turner et al. 2011.
26. See Antonio 2002.
27. See Cleveland, 2004, Cresswell et al. 1999, Gold 2008, Stanley 2006.
28. See Bernal & Villalpando 2002, Turner & Myers 2000.
29. See Stanely 2006, Turner 2003.
30. See Mengel et al. 2017, Pabon & Basile 2019, Reid 2010.
31. See Childers-McKee & Hytten 2015; Littleford et al. 2010, Ford 2011, Pitman 2010.
32. See hooks 1992/2015, Riggs 1987.
33. See Hornstein 2017, Tuitt et al. 2009, Thompson 2008.
34. See Littleford et al. 2010.
35. Perry et al. 2015, 29.
36. See Littleford et al. 2010, 231.
37. See Bavishi et al., 2010.
38. See Bavishi et al. 2010, 252.
39. In his June 8, 2020, Titian Talk, Derrick Tillman shared that systemic racism includes policies and practices entrenched in established institutions like colleges and universities which result in the exclusion or promotion of designated groups. Systemic racism differs from overt discrimination in that no individual intent is required
40. See Linse 2017.
41. See Aruguete et al. 2017.
42. See Diggs 2009, Flaherty 2015, Seldin 1993.
43. See King 1991.
44. See ASA 2019, Hornstein 2017.
45. See Bhattaacharya 2017, Messner 2020.
46. See Denzin 2018.
47. See Andreotti 2016, Love 2019, Grande 2015.
48. See Lebakeng et al. 2006.
49. See Basow et al. 2013, Boatright-Horowitz & Soeung 2009, Huston 2006, Merritt 2008, Reid 2010, Smith & Hawkins 2011.
50. See Berk 2013, Feldman 2007.
51. See Shakur 2007.
52. See King 1991.
53. See Mengel et al. 2017, Pabon & Basile 2019, Reid 2010.

REFERENCES

Ahmad-Noor, F. 2020. "Why is colonialism (still) romanticized?" Video File. Accessed December 6, 2020. https://www.ted.com/talks/farish_ahmad_noor_why

_is_colonialism_still_romanticized?utm_campaign=daily&utm_content=button_ _2020-06-23&utm_medium=email&utm_source=newsletter_daily.

Andreotti, Vanessa. 2016. "(re) imagining education as an un-coercive re-arrangement of desires." *Other Education* 5: 79–88.

Antonio, Anthony. 2002. "Faculty of color reconsidered: Reassessing contributions to Scholarship." *The Journal of Higher Education* 73:582–602. doi:10.1080/0022 1546.2002.11777169.

Aruguete, Mara S., Joshua Slater, Sekela R. Mwaikinda 2017. "The effects of professors' race and clothing style on student evaluations." *The Journal of Negro Education* 86: 494–502.

Berk, Ronald A. 2013. *Top 10 Flashpoints: In Student Ratings and the Evaluation of Teaching: What Faculty and Administrators Must Know to Protect Themselves in Employment Decision.* Sterling, VA: Stylus Publishing.

Bernal, Dolores D., Octavio Villalpando. 2002. "An apartheid of knowledge in academia: The struggle over the 'legitimate' knowledge of faculty of color." *Equity & Excellence* 135: 169–189. doi:10.1080/173845282.

Bhattacharya, Tithi (ed.). 2017. *Social reproduction theory: Remapping class recentering oppression.* London: Plato Press.

Boatright-Horowitz, Su L., Sojattra Soeung. 2009. "Teaching white privilege to white students can mean saying good-bye to positive student evaluations." *American Psychologist* 64: 574–575.

Borting Anne. 2017. "Gender bias in student evaluations of teaching." *Journal of Public Economics* 145: 27–41.

Chapman, Diane D., Jeffrey A. Jones. 2017. "Strategies for increasing response rates for online end-of-course evaluations." *International Journal of Teaching and Learning in Higher Education* 29: 47–60.

Childers-McKee, Ccherese D., Kathy Hytten. 2015. "Critical race feminism and the complex challenges of educational reform." *The Urban Review* 47: 393–412.

Clayson Dennis E. 2020. "Student perception of instructors: The effect of age, gender and political leaning." *Assessment & Evaluation in Higher Education* 45: 607–616.

Clayson, Dennis E., Mary J. Sheffet. 2006. "Personality and the evaluation of teaching." *Journal of Marketing Education* 28: 149–160. doi:10.1177/0273475306288402.

Cleveland, Darell. 2004. *A Long Way to Go: Conversations about race by African American Faculty and Graduate Students.* New York: Peter Lang.

Denzin, Norman K. 2014. *Interpretive Autoethnography.* 2nd Edition. Washington, DC: SAGE.

Diggs, Gregory, Dorothy F. Garrison-Wade, Diane Estrada, Rene Galindo. 2009. "Smiling faces and colored spaces: The experience of faculty of color pursuing tenure in the academy." *The Urban Review* 41: 312–0333.

Erikson, Malgorzata, Martin G. Erikson, Elisabeth Punzi. 2016. "Student responses to a reflective course evaluation." *Reflective Practice* 17: 663–675. doi:10.1080/14623943.2016./206.

Fenton, James, John Mitchell, Michael Stinson. 2004. "Web-based student evaluations of professors: The relations between perceived quality, easiness and sexiness." *Assessment & Evaluation in Higher Education* 29: 91–108.

Felton, James, Peter T. Koper, John Mitchell, Michael Stinson. 2008. Attractiveness, easiness and other issues: Student evaluations of professors on Ratemyprofessors.com." *Assessment & Evaluation in Higher Education* 33: 45–61. doi: 10.1080/02602930601122803.

Feldman, Kenneth A. 2007. Identifying exemplary teachers and teaching: Evidence from student ratings. In. *The Scholarship of Teaching and Learning in Higher Education: An Evidence-Based Perspective*, edited by Raymond P. Perry, John C. Smart, 93–143. New York, NY: Springer.

Flaherty, Colleen 2015. "Flawed evaluations." *Inside Higher Education*, June 10, 2015. Accessed December 6, 2020. https://www.insidehighered.com/news/2015/06/10/aaup-committee-survey-data-raise-questions-effectiveness-student-teaching

Ford, Kristie A. 2011. "Race, gender, and bodily (mis)recognitions: Women of color faculty experiences with White students in the college classroom." *The Journal of Higher Education* 82: 444–478. doi:10.1080/00221546.2011.11777212.

Gold, Rachelle S. 2008. *Outsider within African American Professors and their Experiences at Predominately White Universities: A Narrative Study* (doctoral dissertation). UNC Chapel Hill, Chapel Hill, North Carolina.

Gorry, Devon. 2017. "The impact of grade ceilings on student grades and course evaluation: Evidence from a policy change." *Economics of Education Review* 56: 133–140.

Grande, Sandy. 2015. *Red pedagogy: Native American social and political thought*. Landham, MD: Rowman & Littlefield.

Gurung, Regan, Kriston Vespia. 2007. "Looking good, teaching well? Linking liking, looks and learning." *Teaching of Psychology* 34: 5–10. doi:10.1080/00986280709336641.

Hendrix, Katherine G. 1998. "Student perceptions of the influence of race on professor Credibility." *Journal of Black Studies* 28: 738–763.

Ho, Arnold K., Lotte Thomsen, Jim Sidanius. 2009. "Perceived academic competence and overall job evaluations: Students' evaluations of African American and European American professors." *Journal of Applied Social Psychology* 39: 389–406.

hooks, bell.1992/2015. *Black looks: race and representation*. New York: Routledge.

Hornstein, Henry. 2017. "Student evaluations of teaching are an inadequate assessment tool for evaluating faculty performance." *Cogent Education* 4: 1–8. http://doi.org/10.1080/2331186X.2017.1304016.

King, Joyce E. 1991. "Dysconscious racism: Ideology, identity, and the miseducation of teachers." *The Journal of Negro Education* 60: 133–146.

Larke, Patricia, Alvin Larke. 2009. "Teaching diversity/multicultural education courses in the academy: Sharing the voices of six professors." *Research in Higher Education* 13: 1–8.

Littleford, Linh N., Katherine S. Ong, Andy Tseng, Jennifer C. Milliken, Sonya L. Humy. 2010. "Perceptions of European American and African American instructors teaching race-focused courses." *Journal of Diversity in Higher Education* 3: 230–244.

Linse Angela R. 2017. "Interpreting and using student ratings data: Guidance for faculty serving as administrators and on evaluation committees." *Studies in Educational Evaluation* 54: 94–106.

Lebakeng, J. Teboho, M/ Manthiba Phalane, Nase Dalindjebo. 2006."Epistemicide, institutional cultures and the imperative for the Africanisation of universities in South Africa" *Alternation* 13: 70–87.

Love, Bettina. 2019.*We Want to Do More Than Survive: Abolitionist Teaching and the Pursuit of Educational Freedom.* Boston: Beacon Press.

Ludwig, Jeanette M., John A. Meacham. 1997."Teaching controversial courses: Student evaluations on instructors and content." *Educational Research Quarterly* 23: 27–38.

Marks, Roland G. 2000. "Determinants of student evaluations of global measures of instructor and course value." *Journal of Marketing Education* 22: 108–119. doi:10.1177/027347530022205.

Martin, Lisa L. 2016. "Gender teaching evaluations and professional success in political science." *PS: Political Science & Politics* 49: 313–319.

Mengel, Frederike, Jan Sauermann, Ulf Zölitz. 2017. Gender bias in teaching evaluations." *IZA Discussion Paper No. 11000.* https://papers.ssrn.com/sol3/papers.cfm?abstract_id=3037907.

Messner, MichaelA. .2000. "White guy habitus in the classroom: challenging the reproduction of privilege." *Men and Masculinities.* 2: 457–469.

Miles, Patti, Deanna House. 2015.. "The tail wagging the dog: An overdue examination of student teaching evaluations." *International Journal of Higher Education* 4: 116–126.

Miller, JoAnn, Marilyn Chamberlin. 2000. "Women are teachers, men are professors: A study of student perception." *Teaching Sociology* 28: 238–298.

Mohr, Kathleen A. J., Eric S. Mohr 2016. "Understanding generation z students to promote a contemporary learning environment." *Journal on Empowerment Teaching Excellence* 1: 84–94.

National Association for the Advancement of Colored People. N.D. Criminal Justice Fact Sheet. National Association for the Advancement of Colored People. Accessed December 6, 2020. https://www.naacp.org/criminal-justice-fact-sheet.

Perry, Armon, Sherri L. Wallace, Sharon E. Moore, Gwendolyn D. Perry-Burney. 2015. "Understanding student evaluations: a black faculty perspective." *Reflections: Narratives of Professional Helping* 20: 29–35. Accessed December 6, 2020. https://ir.library.louisville.edu/cgi/viewcontent.cgi?article=1014&context=faculty .

Peters, Jeremy W. .2020. Asked About Black Americans Killed by Police Trump Says, 'So Are White People'. *The New York Times*, July 14, 2020. Accessed December 6, 2020. https://www.nytimes.com/2020/07/14/us/politics/trump-white-people-killed-by-police.html.

Reid, Robin, Kyra Garson. 2017. "Rethinking multicultural group work as intercultural learning." *Journal of Studies International Education* 21: 195–212.

Riggs, M. (director). 1987). *Ethnic notions.* California Newsreel.

Shakur, Tupac A. 2007. "Tupac explains thug life." YouTube Video, 0:19, https://www.youtube.com/watch?v=0TfEr_BLW30.

Shakur Tupac A. 1994. "From the cradle to the grave." Track 9 on *Thug Life Volume 1*, Interscope Records, compact disc.

Smith, Bettye P., Billy Hawkins. 2011. "Examining student evaluations of Black college faculty: Does race matter?" *The Journal of Negro Education* 80: 149–162.

Stroebe, Wolfgang. 2016. "Why good teaching evaluations may reward bad teaching: On grade inflation and other unintended consequences of student evaluations." *Perspectives on Psychological Science* 11: 800–816.

Subbaye, Reshma, Renuka Vithal. 2017. "Gender teaching and academic promotion in higher education." *Gender and Education* 29: 926–951.

Tatum, everly D. 2007. *Can We Talk About Race: And Other Conversations in an Era of School Resegregation*. Boston: Beacon Press.

Thompson, Chasity Q. 2008. "Recruitment, retention, and mentoring faculty of color: The chronicle continues." *New Directions for Higher Education*, 143: 47–54. doi:10.1002/he.312.

Tillman Jr., George. 2018. *The Hate U Give*. Fox 2000 Pictures, Temple Hill Entertainment, State Street Pictures.

Tillman-Kelly, Derrick L. 2020. "Titan Talk - Dialogue and Discussion on "How We Got Here: Racism + Higher Education" YouTube Video, 1:02:30. June 19, 2020. https://www.youtube.com/watch?v=sbCz6Ph2hTc.

To, W. M., Margaret N. F. Tang. 2019. "Computer-based course evaluation: An extended technology acceptance model." *Educational Studies* 4: 131–144.

Tuitt, Frank, Michele Hanna, Lisa M. Martinez, Maria del Carmen Salazar, Rachel Griffin. 2009. "Teaching in the line of fire: Faculty of color in the academy." *Thought & Action: NEA Higher Education Journal* Fall 2009: 65–74.

Turner, Caroline S. V. 2002. "Women of color in academe: Living with multiple marginality." *The Journal of Higher Education* 173: 74–93. doi:10.1080/00221546.2002.11777131.

Turner, Caroline S. V. 2003. "Incorporation and marginalization in the academy: From border toward center for faculty of color." *Journal of Black Studies* 34: 122–125. doi:10.1177/0021934703253689.

Turner, Caroline S. V., Juan C. González, Kathleen Wong. 2011. "Faculty women of color: The critical nexus of race and gender." *Journal of Diversity in Higher Education* 4: 199–211. doi:10.1037/a0024630.

Uttl, Bob, Camela A. White, Daniela Wongv Gonzalez. 2017. "Meta-analysis of faculty's teaching effectiveness: Student evaluations of teaching rating student learning are not related." *Studies in Educational Evaluation* 54: 22–42.

Valencia, Edgar. 2020. "Acquiescence, instructor's gender bias and validity of student evaluation of teaching." *Assessment & Evaluation in Higher Education* 45: 483–495.

Volkwein, J. Fredericks. 2010. "The assessment context: Accreditation, accountability and performance." *New Directions for Institutional Research* 51: 3–12.

Chapter 1

Their Voices Must be Heard

LaVada U. Taylor

Providing information regarding the relevance of course evaluations, a Mid-Western University's Strategic Resource Allocation (SRA) findings notes the following:

> Student feedback on course instruction is critical. Our student experiences matter and their voices must be heard. For course evaluations to be effective, faculty must value the feedback they receive and make adjustment to their teaching based on this information. In order for course evaluations to be essential, faculty as a whole, must buy-in to the assessment and they do not currently. This function lacks quality measures associated with the effectiveness of the instrument used and feedback received. Appropriate consideration should be given to the most effective way to receive and incorporate student feedback. It is also critical to understand that because of implicit bias, course evaluations are typically biased against person of identities underrepresented in the faculty.[1]

In the above SRA report, students' experiences matter. Faculty and administrators must hear students' voices. Student feedback on-course instruction is critical. Specifically, the report shares the need for faculty buy-in in support of student evaluation of teaching while glossing over the role race and racism play in shaping the ways students make meaning of their teaching and learning situations. Though the information is noteworthy in revealing that course evaluations are typically biases against minority faculty, the story fails to acknowledge who underrepresented faculty members are and why student evaluations of teaching (SETs) are biased against them? In so doing, the report silences "why" by normalizing implicit bias as a happenstance for persons of identities underrepresented in the faculty. In 2018, the U.S. Department of Education found that out of 1.5 million faculty in degree-granting postsecondary institutions: 41 percent were White males; 35 percent White were females; 6 percent were Asian/Pacific Islander male; 4 percent were Asian/Pacific Islander female; 3 percent each were Black males, Black females, and Hispanic males; 2 percent were Hispanic females; and 1 percent constituted those who identified as American Indian/Alaska Native or of two or more races.[2]

Student evaluations of teaching are subjective measures of teaching performance. Student evaluations of teaching situated within a historical sociopolitical context are mere reflections naming the objective/subjective selves of both the student and the teacher. Referring to the dialectical relationship between the objective and the personal, Friere writes: "One cannot conceive objectivity without subjectivity."[3] In other words, one's ability to name objectively any moment in time is impossible because, in the very act of naming, a subject is formed.[4] In this process of naming, Friere notes:

> Every prescription represents the imposition of one individual's choice upon another, transforming the consciousness of the person prescribed to into one that conforms with the prescriber's consciousness.[5]

Thus, the subject and one's experience with him/her is born through its viewer's imagination. This imagination, located within a historical sociopolitical context, attempts to frame relationships through perceived binaries: oppressor/oppressed; dominate/marginalized; human/dehumanized.[6] Consequently, omitted in an analysis of student evaluations of teaching are complicated contradictions embedded with naming experiences with a professor who also represents a historically marginalized group and situated as persons whose identities are underrepresented in the faculty.

Historicizing implicit biases shrouding student course evaluations of BIPOC faculty, this work draws on critical race theory (CRT) to illuminate counter-narratives in an attempt to understand better: why are course evaluations typically biased against persons of identities underrepresented in the faculty.[7] This analysis is made possible through memoirs,[8] course evaluation responses, research on students' perceptions of BIPOC, Faculty of Color course evaluations,[9] and research on the attributes of BIPOC teaching on college and university campuses to unpack implicit bias, racism, privilege, knowing, and students evaluations of BIPOC faculty in the academy.[10] To this end, the work contains the following sections: On Race/ism, CRT, Counter-Storytelling, Until the Lion Tells the Story, Their Voices Must be Heard, A Tale by the Lion: Analysis, and Conclusion. Entitled: *On Race/ism*, the following section defines meanings of race and racism to contextualize notions of implicit biases in student evaluations of teaching.

ON RACE/ISM

What is race? According to Stuart Hall, race is a concept used to classify systems of difference operating in human society.[11] Hall holds that race is neither essential nor biologically determined; instead, race is discursive. As a discourse, race mirrors language as a subject in a constant process of redefinition and appropriation. Michael Omi and Howard Winant likewise hold race is a socio-cultural construction.[12] However, race differs from racism. Whereas race is a floating signifier, racism is an experience. Racism consists of experiences through structural and institutional practices used to elevate or advantage one race while depressing or subordinating others.[13] Solórzano and Yosso hold that racism is made possible through three systems of behavior:

1) One group deems itself superior to all others.
2) The select group has the power to carry out racist behavior.
3) Racism benefits only one group while negatively affecting other racial and ethnic groups.[14]

Through Solórzano's and Yosso's claims, racism embodies the personal, the powerful, and the systemic. James Banks argues that racism is a Eurocentric version of U.S. history that reveals race as a socially constructed category, created to differentiate racial groups and to show the superiority or dominance of one race over another.[15] Racism is experienced with food deserts, health care inequity, poverty, unemployment, housing discrimination, re-segregated schools, opportunity gaps, and the unequal distribution of resources. Circumstances created by racial divides that are used to execute individuals dictates of others who are prejudiced, and are realized through routine operations used to exclude members from a particular racial group from significantly participating in society.[16]

Manning Marable offers that racism is the system of ignorance, exploitation, and power used to oppress African Americans, Latinos, Asian Pacific Americans, and Native Americans (BIPOC) based on ethnicity, culture, mannerisms, and skin color.[17] Claud Anderson maintains that racism is a competitive relationship between five European nations—England, Spain, Italy, Portugal, and France.[18] These countries competed in a race advanced through the forced labor of Black, Yellow, Red, and Brown people (BIPOC) for ownership and control of resources, wealth, and power in the following western world: North America, Central America, South America, and the Pacific Islands. Like Anderson, many scholars argue that racism is an invention of European colonization.[19]

In this invention, dominant theory couched in European Imperialism justified colonial conquest and the enslavement and subjugation of BIPOC as an ordained act of god. This position has origin in the Great Chain of Being, which held that colonialists could categorically classify human species by lining them up vertically with the most superior at its top wearing a designation of nearly superhuman and lying just below god's angels.[20] This thought also determined the most inferior species as those resting at the bottom of the chain mirroring the appearance and assigned the intellectual aptitude just above animals, the ape three-fifths of a human, those designated enslaved.[21] This tale created through Renaissance imagination named Europeans at the top of the hierarchy and BIPOC at its bottom. Ordained by their god, race became a mode of being naming European colonizers superior to their colonized and enslaved Black and Ingenious subjects—a belief informing implicit biases to this very day.

Since colonizers created categorical hierarchies, Frantz Fanon held that colonialized subjects needed to be convinced of their subordination.[22] In other words, for the invention to work, they too had to believe in their inferiority. Carter G. Woodson argued that modern education made this inferiority complex possible. He states:

> The same educational process which inspires and stimulates the oppressor with the thought that he is everything good and has accomplished everything worthwhile, depresses and crushes at the same time the spark of genus in the Negro by making him feel that his race does not amount to much and never will measure up to the standards of other peoples.[23]

Woodson held that modern education's teachings in its celebration of whiteness served a dual purpose: re-inscribing the white race's genius while crushing the ingenuity of the Negro race. A cursory examination of a traditional U.S. history book helps one to understand better. In its many pages there you will see recognition of centuries of systematic oppression experienced by BIPOC in the United States through terror, trauma, violence, colonization, enslavement, forced relocation, and segregation. For many, the historic subjugations of Black, Red, and Brown people are undeniable and made fact neatly in pages of U.S. history textbooks.[24] As these meta-narratives —supported through dominant discourses are shared, implicit bias couched in race and racism is formed through the imagery of weakness, conquest, and inferiority, a history of oppression experienced by Native Americans, African Americans, Latino Americans, and Pacific Asian Americans. These images and truths juxtaposed an understanding of how this same history privileges the experiences of those racially designated as white.[25] Students learn that colonizers did not enslave white people. White people did not experience forced relocation, were neither denied education nor access to their history, and in some way real or imagined are superior to BIPOC. As a consequence, in *The Miseducation of the Negro,* Woodson writes: "The so-called modern education, with all its defects, however, does others so much more good than it does the Negro, because it has been worked out in conformity to the needs of those who have enslaved and oppressed weaker people."[26] These lessons lay the foundation for implicit bias that dysconsciously influence students' perceptions of and experiences with BIPOC faculty.[27]

However, understanding that race has no biological credence yet instead is a socially constructed category as Stuart Hall argued, scholars employ CRT to disrupt and transform racialized practices in education.[28] In so doing, CRT provides a lens to problematize students' perception of BIPOC faculty in their teaching evaluation. The next section explores CRT as a research tool.

CRITICAL RACE THEORY

CRT is an approach seeking to identify, analyze, and transform structural and cultural aspects of education that maintain subordinate and dominant racial positions in and out of the classroom settings.[29] Solórzano and Yosso argue that the following are five critical components of CRT: the centrality of race, a commitment to social justice, experiential knowledge, transdisciplinary perspectives, and a call to challenge dominant ideology.[30] Below, each element is considered:

The Centrality of Race

CRT holds that race and racism are central in defining and naming individual experiences. CRT recognizes the intersectionality of race with other forms of systemic oppression, sexism and classism, and maintains race is significant in shaping meaning in and through the intersections of these experiences. With an examination of race whose tentacles crossover and embed in other forms of oppression, critical race theorists search for answers to theoretical, conceptual, and pedagogical questions.

Commitment to Social Justice

CRT is committed to social justice. As praxis, CRT illuminates systemic forms of oppression by revealing breaks and ruptures as opportunities to incite social change (Fanon, 1963/2004; Freire, 2000/2017).

Experiential Knowledge

Understanding that those who benefit most from systems of oppression is least likely to recognize the oppressive experiences of others. A situation

I name the blind spot, CRT holds that the lived experiences of BIPOC are legitimate and necessary when providing a lens to explain subordination, domination, and privilege.

Transdisciplinary Perspective

CRT uses transdisciplinary knowledge, in the fields of history, ethnic studies, women's studies, sociology, and law to illuminate intersections of race, class, language, and gender oppression as lived experiences of BIPOC.[31]

Challenge to Dominant Ideology

CRT challenges dominant notions of race/racism; sex/sexism; and class/classism as fixed categories. Through disruptions of dichotomous discursive practices—rich/poor; male/female; Black/white as static notions this challenge is made possible through language and universal claims to truth (Delgado & Stefancic, 2000; Lawrence & Tatum, 1998). These are dominant discourse narratives that privilege white, Anglo-Saxon, male, middle- and upper-class, and protestant ways of knowing and being by claiming these social locations as racially neutral and therefore an expected point of reference (hooks, 2013; Love, 2018).

In contradiction, centering the voices and experiences of people of color from the margins, CRT challenges dominant notions of race/racism, sex/sexism, and class/classism as fixed categories. CRT forefronts the history and sociopolitical awareness of BIPOC through storytelling techniques. Thus, their voices and unique perspectives serve as counter-narratives to dominant claims to truth. Counter-storytelling, as a CRT approach, is explained in the next section.

COUNTER-STORYTELLING

Solórzano and Yossso define counter-storytelling as "a method of telling the stories of people whose experiences are not often told from their perspectives—including people of color, women, gay, and the poor."[32] Counter-stories challenge dominant discourse by disrupting social, political, and cultural norms with voices and perspectives of those historically situated in the margins.[33] At its core, counter-storytelling exposes race-neutral rhetoric by revealing how racism operates in fundamental ways to organize society by reinforcing and maintaining unequal distributions of power as well as systems of privilege and oppression.[34] BIPOC, who share their experiences through storytelling, provides critical insights to narrate counter-stories in and through CRT. Embraced in African, African

American, Chicana/Chicano, and Native American communities, storytelling is a tool used to create meaning by people of color as public self-authors of their experiences.[35] An intricate part of counter-storytelling is its root: storytelling. As the lion and the hunter asserts until the lion tells the story, the hunter will always be the hero.[36] Counter-stories center the memories and experiences of those often silenced or ignored in dominant discourse. The next section entitled "Until the Lion Tells the Story" illuminates possibilities in counter-storytelling in helping readers understand why student evaluations of teaching bias BIPOC faculty can have positive and negative repercussions.

UNTIL THE LION TELLS THE STORY

Our opening discussion concerning SRA's support of student evaluation of teaching (SETs) despite implicit biases imposed on BIPOC faculty experience through SETs serves as the impetus for our tale. In this narrative, student feedback via course evaluations is critical. They provide a platform for students' voices. The report beckons readers to consider the most effective ways to incorporate student feedback when modifying their teaching based on students' responses. Finally, the narrative ends with a profound acknowledgment: "It is also critical to understand that because of implicit bias, course evaluations are typically bias against persons of identities underrepresented in the faculty"—the mic drops. The SRA silently reminds its audience that student evaluations of teaching are pivotal in promotion and tenure decisions, merit increases, and contract renewals. Yes, student evaluation of instruction is laden with implicit biases nonetheless the instrument is invaluable and BIPOC faculty are not. The proverb of the lion and the hunter resonates here. Until those historically marginalized tell their stories, those who colonize will remain the hero.

CRT employs one of three forms of counter-storytelling in its quest to center the experience of those historically marginalized: personal stories, other people's stories, or composite stories.[37] Personal stories share personal experiences with various forms of racism, classism, and sexism. These narratives are told by situating a narrator's accounts with critical interpretations of the law to reveal the meaning of experiences through a more extensive social critique. Other people's stories are written in a third-person voice. These narratives reveal experiences and shared responses to race, sex, and class oppression. Composite accounts are created from data sources like memoirs, existing literature on the subject, personal and professional situations to recount the experiences of those historically marginalized. Through these data sources, the author(s) creates composite characters and places them in social, historical, and political situations to describe collective experiences with racism, sexism, and classism.

In what follows entitled "Their Voices Must be Heard" are composite stories of Skylar Jacob, a white middle-class daughter of an engineer of a local oil refinery, an aspiring teacher, and a first-generation college student; Dr. Lydia Green, also a first-generation college student, a working-class African American middle-aged woman, and tenured associate professor; Angelina Sanchez, a first-generation student of mixed Irish and Mexican ancestry. She, too, is an aspiring teacher with a 4.0 GPA. Their narratives created through memoirs, course evaluations, and research on the experiences of faculty of color in the academy reveal why student course evaluations bias BIPOC faculty.

THEIR VOICES MUST BE HEARD

Skylar Jacob

Dr. Green is very well educated and certainly knows what she is talking about in terms of multiculturalism and social studies from that perspective. I did feel that this was more of a one-sided politics class rather than looking at education. I was hoping to learn more about how to work in a diverse classroom. I think this class needs to spend more time looking at how these issues affect how we teach rather than how education is affected by history. The course was also poorly set up and needed a lot of improvement. This course, in theory, should be a well-rounded semester filled with learning strategies and positive feedback that allows students to grow and learn to become effective teachers. Without Amy, I would not have done as well this semester. Dr. Green did not promote my learning and did not help me further my teaching career in this course. It was incredibly frustrating when Dr. Green would say one thing, and Amy would contradict her, and the classes tie together. There needs to be more communication between Dr. Green and Dr. Amy Sullivan because their lack of communication makes essential parts of the course very confusing. Instead, this course is disorganized, and Dr. Green is ridiculously unprepared to be a teacher. Students are given unrealistic expectations, like connecting the content to student's lives, with no direction and are talked down to frequently.

After her lectures, Dr. Green asks questions and expects us to respond with a specific answer from the book instead of letting the discussion flow naturally. She would immediately turn down any plausible answer and wanted us to reference the book. That did not help with the conversation and just caused a stop in discussion. By the end of the semester, students are completely unprepared to go into the education profession due to her rude and callous nature. Dr. Green is also inconsistent with instruction and what she expects of students. Different groups of students receive different information/directions from her about assignments and not in a "differentiation of learning" type of way. Her instructions confuse everyone in the class. For example, she shared the need to differentiate instruction based on Visual, Aural, Reading/Writing, and Kinesthetic (VARK) learning modalities to address how students receive information and the need for us to use culturally relevant pedagogy to couch lessons in student's life experiences so that information learned is meaningful.

I'm not from my students' community, and I don't know their home life. On one occasion, a classmate did a lesson on Blues music during Black History Month. All the artists were from Chicago. In front of the entire class, Dr. Green asked her about Black and Brown blues artists and why it might be essential to add those artists to her lesson. She was crushed. Also, there is apparent favoritism taking place, which is reflected in the scores on our assignments. She has made several students cry throughout the semester because of the way she has ripped apart our lessons in front of our entire class with all these questions that she calls feedback. In my opinion, Dr. Green has been unprofessional and inappropriate, and I wouldn't be surprised if we are not asked to come back to our current field site next semester. I feel like I have gotten absolutely nothing out of this semester in her class. I urge someone to find a new professor to take her place so that future students can benefit from this class. I am very thankful this is my last class with this professor. Students have been unhappy with her for a long time.

Dr. Lydia Green

After reading my course evaluation comments, I was shocked. None of my students shared with me any dissatisfaction with the course. I asked my director—my colleague who taught the corresponding course in the block, and the principal of our host school if any of them had received any negative comments about my teaching? Each replied no.

I must admit having served as an urban educator for thirty years, and in higher education, nearly twenty of those thirty years, the comments were hurtful. I believe that they were hurtful not because this, in fact, may be candidates' perception of my teaching. The words were hurtful because they were couched in falsehoods that sought to discredit me as an educator and shape my relationship with teachers and administrators of Black and Brown children in one of the most racially and ethnically diverse communities in our region and a place that I call home. It is my belief that their intentions were malicious. I have often wondered where and from whom did candidates learn that it was okay to attack a professor through course evaluations? I am mindful of the role implicit biases play in naming experience. Yet, I believe the way in which candidates choose to share their dissatisfaction with me was both learned and supported by my peers and members of our faculty. But, why would they do that? Though I cannot name their teachers, those who helped facilitate this learning process, I can provide maybes. Maybe it is fellow colleagues whom students look up to and, like me, know the importance of student course evaluations? Maybe it was administrators who dismissed faculty of color because in the past all a student had to say was that they did not like a faculty and being untenured the faculty would lose his or her job. Or, just maybe it's me as I sit among fellow faculty members voting to approve candidates' spring graduation while fully aware that there are deeply rooted dispositions that may inhibit their ability to respect and/or teach children of color.

Over the years I have watched many African American instructors and/or faculty members of color come in and walk out of the doors of our university with the perception looming over them that they simply could not teach.

Angelina Sanchez

As an education major, I loved this course. It allowed us to discuss and learn about "controversial" topics like race, class, gender, and language and how these concepts manifest in and through education. I believe that these topics are fundamental especially for teachers. This course allowed us to see that our students come from different economic situations, different ideologies, and races. I enjoyed the content of the course and learned to be more aware of the students that will be in my classroom and to question everything. The course was very educational and helpful; as a future educator, it is very important that I understand and learn subjects like multiculturalism. I think Dr. Green is a great professor. I enjoyed her lectures and the conversations we had in class. She is very open minded and understanding. When having discussions, she made everyone in her class feel safe. In her social studies methods class, Dr. Green provided ample time for us to grow as teachers. Instead of lecturing too often, she provided creative opportunities through mock lesson presentations for us to become better teachers. Often after lesson presentations, she would pose the question to us . . . so what . . . in reference to our lesson and its connection to our students. The questions were intended to make us think what we can do to make the lesson more meaningful. I learned a lot about understanding design and how to create a unit. More importantly, I learned how to create lessons couched in students' interests and experiences. I had a great time in this course, and I was happy with the set-up and field placements. Dr. Green is a GREAT teacher, and she knows her stuff about social studies. She is very positive and willing to work with you through email, phone calls, and office hours. I requested feedback on all my lessons and received quality responses from Dr. Green each time. She gives great feedback that I believe is beneficial to my students now and in the future. I admire this about her. She is very supportive and willing to meet individually and provides unyielding support to her students. I learned a great deal in this class. I learned to research and examine a topic to meet the standards while connecting concepts to the lived experiences of my students. I also learned to trust my own thoughts and to follow my thinking throughout my entire lesson and not to insert random ideas that are disconnected and may confuse students.

The above testimonies share perspectives of BIPOC faculty and the students they teach to contextualize the questions: why are course evaluations typically biased against faculty whose identities are underrepresented in the academy—African American, Latino Americans, Asian/Pacific Islanders, and Native Americans. The next section entitled "A Tale by the Lion: An Analysis" situates their narratives within a historical sociopolitical context of schooling to answer these questions and to examine why are BIPOC faculty bias by student evaluations of teaching.

A TALE BY A LION: AN ANALYSIS

The American Sociological Association notes that teaching evaluations are both invalid and unreliable teacher performance measures.[38] Student evaluations are then best understood in a historical sociopolitical context as situated reflections naming the objective/subjective selves of both students and their teachers.[39] Referring to the dialectical relationship between the objective and the personal, Freire writes: "One cannot conceive objectivity without subjectivity"[40] In other words, one's ability to name objectively any moment in time is impossible because, in the very act of naming, a subject is formed.[41] Further, Freire states:

> Every prescription represents the imposition of one individual's choice upon another, transforming the consciousness of the person prescribed to into one that conforms with the prescriber's consciousness.[42]

Thus, subjects name its object. In student evaluations of teaching, binary subjectivities informed by race—influence meanings that students provide in teaching and learning situations.[43] Skylar's evaluation of Dr. Green's is made meaningful through an understanding of Dr. Green's race and social class positionality. Dr. Greene is both African American and working class. Perry et al. write that when a professor represents a historically marginalized group, then students believe that the information taught is both factual and biased.[44] The professor cannot be impartial, scholarly, or credible.[45] Reflecting on this position, Skylar notes:

> Dr. Green did not promote my learning and did not help me further my teaching career in this course. It is incredibly frustrating when Dr. Green would say one thing, and Amy would contradict her, and the classes tie together
>
> This course is disorganized, and Dr. Green is ridiculously unprepared to be a teacher.
>
> I did feel that this was more of a one-sided politics class rather than looking at education.
>
> This class needs to spend more time looking at how these issues (race, class, gender, language, and religion) affect education rather than how education is affected by history.[46]
>
> Noting this phenomenon in their work, Perry et al. concluded the following: students' first impression of their professors, even when they are based solely on their instructors' race, do influence their judgments of the professors' perceived bias and consequently, their perceptions of professors' subjectivity and expertise; thus, a professor's race/ethnicity can directly influence student evaluations.[47]

Referring to race/ism as the "source effects," Litterford et al. found that source effects also apply to European American instructors.[48] However, unlike their African American counterparts, who likewise teach similar subject matter, White teachers are more often deemed credible because they are mirror dysconscious, meaning students apply to European American professors.[49] Skylar writes:

> Without Amy, I would not have done as well this semester. Dr. Green did not promote my learning and did not help me further my teaching career in this course. It was incredibly frustrating when Dr. Green would say one thing, and Amy would contradict her, and the classes tie together. There needs to be more communication between Dr. Green and Dr. Sullivan because their lack of communication makes essential parts of the course very confusing. Dr. Gree is ridiculously unprepared to be a teacher.[50]

Here race and legitimacy are paramount in Skylar's reflection. Dr. Amy Sullivan is a non-tenured white professor, and Dr. Green is a tenured African American professor. Skylar cites familiarity with Amy as she refers to her professor by her first name. She also notes that without Amy's competency, she would not have learned anything to advance her professionally in Dr. Green's class. African American women stereotyped perceptions as Black (illegitimate nor deserving of your position as well as difficult/aggressive and incompetent) and woman (communal, mothering, gentle and amicable) often provide complicated contradictions in their social construct as raced illegitimate, difficult/aggressive while gendered kind, demure and ultimately less academic than their white peers.[51] Illuminating these complicated paradoxes through each narrative couched in stereotypical representations, Skyler and Angelina note the following:

Angelina

The course was very educational and helpful; as a future educator it is very important that I understand and learn subjects like multiculturalism.

[Dr. Green] is very open minded and understanding. When having discussions, she a made everyone feel safe.

She is very supportive and willing to meet individually and provides unyielding support to her students.

I requested feedback on all my lessons and received quality responses from Dr. Green each time.

Skyler:

This course is disorganized, and Dr. Green is ridiculously unprepared to be a teacher.

Students are given unrealistic expectations, like connecting the content to student's lives, with no direction and are talked down to frequently.

Dr. Green did not promote my learning and did not help me further my teaching career in this course.

Students are entirely unprepared to go into the education profession due to her rude and callous nature.

In their research entitled *The Effect of Professor Ethnicity and Gender on Student Evaluations: Judged before Met*, Bavishi et al. note that female African American professors were rated the lowest on competence, interpersonal skills, and legitimacy scales, compared to all other groups.[52] They share that the complexities of being women, Black, and professors often create a double bind syndrome. Women of color face multiple stigmas as less qualified, insensitive, rude, and are often evaluated poorly for being both a woman and a person of color.

Seemingly dismal, faculty of color can also be an attribute to students in college and university settings. Madyun et al. note benefits for having BIPOC who in positions of authority, as teacher, challenge students' perceptions of race in relation to self, power, and knowing.[53] These interactions, though likewise are initially informed by perception and race/ism, help students to develop new understandings of and appreciation for race, culture and difference.

Angelina writes:

> As an education major, I loved this course. It allowed us to discuss and learn about "controversial" topics like race, class, gender, and language and how these concepts manifest in and through education. I believe that these topics are fundamental especially for teachers. This course allowed us to see that our students come from different economic situations, different ideologies, and races. I enjoyed the content of the course and learned to be more aware of the students that will be in my classroom, and to question every assumption.

Baxter-Magolda notes that through lived experience and scholarship focusing on the lives of people of color, BIPOC broadens students' perspectives and helps students become self-authors of their experiences.[54] In classroom settings, taught by BIPOC faculty, self-authorship affords spaces where implicit notions of race/sim are questioned and sometimes challenged. In teaching and learning situations, as a skill set, self-authorship requires students to problematize preconceived notions of what it means to be a racialized other by taking seemingly disjointed fact and recreating meanings of being for themselves. Angelina notes:

> Instead of lecturing too often, [Dr. Green] provided creative opportunities through mock lesson presentations for us to become better teachers. Often after lesson presentations, she would pose the question to us . . . so what in reference to our lesson and its connection to our students. The questions were intended to elicit us to think what can we do to make the lesson more meaningful.

Although self-authorship provides multiple possibilities for teachers teaching in diverse communities, the journey of gaining self-authorship is not necessarily comfortable. One difficulty lies in students' unwillingness to let go of preconceived assumptions and more prejudice and racist beliefs. Students may feel that their opinions and worldviews are being personally challenged and thus disengage with instruction.[55] Skylar shares:

> I did feel that this was more of a one-sided politics class rather than looking at education. I was hoping to learn more about how we work with a diverse classroom. This class needs to spend more time looking at how these issues affect education rather than how education is affected by history.
>
> [Dr. Green] always shares the need to differentiate instruction based on Visual, Aural, Reading/Writing, and Kinesthetic (VARK) learning modalities to address how students receive information and the need for culturally relevant pedagogy to couch lessons in student's life experiences so that information is

relevant and meaningful. But, I'm not from their community, and I don't know their home life.

Stated simply, in the process of moving toward self-authorship, students may encounter crossroad experiences. Citing Baxter-Magolda's argument, Madyun et al. hold that

> before a student can adopt an identity informed by an internal mechanism, she or he typically must encounter a rich experience that is termed "the crossroads." Like many ethnic identity models, the crossroads is the point at which an individual recognizes a flaw or incompleteness in the external definition of a phenomenon.[56]

BIOPC faculty whose lived experiences and epistemological ways of understanding the world and being in the world may contradict more prejudicial assumptions of what it means to be Black, woman, and professor.[57] It is here in these contradictions that crossroad experiences occur and, depending on the receiver, can lead to more negative experiences. As Skylar writes:

> I feel like I have gotten absolutely nothing out of this semester in her class. I urge someone to find a new professor to take her place so that future students can benefit from this class. I am very thankful this is my last class with this professor. Students have been unhappy with her for a long time.[58]

Or crossroad experiences can lead to a more positive experience, as Angelina explains:

> The course was very educational and helpful; as a future educator, I must understand and learn multiculturalism subjects. I think Dr. Green is a great professor. I enjoyed her lectures and the conversations we had in class. She is very open-minded and understanding when having discussions. She made everyone in her class feel safe.[59]

Crossroads can also cause cracks through its intersection between a known process of understanding that forges new possibilities for self-authorship. Engaged in teaching/learning relationships with BIPOC faculty, through crossroad experiences, students can begin to problematize prejudice and implicit notions of race/ism informing their learning experiences.[60] Students become self-authors as "[they] move from passively accepting external definitions of the world to critically examining definitions and developing the capacity to measure them against their own belief" and make meaning for themselves.[61] Sharing her crossroad experience Angelina continues:

I learned a great deal in this class. I learned to research and examine a topic to meet the standards while addressing my students' needs. I also learned to trust my thoughts and follow my thoughts throughout my entire lesson and not insert random ideas that are disconnected and may confuse my students.[62]

Through these teaching and learning situations, students become self-authors as they understand "that different people hold different world views for legitimate reasons."[63] Students begin to appreciate learning, knowing, and possibilities for being different.[64] The following concludes this piece.

CONCLUSION

Advocating for student evaluations of teachings to provide critical feedback when students evaluate their teaching and learning experiences, the SRA report neglects to account for the historical influence of race and racism in student course evaluations.[65] Consequently, the information fails to mention systems and institutional practices that use course evaluations—in very punitive ways, that is, promotion and tenure decision—to further marginalizing faculty of color by relying on a very subjective measure of teaching effectiveness. Though not a reliable instrument for determining the quality of instruction, course evaluations are useful in revealing the influence of race and racism as students make meaning of teaching and learning situations with BIPOC faculty.[66]

Contextualizing the question: why are student course evaluations typically biased against BIPOC faculty? This piece offers the following findings: (1) The presence and epistemology of BIPOC faculty in the academy can disrupt notions of a racialized other understood in relation to a self, power, authority, knowing, and being. (2) Cultural dissonance or disruption experienced by students during interactions with BIPOC faculty may materialize as fear, loss of control, a threat to a core self, or as an opportunity for self-authorship. (3) The presence of faculty of color in college and university spaces can create disruptions while also forging new possibilities for consciousness, decolonization, and liberation with the students they teach. (4) Students' responses to these disruptions can lead to either negative or positive experiences and positive or negative course evaluations.

Understanding why student evaluation of teaching is typically biased against BIPOC faculty is invaluable, particularly when exploring the historical sociopolitical contexts of race. This knowing lends itself to a better understanding of how race, as well as racism, informs the way students make meaning of their teaching and learning situations with BIPOC faculty. Perhaps most importantly, this lens provides an analysis for how these relationships forge new possibilities in knowing, being, and experiencing difference. Though an ending, this conclusion is not a final thought. Instead, I pose future research consideration below:

1. Can social psychologists aid us in understanding how more racist colonial memory as lived experiences today is re-imagined as an impetus to change patterns of social behaviors in teaching and learning contexts tomorrow?
2. Why would any institution use course evaluations to measure teaching effectiveness, to inform promotion and tenure decisions, and in determining merit raise justification when it is known that student course evaluations are subjective and are typically biased against BIPOC?
3. What role does the academy play in perpetuating discursive practices of binary opposition's rich/poor; white/a person of color, right/wrong as real and fixed concepts?
4. How do these practices inform the perpetuation of BIPOC as underrepresented members on college and university campuses?

NOTES

1. Anonymous (2019), 38.

2. United States Department of Education, *Characteristics of Postsecondary Faculty; The Condition of Education* (Washington, DC: National Center for Education Statistics, 2018).

3. Paulo Friere, *Pedagogy of the Oppressed*, trans. Myra Bergman Ramos (New York, NY: Bloomsbury Academic, 2000), 50.

4. See: Paul Ricour, *Time and Narrative*, trans. Paul Blamey and Kathleen Pellauer (New York: Cobble Hill Books, 1988).

5. Friere, *Pedagogy of the Oppressed*, 49.

6. Franz Fanon, *Black Skin, White Masks*, trans. Richard Philcox (New York, NY: Grove Press, 1967/2008).

7. See, for instance: Richard Delgado and Jean Stefanci, *Critical Race Theory: The Cutting Edge* (Philadelphia, PA: Temple University Press, 2017); Gloria Ladson-Billings and William F. Tate, IV, "Toward a Critical Race Theory of Education," in *Critical Race Theory in Education*, ed. Adrienne D. Dixson and Celia K. Rousseau (New York, NY: Routledge Press, 2006), 11–30.

8. See, for instance: Theodora Berry and Nathalie Mizelle, eds. *From Oppression to Grace: Women of Color and Their Dilemmas within the Academy* (Sterling, VA: Stylus, 2006); R. Harlow, "'Race Doesn't Matter, but . . .': The Effect of Race on Professor's Experiences and Emotional Management in Undergraduate College Classrooms," *Social Psychology Quarterly* 66, no. 41 (2003): 348–67; Christine Stanley, ed., *Faculty of Color: Teaching in Predominantly White Colleges and Universities* (Bolton, MA: Anker Publishing Company, 2006); Frank Tuitt et al.,

"Teaching in the Line of Fire: Faculty of Color in the Academy," *Thought and Action: NEA Higher Education Journal* (Fall 2009): 65–74; Caroline Turner, Juan Carlos González, and Kathleen Wong, "Faculty Women of Color: The Critical Nexus of Race and Gender," *Journal of Diversity in Higher Education* 4, no. 4 (2011): 199–211.

9. Anish Bavishi, Juan Madera, and Michelle Hebl "The Effect of Professor Ethnicity and Gender on Student Evaluations: Judge Before Met," *Journal of Diversity in Higher Education* 3, no. 4 (2010); Linh Littleford et al., "Perceptions of European American and African American Instructors Teaching Race-focused Courses," *Journal of Diversity in Higher Education* 3, no. 4 (2010): 230–44.; Armon Perry, Sherri Wallace, Sharon Moore, and Gwendolyn Perry-Burney, "Understanding Student Evaluations: A Black Faculty Perspective," *Faculty Scholarship* 15 (2015): 1–7.

10. Stephanie Adams, "Succeeding in the Face of Doubts," in *Faculty of Color: Teaching in Predominantly White Colleges and Universities*, ed. Christine Stanley (Bolton, MA: Anker Publishing Company, 2006), 30–40; Denise Bane, "Free To Be the Me You See: Discovering the Joy of Teaching," in *Faculty of Color: Teaching in Predominantly White Colleges and Universities*, ed. Christine Stanley (Bolton, MA: Anker Publishing Company, 2006), 54–67; Na'im Madyun et al., "On the Importance of African American Faculty in Higher Education: Implications and Recommendations," *Educational Foundations* Fall/Summer (2013): 65–82.

11. Stuart Hall, *Race: The Floating Signifier* (North Hampton, MA: Media Education Foundation, 1996).

12. Michael Omi and Howard Winant, *Racial Formation in the United States*, 3rd ed (New York, NY: Routledge, 2015).

13. Audre Lorde, *Sister/Outsider: Essays and Speeches* (New York: Random House, 1984/2007); Derrick Tillman-Kelly (2020). How we got here: Racism + higher education [PowerPoint slides]. https://www.youtube.com/watch?v=sbCz6Ph2hTc.

14. Daniel Solórzano and Tara J. Yosso, "Critical Race Methodology: Counter-Storytelling as an Analytical Framework for Education Research," *Qualitative Inquiry* 8, no. 23 (2002): 24.

15. James Banks, *Cultural Diversity and Education: Foundations, Curriculum and Teaching*, 5th ed. (Boston. Massachusetts: Pearson, 2005).

16. Bettina Love, *We Want to Do More Than Survive: Abolitionist Teaching and the Pursuit of Educational Freedom* (Boston: Beacon Press, 2019). See also: Tillman-Kelly.

17. Manning Marable, *Speaking Truth to Power: Essays on Race, Resistance, and Radicalism* (Boulder, CO: Westview Press, 1996).

18. Claud Anderson, *Black Labor, White Wealth: The Search for Power and Economic Justice* (Englewood, MD: Duncan & Duncan, 1994).

19. See for instance: Fanon, *Black Skin, White Masks*; Simon Schama, *Rough Crossings: Britain, the Slaves and the American Revolution* (New York, NY: Ecco Press, 2006); Farish Ahmad-Noor, *What Your Teacher Didn't Tell You*, vol. 1, 4th ed. (Jaya, Malaysia: Matahari Books, 2010); Jane Hiddleston, *Understanding Postcolonialism* (New York, NY: Routledge Press, 2014).

20. Robert Gordon, "The Venal Hottentot Venus and the Great Chain of Being" *African Studies* 51, no. 2 (1992).

21. Edward Lurie, "Louis Agassiz and the Races of Man," *The University of Chicago Press on Behalf of the History of Science Society* 45, no. 3 (1954): 227–242.

22. Frantz Fanon, *The Wretched of the Earth*, trans. Richard Philcox (New York, NY: Grove Press, 2004).

23. Carter G. Woodson, *The Miseducation of the Ne*gro (Trenton, NJ: Africa World Press, 1933/1998). xiii.

24. James Loewen, *Lies My Teacher Told Me: Everything Your American History Text Got Wrong* (New York, NY: New York Press, 1996/2018).

25. Woodson, The Miseducation of the Negro, 7–11.

26. Woodson, The Miseducation of the Negro, xii.

27. See, for instance: Joyce E. King, "Dysconscious Racism: Ideology, Identity, and the Miseducation of Teachers," *Journal of Negro Education*, 60, no. 2 (1991): 133–46; bell hooks, *Black Looks: Race and Representation* (New York: Routledge Press, 2015); Henrt Hornstein, "Student Evaluations of Teaching Are an Inadequate Assessment Tool for Evaluating Faculty Performance," *Cogent Education* 4, no. 1 (2017).

28. Gloria Ladson-Billings and William Tate, "Toward a Critical Race Theory of Education," *Teachers College Record* 97, no. 1 (1995): 47–67; Christine Sleeter, "Critical Race Theory and the Whiteness of Teacher Education," *Urban Education* 52, no. 2 (2017): 155–69.

29. Richard Delgado and Jean Stefancic, *Critical Race Theory* (New York, NY: New York University Press, 2017), 63–66.

30. Solórzano and Yosso, "Critical Race Methodology," 25–27.

31. Love, *We Want to Do More Than Survive*, 136.

32. Solórzano and Yosso, "Critical Race Methodology, 26.

33. Delgado and Stefancic, *Critical Race Theory*, 49; Solórzano and Yosso, "Critical Race Methodology, 32.

34. Derrick Bell, Faces at the Bottom of the Well: The Permanence of Racism (New York: Basic Books, 1992. 163–164.

35. Richard Delgado, "Storytelling for Oppositionists and Others: A Plea for Narrative," *Michigan Law Review* 87, no. 8 (1989): 2411–41.

36. Abagba, Simeon. "African Proverbs, Sayings, and Stories," AFRIPROVE. ORG, March 23, 2021, https://afriprov.org/april-2006-proverb-quntil-the-lion-has-his-or-her-own-storyteller-the-hunter-will-always-have-the-best-part-of-the-storyq-ewe-mina-benin-ghana-and-togo.

37. Delgado and Stefanci, *Critical Race Theory*, 46–50.

38. American Sociological Association, "Statement on Student Evaluations of Teaching," *The American Sociological Association* (September 2019).

39. Kristine Ford, "Race, Gender, and Bodily (Mis)Recognitions: Women of Color Faculty Experiences with White Students in the College Classroom," *The Journal of Higher Education* 82, no. 4 (2011): 444–478.

40. Paulo Friere, *Pedagogy of the Oppressed*, 50.

41. LaVada Taylor Brandon, "Navigating Knowing/Complicating Truth: African American Learners Experiencing Oral History as Real Education" (PhD dissertation, Louisiana State University, Baton Rouge, 2001).

42. Friere, *Pedagogy of the Oppressed*, 47.

43. Kamini Grahame, "Contesting Diversity in the Academy: Resistance to Women of Color Teaching Race, Class, Gender," *Race, Gender, and Class in Education* 11, no. 3 (2004): 54–73; Litterford et al., "Perceptions of European American and African American Instructors," 230–244; Caroline Turner, "Incorporation and Marginalization in the Academy: From Border Toward Center for Faculty of Color," *Journal of Black Studies* 34, no. (2003): 122–125.

44. Perry et al., "Understanding Student Evaluations," 29.

45. Perry et al., "Understanding Student Evaluations," 230–244.

46. Skylar, anonymous compilation of student course evaluations

47. Perry et al., "Understanding Student Evaluations," 29.

48. Litterford et al., "Perceptions of European American and African American Instructors," 231.

49. Joyce King, "Dysconsious Racism," 135.

50. Skylar, anonymous composite of student course evaluations.

51. Bavishi, Madera, and Hebl "The Effect of Professor Ethnicity and Gender."

52. Bavishi, Madera, and Hebl, "The Effect of Professor Ethnicity and Gender," 252.

53. Madyun et al., "On the Importance of African American Faculty," 69.

54. Marcia Baxter-Magolda, "Three Elements of Self-Authorship," *Journal of College Student Development* 49, no. 4 (2008): 269–284.

55. Gloria Boutte and Tambra Jackson, "Advice to White Allies: Insight from Faculty of Color," *Race, Ethnicity, and Education* 17, no. 5 (2014): 623–642; Baxter-Magolda, "Three Elements of Self-Authorship."

56. Madyun et al., "On the Importance of African American Faculty," 71.

57. Ford, "Race, Gender, and Bodily (Mis)Recognitions."

58. Skylar, anonymous composite story of student evaluations of teaching

59. Angelina, composite story of student evaluations of teaching

60. Caroline Turner, "Women of Color in Academe: Living with Multiple Marginality," *The Journal of Higher Education* 173, no. 1 (2002): 74–93.

61. Madyun et al., "On the Importance of African American Faculty," 70.

62. Angelina, composite story of student evaluations of teaching

63. Madyun et al., "On the Importance of African American Faculty," 70.

64. Banks, *Cultural Diversity and Education*.

65. Mara Aruguete, Joshua Slater, and Sekela Mwaikinda, "The Effects of Professors' Race and Clothing Style on Student Evaluations," *The Journal of Negro Education* 86, no. 4 (2017): 495.

66. American Sociological Association, "Statement on Student Evaluations of Teaching," 1–4; Hornstein, "Student Evaluations of Teaching," 1–8.

REFERENCES

Adagba, Simeon. African Proverbs, Sayings and Stories," AFRIPROV.ORG. https://afriprov.org/april-2006-proverb-quntil-the-lion-has-his-or-her-own-storyteller-the-hunter-will-always-have-the-best-part-of-the-storyq-ewe-mina-benin-ghana-and-togo (accessed March 23, 2021).

Ahmad-Noor, Faris. *What Your Teacher Didn't Tell You*. Vol. 1. 4th ed. Jaya, Malaysia: Matahari Books, 2010.

Adams, Stephanie. "Succeeding in the Face of Doubts." In *Faculty of Color: Teaching in Predominantly White Colleges and Universities*, edited by Christine Stanley, 30–40. Bolton, MA: Anker Publishing Company, 2006.

American Sociological Association. "Statement on Student Evaluations of Teaching." *The American Sociological Association*, Month Date, 2019. https://www.historians.org/news-and-advocacy/aha-advocacy/aha-signs-onto-asa-statement-on-teaching-evaluations.

Anderson, Claud. *Black Labor, White Wealth: The Search for Power and Economic Justice*. Englewood, MD: Duncan & Duncan, 1994.

Anonymous. Final Report of the Support Functions Taskforce. 2018–2019 *Strategic Resource Allocation*, 2019.

Aruguete, Mara, Joshua Slater, and Sekela Mwaikinda. "The Effects of Professors' Race and Clothing Style on Student Evaluations." *The Journal of Negro Education* 86, no. 4 (2017): 494–502.

Bane, Denise. "Free To Be the Me You See: Discovering the Joy of Teaching." In *Faculty of Color: Teaching in Predominantly White Colleges and Universities*, edited by Christine Stanley, 54–67. Bolton, MA: Anker Publishing Company, 2006.

Banks, James. "The Historical Reconstruction of Knowledge about Race: Implications for Transformative Teaching." *Educational Researcher* 24, no. 2 (1995): 15–25. doi:10.3102/0013189x024002015.

Banks, James. *Cultural Diversity and Education: Foundations, Curriculum and Teaching*. 5th ed. Boston, MA: Pearson, 2005.

Bavishi, Anish, Juan Madera, and Michelle Hebl. "The Effect of Professor Ethnicity and Gender on Student Evaluations: Judge Before Met." *Journal of Diversity in Higher Education* 3, no. 4 (2010): 245–56. doi:10.1037/a0020763.

Baxter-Magolda, Marcia. "Three Elements of Self-Authorship." *Journal of College Student Development* 49, no. 4 (2008): 269–84. doi:10.1353/csd.o.0016.

Bernal, Dolores. "Using a Chicana Feminist Epistemology in Educational Research." *Harvard Educational Review* 68, no. 4 (1998): 555–83. doi:10.17763/haer.68.4.5wv1034973g22q48.

Bernal, Dolores and Octavio Villalpando. "An Apartheid of Knowledge in Academia: The Struggle over the 'Legitimate' Knowledge of Faculty of Color." *Equity and Excellence* 135, no. 2 (2002): 169–89. doi:10.1080/173845282.

Berry, Theadora and Nathalie Mizelle, eds. *From Oppression to Grace: Women of Color and Their Dilemmas within the Academy*. Sterling, VA: Stylus, 2006.

Boutte, Gloria and Tambra Jackson. "Advice to White Allies: Insight from Faculty of Color." *Race, Ethnicity, and Education* 17, no. 5 (2014): 623–42. doi:10.1080/13613324.2012.759926.

Brandon, LaVada Taylor. "Navigating Knowing/Complicating Truth: African American Learners Experiencing Oral History as Real Education." PhD diss, Louisiana State University, Baton Rouge, 2001. LSU Historical Dissertations and Thesis, 395.

Childers-McKee, Cherese, and Kathy Hytten. "Critical Race Feminism and the Complex Challenges of Educational Reform." *The Urban Review* 47, no. 3 (2015): 393–412.

Clayson, Dennis, and Mary Jane Sheffet. "Personality and the Evaluation of Teaching." *Journal of Marketing Education* 28, no. 2 (2006): 149–60. doi:10.1177/0273475306288402.

Cleveland, Darrell. *A Long Way to Go: Conversations about Race by African American Faculty and Graduate Students*. New York, NY: Peter Lang, 2004.

Delgado, Richard. "Storytelling for Oppositionists and Others: A Plea for Narrative." *Michigan Law Review* 87, no. 8 (1989): 2411–41. doi:10.2307/1289308.

Delgado, Richard, and Jean Stefanci. *Critical Race Theory: An Introduction*. 3rd ed. New York: New York University Press, 2017.

Delgado, Richard, and Jean Stefanci. *Critical Race Theory: The Cutting Edge*. Philadelphia, PA: Temple University Press, 2017.

Delgado, Richard, and Jean Stefanci, eds. *Critical White Studies: Looking Behind the Mirror*. Philadelphia, PA: Temple University Press, 1997.

Delucci, Michael. "Don't Worry, Be Happy: Instructor Likability, Student Perceptions of Learning, and Teacher Rating in Upper Level Sociology Courses." *Teaching Sociology* 28, no. 3 (2000): 220–31. doi:10.2307/1318991.

Diggs, Gregory, Dorothy Garrison-Wade, Diane Estrada, and Rene Galindo. "Smiling Faces and Colored Spaces: The Experience of Faculty of Color Pursuing Tenure in The Academy." *The Urban Review* 41, no. 4 (2009): 312–33.

Fanon, Frantz. *The Wretched of the Earth*. Translated by Richard Philcox. New York, NY: Grove Press, 2004.

Fanon, Frantz. *Black Skin, White Masks*. Translated by Richard Philcox. New York, NY: Grove Press, 1967/2008.

Ford, Kristine. "Race, Gender, and Bodily (Mis)Recognitions: Women of Color Faculty Experiences with White Students in the College Classroom." *The Journal of Higher Education* 82, no. 4 (2011): 444–78. doi:10.1080/00221546.2011.11777212.

Freire, Paulo. *Pedagogy of the Oppressed*. Translated by Myra Bergman Ramos. New York, NY: Bloomsbury Academic, 2000.

Flaherty, Colleen. "Flawed Evaluations." *Inside Higher Education*, June 10, 2015. https://www.insidehighered.com/news/2015/06/10aaup-committee-survey-data-raise-questions-effectiveness-student-teaching.

Gold, Rachelle. "Outsider Within: African American Professors and Their Experiences at Predominately White Universities: A Narrative Interview Study." PhD diss, University of North Carolina, Chapel Hill, 2008.

Gordon, Robert. "The Venal Hottentot Venus and the Great Chain of Being." *African Studies* 51, no. 2 (1992): 185–201.

Grahame, Kamini "Contesting Diversity in the Academy: Resistance to Women of Color Teaching Race, Class, Gender." *Race, Gender, and Class in Education* 11, no. 3 (2004): 54–73.

Gurung, Regan, and Kristin Vespia. "Looking Good, Teaching Well? Linking Liking, Looks and Learning." *Teaching of Psychology* 34, no. 1 (2007):185–201. doi:10.1080/00986280709336641.

Hall, Stuart. *Race: The Floating Signifier.* North Hampton, MA: Media Education Foundation, 1996.
Harlow, Roxanna "'Race doesn't matter, but . . .': The Effect of Race on Professor's Experiences and Emotional Management in Undergraduate College Classrooms." *Social Psychology Quarterly* 66, no. 41 (2003): 348–67.
Hiddleston, James. *Understanding Postcolonialism.* New York, NY: Routledge Press, 2014.
hooks, bell. *Writing Beyond Race.* New York, NY: Routledge Press, 2013.
hooks, bell. *Black Looks: Race and Representation.* New York: Routledge Press, 2015.
Hornstein, Henry. "Student Evaluations of Teaching Are an Inadequate Assessment Tool for Evaluating Faculty Performance." *Cogent Education* 4, no. 1 (2017): 1–8. doi:10.1080/2331186X.2017.1304016.
James, Denise. "Playing the Race Game: A Response to Thandeka's 'Whites: Made in America.'" *The Pluralist* 13, no. 1 (2017): 51–8. doi:10.5406/pluralist.13.1.0051.
King, Joyce E. "Dysconscious Racism: Ideology, Identity, and the Miseducation of Teachers." *Journal of Negro Education*, 60, no. 2 (1991): 133–46.
Ladson-Billings, Gloria "The (R)evolution Will Not Be Standardized: Teacher Education, Hip Hop Pedagogy, and Culturally Relevant Pedagogy 2.0." In *Culturally Sustaining Pedagogies*, edited by Django Paris and H. Samy Alim, 141–56. New York, NY: Teachers College Press, 2017.
Ladson-Billings, Gloria and William F. Tate IV. "Toward a Critical Race Theory of Education." In *Critical Race Theory in Education: All God's Children Got a Song*, edited by Adrienne D. Dixson and Celia K. Rousseau, 11–30. New York, NY: Routledge Press, 2006.
Littleford, Linh Nguyen, Katherine, Ong, Andy Tseng, Jennifer Milliken, and Sonya Humy. "Perceptions of European American and African American Instructors Teaching Race-focused Courses. *Journal of Diversity in Higher Education* 3, no. 4 (2010): 230–44. doi:10.1037/a0020950.
Loewan, James W. *Lies My Teacher Told Me: Everything Your American History Text Got Wrong.* New York, NY: New York Press, 1996/2018.
Lorde, Audre. *Sister/Outsider: Essays and Speeches.* New York, NY: Random House, 1984/2007.
Love, Bettina. *We Want to Do More Than Survive: Abolitionist Teaching and the Pursuit of Educational Freedom.* Boston, MA: Beacon Press, 2019.
Lurie, Edward. "Louis Agassiz and the Races of Man." *The University of Chicago Press on Behalf of the History of Science Society* 45, 3 (1954): 227–42.
Madyun, Na'im, Sheneka M. Williams, Ebony O. McGee, and H. Richard Milner. "On the Importance of African American Faculty in Higher Education: Implications and Recommendations." *Educational Foundations* Summer/Fall (2013): 65–82.
Marable, Manning. *Speaking Truth to Power: Essays on Race, Resistance, and Radicalism.* Boulder, CO: Westview Press, 1996.
Marks, Ronald B. "Determinants of Student Evaluations of Global Measures of Instructor and Course Value." *Journal of Marketing Education* 22, no. 2 (2000): 108–19. doi:10.1177/027347530022205.

Mengel, Friederike, Jan Sauremann, and Ulf Zölitz. "Gender Bias in Teaching Evaluations." Discussion Paper Series 11000, IZA Institute of Labor Economics, Bonn, Germany September 2017.

Modica, Jonathon L, and Ketevan Mamiseishvili. "Black Faculty at Research Universities: Has Significant Progress Occurred?" *Negro Educational Review* 61, no. 1–4 (2010): 107–22.

Myers, Samuel L. and Caroline S. Turner. "The Effects of PhD Supply on Minority Faculty Representation." *American Economic Review* 94, no. 2 (2004): 296–301.

Omi, Michael, and Howard Winant. *Racial Formation in the United States*. 3rd ed. New York, NY: Routledge, 2015.

Pabon, Amber, and Vincent Basile. "Can We Say the 'R' Word?: Identifying and Disrupting Colorblind Epistemologies in a Teacher Education Methods Course." *Educational Studies* 55, no. 6 (2019): 633–50. doi:10.3102/00131946.2019.1674312.

Perry, Armon, Sherry Wallace, Sharon Moore, and Gwendolyn Perry-Burney. "Understanding Student Evaluations: A Black Faculty Perspective." *Faculty Scholarship* 15 (2015). http//ir.library.louisville.edu/faculty/15.

Pittman, Chavella. "Race and Gender Oppression in the Classroom: The Experiences of Women Faculty of Color with White Male Students. *Teaching Sociology* 38, no. 3 (2010): 183–96. doi: 10.1177/0092055x10370120.

Reid, Landon D. "The Role of Perceived Race and Gender in the Evaluation of College Teaching in Ratemyprofessors.Com." *Journal of Diversity in Higher Education* 3, no. 3 (2010): 137–52.

Riggs, Marlon. (Producer/Director). (1987). Ethnic notions [Video]. Available from California Newreel, 149 9th Street/420, San Francisco CA 94103.

Seldin, Peter. "When Students Rate Professors." *The Chronicle of Higher Education*, July 21, 1993.

Shujaa, Mwalimu, ed. *Too Much Schooling, Too Little Education: A Paradox of Black Life in White Societies*. Trenton, NJ: African World Press, 1995.

Schama, Simon. *Rough Crossings: Britain, the Slaves and the American Revolution*. New York, NY: Ecco Press, 2006.

Sleeter, Christine. "Critical Race Theory and the Whiteness of Teacher Education." *Urban Education* 52, no. 2 (2017): 155–69. doi:10.1177/0042085916668957.

Solórzano, Daniel G., and Tara J. Yosso. "Critical Race Methodology: Counter-Storytelling as an Analytical Framework for Education Research." *Qualitative Inquiry* 8, no. 1 (2002): 23–44. doi:10.1177/107780040200800103.

Stanley, Christine, ed. *Faculty of Color: Teaching in Predominantly White Colleges and Universities*. Bolton, MA: Anker Publishing Company, 2006.

Strauss, Anselm., and Juliet Corbin. *Basics of Qualitative Research: Grounded Theory Procedures and Techniques*. Thousand Oaks, CA: Sage Publication, 1990.

Thompson, Chasity Q. (2008). "Recruitment, Retention, and Mentoring Faculty of Color: The Chronicle Continues." *New Directions for Higher Education* 143 (2008): 47–54. doi:10.1002/he.312.

Tillman-Kelly, Derrick. (2020). How we got here: Racism + higher education [PowerPoint slides]. https://www.youtube.com/watch?v=sbCz6Ph2hTc.

Tuitt, Frank, Michele Hanna, Lisa Martinez, María del Carmen Salazar, and Rachel Griffin. "Teaching in the Line of Fire: Faculty of Color in the Academy." *Thought and Action: NEA Higher Education Journal* (Fall 2009): 65–74. http://beta.nsea-nv.org/assets/docs/HE/TA09LineofFire.pdf.

Turner, Caroline Sotello Viernes "Women of Color in Academe: Living with Multiple Marginality." *The Journal of Higher Education* 173, no. 1 (2002): 74–93. doi:10.1080/00221546.2002.11777131.

Turner, Caroline Sotello Viernes. "Incorporation and Marginalization in the Academy: From Border Toward Center for Faculty of Color." *Journal of Black Studies* 34, no. (2003): 122–5. doi:10.1177/0021934703253689.

Turner, Caroline Sotello Viernes, Juan Carlos González, and Kathleen Wong. "Faculty Women of Color: The Critical Nexus of Race and Gender." *Journal of Diversity in Higher Education* 4, no. 4 (2011): 199–211. doi:10.1037/a0024630.

Woodson, Carter Godwin. *The Miseducation of the Ne*gro. Trenton, NJ: Africa World Press, 1933/1998.

United States Department of Education. *Characteristics of Postsecondary Faculty; The Condition of Education*. Washington, DC: National Center for Education Statistics, 2018. https://nces.ed.gov/fastfacts/display.asp?id=61.

Chapter 2

Dismantling the Architecture of "Good" Teaching

Donyell L. Roseboro

For the past several decades, researchers have disrupted the notion that course evaluations are objective measures of student learning. Early research on student evaluations suggested that such evaluations were consistent, stable over time, and reliable indicators of student learning.[1] More recent research suggests that they are, instead, subjective indicators of student perceptions of learning,[2] perceptions that are inherently bound by the implicit biases students bring to the classroom with respect to gender and race.[3] The validity and integrity of student course evaluations matters most when such ratings factor heavily into tenure and promotion decisions. Indeed, student course evaluations presume all faculty teach from a perceived position of intellectual competence.

For Black faculty who teach with the legacy of eugenics, the act of teaching has been and continues to be a political one to counter assumptions of intellectual inferiority.[4] Knowing that promotion and tenure often depends upon students' course evaluations and that these evaluations cannot be unequivocally disconnected from the biases that students bring to the classroom, I turn to the question—how do Black faculty members enter this evaluative space when white students disassociate Black racial identity from intellectualism and, by extension, collegiate teaching competence? This chapter thus grapples with stereotype congruence as a perpetually reproductive narrative. In defining stereotype congruence, Aruguete, Slater, and Mwaikinda note:

> For example, seeing a Black professor might elicit the stereotype that African Americans lack intellectual competence. Once the stereotype is elicited, the student may be more likely to search for and remember negative aspects of the professor's behavior (stereotype congruent information). The influence of

the stereotype is not conscious or deliberate, and is therefore hard to control. (Dovidio & Gaertner, 2004)[5]

Absent a complete eradication of systemic racism, particularly those ideologies strengthened by eugenics 2.0, we face the very real possibility that student perceptions of teaching not only do not measure "good" teaching but actually reinforce assumptions about who is smart/qualified/capable enough to teach in the academy.[6] It is this reproductive element to student course evaluations that perhaps most insidiously undermines Black faculty members at predominantly white institutions.

As a Black teacher educator at predominantly white universities for the last sixteen years, I enter this space with certain heaviness, a questioning that troubles my hope. I live the fear I felt as an untenured faculty member finding the courage to read my course evaluations. Having been an administrator for seven and a half years, I have listened to faculty senators debate the value of student course evaluations, cringed when reading particularly vicious comments on those course evaluations, and talked with faculty about identifying alternative evidence to define good teaching. Now, as a full professor, I hear the echo of those defining words wielded with precision to evaluate the teaching of those who seek promotion to full professor. And so, it is this narrative of good teaching, contextualized historically, that I interrogate.

THE HISTORY OF BLACK FACULTY IN ACADEMIA

When in 2007 the *Journal of Blacks in Higher Education* reported on the numbers of African American faculty in academia, the highest percentage of those faculty was 6.8 percent at the University of Alabama, Tuscaloosa. By 2018, there were 1.5 million faculty members in higher education. Of those, 6 percent were Black.[7] When considering academic rank, African Americans were just 4 percent of the population of full professors. At the Assistant Professor rank, we comprised 8 percent of the population. Indeed, Black faculty are more likely to teach at community colleges and Historically Black Institutions. Even when hired at predominantly white four-year institutions, Black faculty often lack the positional authority to affect decision-making processes.[8] They simply are not in positions that could, by virtue of the position, influence change. In as much as representation is critical to how Black folks are interpreted in the world, when and how Black faculty are incorporated into the decision-making structure of the institution thus remains a fundamental question.

When the first Black scholars entered academia in the United States, they did so with formalized racist laws and policies in place in a country with clear disregard for the value of Black intellect. Not only did Supreme Court mandates like *Plessy* v. *Fergusen* normalize segregated facilities, local level translation of that ruling further reinforced the assumptions of inferiority that would justify for white folks the allocation of inferior facilities to Black people. Moreover, housing and schooling practices reinforced the notion that Black Americans were inferior, corporate lending practices limited entrepreneurial opportunities at the same time that white Americans wielded political control to institutionalize white superiority. When Dr. W. E. B. DuBois (1868–1963), Dr. Carter G. Woodson (1875–1950) and Dr. Charles H. Wesley (1891–1967) joined the professorate, they were pioneers and anomalies in the white imagination precisely because they lived an intellectual reality that challenged normative assumptions about Black intellectual inferiority. All received their PhDs from Harvard University. Dubois taught at Atlanta University while Woodson and Wesley taught at Howard, with Wesley going on to serve as president of Wilberforce University and Central State University. All were prolific thinkers and writers whose scope of work fundamentally shaped what we know about the history of African Americans in the United States.

With their lives shaped by Jim Crow segregation and the politics of desegregation, they wrote Black consciousness in historical, sociological, and psychological complexity. In as much as their academic success structured an architectural narrative of Black folks in the United States, that narrative must always include the influence of Georgiana Simpson, Sadie Tanner Mossell Alexander, Eva Beatrice Dykes, and Anna Julia Cooper, the first four Black women to receive PhDs in the United States. Although they may not have gone on to traditional academic careers,[9] their thinking, writing, and teaching shaped the scholarly trajectory of Black people in the United States. Cooper's writing, in particular, inspired Black feminism and called into question the difficulty in privileging identities that marginalize in distinctly different ways. Perhaps most important, her focus on "when and where I enter" lays the groundwork for examining Black faculty in the academy.

Prior to 1930, Dr. David Canton argues that at least fifty-one African Americans had earned PhDs. By 1943, there were more than 300.[10] When Dr. William Boyd Allison Davis earned tenure at the University of Chicago in 1947 and a full professor in 1948, he became the first African American faculty member to achieve those distinctions in academia. Prior to accepting the position at the University of Chicago, Davis earned master's degrees in English and Anthropology from Harvard University, studied at the London School of Economics, taught at Dillard University and later Hampton Institute from 1925 to 1931 and, continued his career for a year at Yale University on a research fellowship. By 1941 his research in Mississippi led to the publication of *Deep South: A Social Anthropological Study of Caste and Class*.

I highlight these accomplishments here and return to the significance of Cooper's epistemological framing of Black faculty in the predominantly white academy. Allison's interdisciplinary academic pedigree crossed the fields of English, Anthropology, and Economics with three graduate degrees from two "prestigious" institutions and a research fellowship from another Ivy League Institution. His *entering* of the academy was predicated on an acquisition of white intellectualism at the same time he used that intellectualism to conduct research that unveiled the structural implications of race and racism, class and classism.

To return to the question—how do Black faculty members enter this evaluative space when white students disassociate Black racial identity from intellectualism and, by extension, collegiate teaching competence? Entering is spatial, bound by time, and connected. When one enters, the characteristics of the space shift. In entering, we move. Our presence changes the sensory landscape, whether that is physical or virtual. When we enter, we do so in time. That entering thus connects us to the moment before we entered, the moment we enter, and, assuming we leave, the moment we depart. In specific ways, entering is infinitely bound by time. There were many moments that led us to that one place at that one time. And those moments live at the intersection of moments, shaped by our connections to others who may have pushed us toward a moment or fought to keep us from it. For Black faculty in academia, it is this entering which marks our presence.

When Cooper asked "What are we worth" in 1892, she coupled the question of entering with one of value. It remains a salient question for any examination of Black faculty in academia. Such a question forces us to examine the intrinsic and extrinsic value and the mechanisms for determining worth. How do we determine that worth over time when it, in this country, is calculated only in tangible terms like property, when that calculation never accounted for the incalculable humanity of Black folks as people? Indeed, "These bodies of ours often come to us mortgaged to their full value," such that our worth is predetermined not just by how we enter, but shaped by the lives, histories, and worth of those that contributed to our genesis.[11] In that, we inherit a certain measure of worth and that measure may differ depending on the perceived worth of the identities we carry; Black academics must habitually confront any inheritance that binds us to servitude and deference because we live with colonizing beliefs that Black is less than, justifiably exploited, and corrupt. Any analysis of student course evaluations in relation to Black academics must, therefore, face these questions of worth and value, both of which sit in the nexus of inheritance and presence. The course evaluations our students complete are thus marked by the beliefs they have inherited in relation to the bodies they interpret when we enter academic space.

THE CONSTRUCTION OF BLACK TEACHER IDENTITIES IN COLONIZING SPACES

Intelligence, Ability, and Eugenics

As we examine the construction of Black teacher identities in the United States, we must deconstruct the evolution of that identity in colonizing space. When Fanon theorized the effects of colonization on Black identity development, he argued that colonization framed Black identity as impure, neurotic, and disordered navigating an inferiority complex created within and because of that colonizing structure.[12] Indeed, coloniality assumes a certain humanity inevitably defined by particular hegemonic "key traits" which establish western (and by implication, whiteness), as superior.[13] The perniciousness of this othered and inferior identity evolved with the continued introduction of research to further nuance, explain, and justify notions of inferiority.[14] The Eugenics movement during the first four decades of the twentieth century, in particular, inspired an ideological shaping of race-based superiority and thus led to the justification of subsequent medical practices that sterilized, disfigured, and, at times, contributed to the deaths of people deemed genetically inferior.

The Tuskegee Syphilis study which occurred from 1932 to 1972 stands as just one example of the ideological assumption that Black folk were inferior, less deserving, and worthy of genetic erasure. Researchers' intentional decision not to treat Black men who were infected with syphilis for the sake of witnessing the progression of the disease left many to die when treatment existed. Subsequent federal hearings and apologies later led to the reform of research protocols to protect human subjects. The persistence of these medical experiments into the 1990s represents the long-lasting dismissiveness of Black bodies and intellect. It represents this dismissiveness and at the same time it fuels distrust among Black folk who see the health care enterprise as indicative of white supremacist structures that reinforce and recast Black people as less than. Indeed,

> the history of medical and research abuse of African Americans goes well beyond Tuskegee. Harriet Washington eloquently describes the history of medical experimentation and abuse, demonstrating that mistrust of medical research and the health care infrastructure is extensive and persistent among African Americans and illustrating that more than four centuries of a biomedical enterprise designed to exploit African Americans is a principal contributor to current mistrust.[15]

It was this assumption that some genes were better than others that laid the foundation for genocide, undergird racial segregation, and solidified white privilege.

Although eugenics was critiqued at the time, its impact on teaching, research, and policy in the United States remains. Its inherent assumptions around intelligence and ability allowed for the passage of legal decisions from slavery to Jim Crow to the *Plessy* v. *Fergusen* Supreme Court decision that policed and segregated Black bodies. The presumed intellectual inferiority of Black folks allowed for what Carter G. Woodson referred to as the "mis-education of the Negro."[16] Although a number of scholars have since recognized the intellectual rigor of Black teaching in segregated schools for Black children (e.g., Vanessa Siddle Walker, Gloria Ladson-Billings, Hilton Kelly, Audrey McCluskey), such schools were notoriously underfunded and under-resourced serving families who were intentionally disenfranchised and socioeconomically disadvantaged. Indeed, when NAACP attorneys argued the Brown case before the Supreme Court, they based their arguments on the assumption that school reputation and teacher quality were intangible characteristics that provided some students with a better education than others. Those arguments, however, unintentionally reinscribed colonizing definitions of intellect, ability, and goodness. With Black people marked as inferior during the colonial occupation of the United States, subsequently relegated to subservient by law and policy, and "scientifically" labeled as worthy of genetic erasure, Black teachers would never have been included in any white narrative of high-quality teacher. Nor would any school serving primarily Black students have been comparatively elevated to higher prestige than a school serving primarily white students.

The ultimate question of inferiority and its complicated entanglement in law, policy, and practice lies at the core of any current debate about how we define good teaching. In its final decision in *Brown* v. *Board of Education*, Chief Justice Earl Warren wrote, "To separate them [children in grade and high schools] from others of similar age and qualifications solely because of their race generates a feeling of inferiority as to their status in the community that may affect their hearts and minds in a way unlikely to ever be undone."[17] That feeling of inferiority existed in tandem with a belief that white students, teachers, and schools were automatically superior. Black teachers and students struggled with and against the psychological effects of these intersecting beliefs. That struggle, however, could not undo the ideological inheritance that remains.

THE MULTIPLIER EFFECT: REPRODUCING WHITENESS

As we examine the socio-historical contexts of Black faculty in academia, it is not enough to consider the history of race relations and racism in the United

States. We must also examine the reproduction of whiteness in current institutional forms and processes. If we consider whiteness as

> a political, economic and cultural system in which Whites overwhelmingly control power and material resources, conscious and unconscious ideas of white superiority and entitlement are widespread, and relations of white dominance and nonwhite subordination are daily reenacted across a broad array of institutions and social settings," then can deconstruct how the ideology becomes systemic and impervious.[18]

As the ideological assumptions are reenacted daily, so do they embed themselves as normative, beyond critique, and consequently become synonymous with inherited goodness. At the core of this examination is this idea that "Whiteness is simultaneously an identity, a status, and a property produced by the ideology of racial hierarchy and inextricably linked to economic benefits legitimized through legal status."[19] It is subsequently reproduced through discursive practice, law, policy, and schooling. It is this reproduction that manifests on college campuses nationwide.

School Identity

Colleges and universities exist within a ranking system that identifies some as prestigious and others as not. Those classifications attempt to capture the intangible, school quality, using quantitative measures like research productivity. Such classifications, when automatically divorced from the colonizing histories that gave birth to them, inevitably reproduce whiteness when they extend hegemonic assumptions about high-quality education and good teaching. When considering university reputation within the ranking system for example,

> As with the Olympic Games, the global university rankings pull together actors who share both an appreciation for the highest levels of performance on a worldwide stage and a drive to compete. Not all entrants in these contests are created equal, however. To perform well in elite competitions such as the Olympic Games and the global university rankings—which require many years of consistently high-quality, specialized training and often the fielding of large, multimember teams, the development of unique strategies, and the reliance on high-cost equipment or facilities—being smart and rich helps. Deep familiarity and experience with the rules of the game is also a key asset, as success often hinges on leveraging key strengths and minimizing weaknesses.[20]

The game metaphor here evokes a critical reminder that any definition of academic quality emerges within linguistic and cultural systems that assign meaning to the constituent parts of that system. When and how we enter the game could have profound implications on how we compete and how we finish. Although intellect matters, knowledge of the rules and structure of the game eliminates hesitation and better positions some to win.

More recent research argues that students base their institution selection on the school's reputation, and reputation is often tied to two particular characteristics—institution size and admission selectivity.[21] Critics of current definitions of reputation or prestige in colleges and universities argue that there are varying models of quality (i.e., resource/reputation, client-centered, strategic investment, and talent development) and different comparative measures (i.e., whole university v. distinct programs or departments). Comparing across different models and measures makes ranking systems problematic. Contextualizing this tension within a colonizing structure that historically privileges western epistemologies illuminates the challenge facing universities that primarily serve underrepresented populations.

If we consider universities as part of a more comprehensive continuum of schooling, then we can examine the extent to which beliefs about school reputation and prestige get inextricably linked to school quality and, in that linking, reinscribe colonizing attitudes that stigmatize Black schools, teachers, and the communities they serve. The de-segregation of schools, including colleges and universities, did not erase centuries of racism grounded in a fundamental assumption about Black intellectual inferiority. Instead, decades post de-segregation, the U.S. educational system has witnessed an ideological entrenchment of those same ideas within the discourse of school choice and neighborhood schools. This discourse dichotomizes schools between the good and the bad, disproportionately ascribing the "bad school" label and, by consequence, what Erving Goffman termed "stigmatized identity"[22] to schools with Black and Brown children.[23] Once assigned, stigmatized identities are difficult to manage. While individuals with stigmatized identities typically navigate by attempting to pass with the stigma, admitting the stigma, or detaching from the stigma, institutions that carry stigmatized identities can transfer that stigma to those who affiliate with the institution. If Blackness carries with it a historicized stigma, then schools that serve Black students can embody that stigma.

If we further contextualize school reputation, prestige, and quality within larger capitalist assumptions surrounding free choice and competition, then we can interrogate the color-blind assumption that market forces improve school quality irrespective of the stigmatized identities that schools serving mostly Black students might carry. Although school choice programs can expand possibilities, those possibilities are not without context and consequence. Indeed, several recent researchers have argued that such programs re-segregate students racially and do little to dismantle the ideology that ascribes intellectual inferiority to Black folks and superior intellect to whites.[24]

Given the complicated relationship between college rankings, reputation, school choice, and identity, teachers who attended institutions that are highly ranked, with good reputations stand to inherit an assumption of intellectual competence that may not be afforded those who attend lesser-known, poorly ranked institutions with no widely known reputation. This inherited intellectual competence opens doors and possibilities. Perhaps most important, it translates such that others may perceive an instructor to have expertise even when that instructor may not. For Black teachers who may not automatically inherit this presumption of competence, the road to proof depends on each classroom interaction, discursive response, and professional experience. When one does not inherit, one must earn the right to enter. Here again, we turn to the question of value raised by Anna Julia Cooper. How do we navigate the tension between inherited intellectual value and earned intellectual value?

Stigmatized Identities, Stereotype Threat, and the Oppositional Gaze

As with any profession, the quality of one's teaching changes over time with some assumption that additional experiences enhance one's teaching abilities. What counts as experience within a colonizing system inevitably reproduces whiteness. Certain experiences are privileged for academic positions and, in as much as hiring committees may claim some sort of objectivity when evaluating candidate experience, it is the assumption about what counts as reputable experience that matters. And when experience requires opportunity and opportunities are wedded to racial hierarchies, entering academia for Black faculty demands a lived experience predicated upon the assumption that one will traverse this opportunity conundrum, that one will find the opportunities within a structure that intentionally withholds them from Black folk.

To speak to the idea of teacher experience, I start with the notion that teachers universally have shared knowledge, pose critical questions, and assess student understanding. Teaching demands a certain level of knowledge or expertise. It requires some significant study. In more recent years, educational theorists have argued that teachers are not merely conveyers of information. To be a "good teacher," we must teach who we are, developing an inward searching compass that can

> project the condition of my soul onto my students, my subject, and our way of being together. The entanglements I experience in the classroom are often no

more or less than the convolutions of my inner life. Viewed from this angle, teaching holds a mirror to the soul. If I am willing to look in that mirror, and not run from what I see, I have a chance to gain self-knowledge—and knowing myself is as crucial to good teaching as knowing my students and my subject.[25]

This definition of teaching differs greatly from those that focus only on the expertise of the instructor, arbiter of information and grades. The kinds of experiences necessary to hone one's craft as intellectual expert differ from those that would make one a better reflective mirror to the soul. How, why, and in what manner instructors define good teaching guide the seeking of particular experiences that will allow us to grow in that image.

When Black faculty enter predominantly white universities, aside from the colonizing expectation that they are intellectually inferior, they also confront expectations about experience that determine what matters in academic space. Who determines which experiences count? And, in that counting, which definitions of good teaching are privileged? In the promotion and tenure process, faculty submit teaching evaluations that are usually based on student perceptions, peer observations that are typically done by colleagues in the department, and examples of professional development related to teaching. For some universities, the only experiences that matter are those that are directly related to acquisition of content, for other universities, improving one's pedagogy is a worthwhile endeavor, while at other institutions, a wide array of activities could count as relevant to improving one's teaching. And while the college teaching environment has certainly changed over the last decade, increasingly, one's experience with online teaching matters. Indeed, virtual spaces in the teaching universe illuminate instructor gifts or shortcomings in equally relevant ways.

Moreover, professional development for instructors typically follows two lines of thinking—on the one hand, we seek to develop the skills of instructors, their ability to facilitate groups, engage the whole class, and listen; on the other hand, we seek to develop their thinking about a problem. In as much as "teaching reflects the intentional effort to influence another human being for the good rather than for the bad," relevant experiences could represent the total of one's lived experience.[26] Lived experience, however, is not counted for promotion and tenure purposes. And while lived experience may not "count" for tenure and promotion purposes, it matters in that it has shaped the trajectory of Black faculty into academia. Those experiences have allowed Black faculty access to certain spaces, opportunities, and discourse such that they can translate themselves to white faculty and within white-dominated power structures.

This translation can come at high cost if Black faculty constantly navigate racially antagonizing spaces, limited opportunities, and demeaning discourse that privileges certain cultural norms.[27] The tax burden of this racially contextualized navigation has persistently disrupted the promotion and tenure track for Black faculty as they engage in research, teaching, service, and unofficial diversity consulting activities that add value to the institution but, more often than not, do not add value according to promotion and tenure parameters. Numerous researchers have cited Black faculty's cultural obligations to engage in service, mentoring, and teaching as a means to uplift the race.[28] When that purpose conflicts with the standardized promotion and tenure guidelines that focus on disciplinary teaching, scholarship, and service, Black faculty face the untenable position of choosing or trying to work toward both. And, if attempting to intersect these purposes with equal force, Black faculty run the risk of appearing ill-prepared, incompetent, and uncommitted.

Confronting these appearances forces Black faculty to constantly face stereotype threat and the myriad of ways it manifests itself in daily professional interactions. Casad and Bryant (2016) suggest that individuals with stigmatized identities function with the notion that those identities may negatively shape certain contexts. In particular, and of importance to the success of Black faculty at predominantly white institutions, "When employees view their personal identity (e.g., woman, African American) as incompatible with their professional identity (e.g., lawyer) because of stereotype threat in the workplace, negative mental health consequences are likely."[29] To survive, faculty may disengage yet that disengagement can further reinforce the stereotype threat and lend credence to colleagues' assumptions that a Black faculty member is unqualified.

When marked as unqualified, Black faculty members do not belong in academia. Belonging implies acceptance, membership, affinity. It suggests that an individual feels valued by the organization and a sense of connection within and to a particular group or institution.[30] The implications of social connectedness can be profound since the lack thereof can impede our ability to self-regulate and increase mortality.[31] If Black faculty's lived experience situates them in the realm of not yet accepted, not quite trusted, or not quite smart enough, then claiming any sense of belonging at the institution could prove impossible. And, perhaps, more important, could be futile. How does one belong within a system designed to cast one's entire race as inferior?

When academic spaces at predominantly white institutions exist as antithetical to belonging for Black faculty members, Black faculty members' lived experience in those spaces stands in a priori opposition. Lived experiences developed in opposition give rise to a double consciousness that mirrors the multiplicative identities with which Black folks exist.[32] With multiplicative identity, the individual identities we claim can be infinite while the whole person with which we enter the world appears as a singular representation. The challenge remains constant for Black faculty living in opposition to put forward a cohesive self to the world despite the spatial structures that diminish, erase, or marginalize. Indeed, living in opposition can give voice and gaze to agency as Black faculty construct third spaces of belonging at PWIs.

When one's professional space does not automatically embrace one's identity, one's responses to that space confronts and contests in its oppositional existence. Behari-Leak and le Roux capture the ways that third spaces can emerge as spaces of possibility in that opposition by outlining the evolution of third space from first and second space,

> Homi Bhabha (1994) first developed the concept of third space as a metaphor for the space in which two cultures meet. Bhabha (1994) identified a dynamic, "in-between space" in which cultural translation takes place. When migrants left their homes (1st place) to settle in a foreign land (2nd place), they defied the notion that a pure, homogeneous cultural place exists. The new "in-between" space shares attributes of both spaces (Saudelli, 2012) and is a generative space where academics combine diverse knowledges into new insights and plans for action. (Bhabha, 1990)[33]

Third spaces cultivate the integration of diverse knowledge into action plans and, in so doing, translate opposition into agency. In as much as third spaces can be conduits for action, for Black faculty working the dichotomy, such spaces demand expertise in each space and identity.

This expertise in translating space and identity comes with an oppositional gaze that allows Black faculty to see the distinctions in and bridges between each space. It is a gaze that allows us to see within, without, and beyond. This oppositional gaze represents a pivot point toward agency, one that binds the past to the present to the future. hooks captures this pivot by noting

> that all attempts to repress our/black peoples' right to gaze had produced in us an overwhelming longing to look, a rebellious desire, an oppositional gaze. By courageously looking, we defiantly declared: "Not only will I stare. I want my look to change reality." Even if the worse circumstances of domination, the ability to manipulate one's gaze in the face of structures of domination that would contain it opens up the possibility of agency.[34]

Oppositional gazes interrogate truth and reality; they displace normative assumptions about what was and visualize what can be. To be born Black, however, does not presume that one inherits an oppositional gaze. Such gazes are learned in spite of colonizing space, discourse, and beliefs that would seek to engender colonized thinking. It is this counter to colonized thinking that signifies the critical capacity of an oppositional gaze.

Working from intersectional perspectives allows us to consider how those points represent the ways in which Black faculty operate with competing epistemologies. These dueling ways of maneuvering through and responding to the world demand attention if universities are to ever embrace the value of Black faculty as more than the limited sum of promotion and tenure criteria. Indeed,

> as the faculty diversifies and brings to the academy different ways of knowing, it is important that they are given the opportunity for individual expression—authentic and spiritual. The literature in this area is growing and indicates the need for departments to recognize the underlying messages conveyed to faculty of color that devalue their research and writing in an oppressive fashion (see Table 30). For example, Louis (2007) urged scholars to accept, as legitimate ways of knowing, "knowledge systems that do not necessarily conform to Western academic standards."[35]

This question of legitimacy with respect to epistemology rests at the core of any examination of Black faculty at predominantly white institutions. How and when "othered" knowledge systems and the lived experiences that give rise to those epistemologies emerge as accepted parts of the dominant promotion and tenure discourse remains a critical question.

COURSE EVALUATIONS AS REPRODUCTIONS OF WHITENESS

Historically, faculty members of color, particularly women of color have received student course evaluations that were lower than those of their white male counterparts.[36] Despite this context, universities continue to engage in the course evaluation process and to centralize course evaluations in the promotion and tenure process. The central role that they continue to play in promotion and tenure allows students who have inherited colonizing attitudes to provide formalized feedback on the quality of an instructor's teaching. The use of course evaluations as evidence of good teaching presumes a neutrality with respect to identity, or it assumes that students who may have unexamined privilege can acknowledge their heteronormative assumptions and actively work against those to provide a fair evaluation of Black faculty. Equally important, seminal scholarship suggests that educational institutions inevitably reproduce societal structures by examining "the ways in which macro-structures play out in the interactions, rituals, and traditions of the classroom."[37] Schools then act as colonizing spaces that reproduce whiteness through their rewards and consequences, rules and procedures, curricula, and leadership structures. For Black faculty to teach within this system requires an understanding of the structure, a willingness to navigate it, and an ability to keep one's self in tack while existing in opposition.

Course evaluations are bound by language. Language is bound by the dominant ideologies that led to its formation. In essence, words are never neutral. They connote, frame, and extend ideas. In my most recent course evaluations, the questions asked students to:

Describe the frequency of your instructor's teaching procedures.

- Displayed a personal interest in students and their learning
- Found ways to help students answer their own questions
- Demonstrated the importance and significance of the subject matter
- Made it clear how each topic fit into the course
- Explained course material clearly and concisely
- Introduced stimulating ideas about the subject
- Inspired students to set and achieve goals which really challenged them

Students' responses to these questions depend entirely on how they translate the concepts. To "display a personal interest in students and their learning" could mean that the instructor reaches out to each student individually several times during the course of the semester, or it could mean that the instructor personalizes feedback. It could mean that the instructor asks students about their long-term academic goals or other coursework. It could mean that the instructor hosts drop-in office hours and spends time talking one-on-one with students. With "explained course materials clearly and concisely," students' perceptions about a faculty member's use of the English language could negatively affect their perception of the instructor's ability to explain course material clearly and concisely. Indeed, even the use of the term concisely comes with an inherent assumption that to explain concisely is somehow better. Dare I add that "stimulating ideas," and "inspire" are equally ambiguous terms that could come with a host of varied interpretations.

Decades of research in critical discourse analysis has demonstrated the ways that language acts as a medium of control, power, and privilege.[38] This research has evolved to iterate several core principles, including that language is a dialectical social construction. In short, language both influences and is influenced by cultural and historical contexts. It is imprecise in as much as it situates meaning. Perhaps more important, discourse is bound to materiality and, in this binding, voice, becomes embodied. Our bodies both shape and are shaped by language, creating a dialectical relationship in which meaning is translated in form. With that said, the significance of Black bodies to the course evaluation process matters. The ways students interpret those bodies lives in the architectural space between dominant and counter-narratives about who can be qualified, intellectual, or pedagogically inspirational, is the question that remains.

SPEAKING OF EXPERIENCE: A CONCLUSION

As a tenured, full professor who has served as a department chair and associate dean, I have witnessed the contradictory interpretations of course evaluations, the challenges faced by faculty of color, and the ways those same faculty are forced to use that which undermines their teaching to support an application for promotion and/or tenure. This usage reinscribes the ideological assumption that Black faculty are inferior in that course evaluations become semi-public knowledge in the promotion and tenure process. Their dissemination through the process, the re-reading that occurs, and the subsequent discussion about how these statements capture this faculty member's teaching inevitably construct a narrative about that faculty member in the academy. For Black faculty members, being forced to analyze and include those course evaluations in the promotion and tenure application may, in fact, re-traumatize. Re-reading and explaining them when they undercut one's ability and intellect requires more than a justification of one's methods. It requires a self-justification of one's right to be. And that prescribed self-justification reinforces the idea that one does not belong.

If we can accept that course evaluations live within a colonizing system that marks whiteness as superior, that this system is structured with language that privileges western ways of speaking, and that course evaluations employ that language as if all interpretations were singular, then we can understand precisely why those evaluations are ill-suited to be included in any promotion and tenure process. In my sixteen years as a tenure-track and tenured professor, not once have I been asked to submit with my course evaluations a statement indicating how I translate the evaluative criteria. Setting that point might just be a new beginning toward an interpretive genealogy that position the faculty member with the criteria—a person in relationship to language as both evolve over time. Using an interpretive genealogy forces us to find the kinship networks in the evaluative language—what speaks to our pedagogy and how does our pedagogy speak to the criteria? Doing so might actually cultivate space for us to map who we are to how we teach.

NOTES

1. Kenneth. A. Feldman, "Effective College Teaching from the Students' and Faculty's' View: Matched or Mismatched Priorities," *Research in Higher Education*

28, no. 4 (1988): 291–344; Nira Hativa, "University Instructors' Ratings Profiles: Stability Over Time, and Disciplinary Differences," *Research in Higher Education* 37, no. 3 (1996): 341–65. Hebert W. Marsh, "Students' Evaluations of University Teaching: Research Findings, Methodological Issues, and Directions for Further Research," *International Journal of Educational Research* 11 (1987): 253–388.

2. John V. Adams, "Student Evaluations: The Ratings Game," *Inquiry* 1, no. 2 (1997); Henry A. Hornstein, "Student Evaluations of Teaching Are an Inadequate Assessment Tool for Evaluating Faculty Performance," *Cogent Education* 4 (2017): 1–8.

3. On gender, see: Lillian MacNell, Adam Driscoll, and Andrea N. Hunt, "What's in a Name: Exposing Gender Bias in Student Ratings of Teaching," *Innovative Higher Education* 40 (2014): 291–303; Ellen M. Key, and Phillip J. Ardoin, "Students Rate Male Instructors More Highly Than Female Instructors. We Tried to Counter That Hidden Bias," *The Washington Post*, August 20, 2019; Suzanne Young, Leslie Rush, and Dave Shaw, "Evaluating Gender Bias in Rating of University Instructors' Teaching Effectiveness," *International Journal for the Scholarship of Teaching and Learning* 3, no. 2 (2009): 1–14. On race, see: Friederike Mengel, Jan Sauermann, and Ulf Zölitz, "Gender Bias in Teaching Evaluations" (discussion paper, Series Title, Institute of Labor Economics, Location, 2017); Katherine G. Hendrix, "Student Perceptions of the Influence of Race on Professor Credibility," *Journal of Black Studies* 28, no. 6 (1998): 738–63; A. K. Ho, Lotte Thomsen, and J. Sidanius, "Perceived Academic Competence and Overall Job Evaluations: Students' Evaluations of African American and European American Professors," *Journal of Applied Social Psychology* 39, no. 2 (2009): 389–406; Landon D. Reid, "The Role of Perceived Race and Gender in the Evaluation of College Teaching on RateMyProfessor.Com," *Journal of Diversity in Higher Education* 3, no. 3 (2010): 137–52.

4. C. Chitty, *Eugenics, Race and Intelligence in Education* (London: Continuum, 2007); Timothy Mccune, "Dewey's Dilemma: Eugenics, Education, and the Art of Living," *The Pluralist* 7, no. 3 (2012): 96–106; Richard J. Hernstein and Charles Murray, *The Bell Curve: Intelligence and Class Structure in American Life* (New York: Free Press Paperbacks, 1994); Jo C. Phelan, Bruce G. Link, and Naumi M. Feldman, "The Genomic Revolution and Beliefs About Essential Racial Differences: A Backdoor to Eugenics?" *American Sociological Review* 78, no. 2 (2013): 167–91.

5. Mara S. Aruguete, Joshua Slater, and S. R. Mwaikinda, "The Effects of Professors' Race and Clothing Style on Student Evaluations," *The Journal of Negro Education* 86, no. 4 (2017): 495.

6. Antonio Regalado, "Eugenics 2.0: We're at the Dawn of Choosing Ebryos by Health, Height, and More," *MIT Technology Review*, November 1, 2017.

7. National Center for Education Statistics, 2019. https://nces.ed.gov/fastfacts/display.asp?id=61.

8. A. B. Assensoh, "Trouble in the Promised Land: African American Studies Programs and the Challenges of Incorporation," *Journal of Black Studies* 34 (2003): 52–62.

9. Cooper served as president of Frelinghuysen University, Simpson taught at Dunbar high school in Washington, D.C. Simpson and Alexander had trouble

securing jobs in academia as Black women. Mossell turned down job offers at HBCUs because she was did not want to leave Philadelphia. After teaching at Dunbar High School, Dykes became a member of the English faculty at Howard University and then accepted a position as Chair of the English faculty at Oakwood College in Huntsville, Alabama. For more information, see Slater, Robert Bruce. "The First Black Faculty Members at the Nation's Highest-Ranked Universities." *The Journal of Blacks in Higher Education*, no. 22 (1998): 97–106. Accessed December 15, 2020. doi:10.2307/2998851.

10. Lois Elfman, "Two History Professors Chronicle the Lives of the First Black Scholars Hired at PWIs," *Diverse Education*, February 13, 2020.

11. Anna J. Cooper, *A Voice from the South* (Place of Original Publication: Original Publisher, 1892; Place of Online Publication, Online Publisher, 2000), 237. Retrieved from https://docsouth.unc.edu/church/cooper/cooper.html.

12. Frantz Fanon (1952/2008). *Black Skin, White Masks*. New York: Grove Press (Richard Philcox, Trans.).

13. Nelson Moldenado-Torres, "On the Coloniality of Human Rights," *Revista Crítica de Ciências Sociais* (2016): 117.

14. Garland E. Allen, "Eugenics and Modern Biology: Critiques of Eugenics 1910–1945," *Annals of Human Genetics 75*, (2011): 314–22; Ingrid Grenon and Joave Merrick, "Intellectual and Developmental Disabilities: Eugenics," *Frontiers in Public Health* 2 (2014); Felipe Vizcrrondo, "Human Enhancement: The New Eugenics," *The Linacre Quarterly* 81, no. 3 (2014): 239–43; Stephen Wilkinson, "'Eugenics Talk' and the Language of Bioethics," *Journal of Medical Ethics* 34 (2008): 467–71.

15. Darcell Scharff et al., "More than Tuskegee: Understanding Mistrust about Participation," *Journal of Health Care for the Poor and Underserved* 21 (2010): 880.

16. Carter G. Woodson, *The Mis-Education of the Negro*, 1933; Trenton, NJ: Africa World Press, 1990.

17. Brown v. Board of Education, 347 U.S. 483 (1953).

18. Francess L. Ansley, "Stirring the Ashes: Race Class and the Future of Civil Rights Scholarship," *Cornell Law Review* 74 (1988): 1024.

19. Marlo G. Hode and Rebecca J. Meisenbach, Rr., "Reproducing Whiteness Through Diversity: A Critical Discourse Analysis of the Pro-Affirmative Action Amicus Briefs in the *Fisher* Case," *Journal of Diversity in Higher Education* 10, no. 2 (2017): 165.

20. Maria Yudkevich, Philip Altbach, and Laura Rumbley, "Global University Rankings: The "Olympic Games" of Higher Education," *Prospects* 45 (2015): 413.

21. Kyle. Sweitzer and J. Fredericks. Volkwein, "Prestige Among Graduate and Professional Schools: Comparing the U.S. News' Graduate School Reputation Ratings Between Disciplines," *Research in Higher Education* 50, no. 8 (2009): 812–36.

22. Erving Goffman, *Stigma: Notes on the Management of Spoiled Identity* (New York, NY: Simon & Schuster, 1963).

23. Nihad Bunar and Anna Ambrose. "Schools, Choice and Reputation: Local Markets and the Distribution of Symbolic Capital in Segregated Cities," *Research in Comparative & International Education* 11, no. 1 (2016): 34–51; Linda

Darling-Hammond, *The Fiat World and Education: How America's Commitment to Equity Will Determine Our Future* (New York, NY: Teachers College Press, 2010); Lisa Delpit, *Multiplication is for White People: Raising Expectations for Other People's Children* (New York, NY: The New Press, 2012); D. Roseboro and C. Thompson, "To Virgo or not to Virgo": Examining the Closure and Reopening of a Neighborhood School in a Predominantly African American Community," *Equity & Excellence in Education* 47, no. 2 (2014): 187–207.

24. Gary Orfield and E. Frankenberg, "Increasingly Segregated and Unequal Schools as Courts Reverse Policy," *Education & Administration Quarterly* 50, no. 5 (2014): 718–34; Marc L. Stein, "Public School Choice and Racial Sorting. An Examination of Charter Schools in Indianapolis." *American Journal of Education* 121 (2015): 597–627.

25. Parker Palmer, "The heart of a teacher: Identify and integrity in teaching," *Site Title*, Date, 1997, 1. https://biochem.wisc.edu/sites/default/files/labs/attie/publications/Heart_of_a_Teacher.pdf.

26. Hansen (2001), 828, cited in E. Campbell, "The Ethics of Teaching as a Moral Profession," *Journal of Curriculum Inquiry* 38, no. 4 (2008).

27. Dade et al., "Assessing the Impact of Racism on Black Faculty in White Academe: A Collective Case Study of African American Female Faculty," *The Western Journal of Black Studies* 39, no. 2 (2015): 134–46; Shametrice Davis and Kelly Brown, "Automatically Discounted: Using Black Feminist Theory to Critically Analyze the Experiences of Black Female Faculty," *International Journal of Educational Leadership Preparation* 12, no. 1 (2017); Parsons et al., "General Experiences + Race + Racism = Work Lives of Black Faculty in Postsecondary Science Education." *Cultural Studies of Science Education* 13 (2018): 371–94; Josê E. Rodriguez, Kendall M. Campbell, Linda H. Pololi, "Addressing Disparities in Academic Medicine: What of the Minority Tax?" *BMC Medical Education* 15, no. 6 (2015): 1–5.

28. Djanna Hill-Brisbane, "Black Women Teacher Educators, Race, Uplift, and the Academic Other-Mother Identity," *Advancing Women in Leadership* 19 1–13; Caroline Turner, Juan González, and J. Luke Wood, "Faculty of Color in Academe: What 20 Years of Research Tells Us," *Journal of Diversity in Higher Education* 1, no. 3 (2008): 139–68.

29. Isis H. Settles, Robert M. Sellers, and Alphonse Damas Jr., "One Role or Two? The Function of Psychological Separation in Role Conflict," *Journal of Applied Psychology* 87, no. 3 (2002): 574–82; Isis H. Settles, "When Multiple Identities Interfere: The Role of Identity Centrality," *Personality & Social Psychology Bulletin* 30, no. 4 (2004): 487–500.

30. Karyn Hall, "Create a Sense of Belonging: Finding Ways to Belong Can Help Ease the Pain of Loneliness," *Psychology Today*, March 24, 2014.

31. Gregory M. Walton et al., "Mere Belonging: The Power of Social Connections," *Journal of Personality and Social Psychology* 102, no. 3 (2011): 513–32.

32. W. E. B. DuBois, "The Souls of Black Folk," in *The Oxford W. E. B. Dubois Reader*, ed. E. J. Sundquist (Oxford, UK: Oxford University Press, 1903), 97–240; Paul Willis, *Learning to Labor: How Working-Class Kids Get Working Class Jobs* (New York: Columbia University Press, 1977).

33. Kasturi Behari-Leak and Nataliele le Roux. "Between a Rock and a Hard Place, Third Space Practitioners Exercise Agency," *Perspectives in Education* 36, no. 1 (2018): 33.

34. bell hooks, *Teaching Community: A Pedagogy of Hope* (New York, NY: Routledge, 2003), 94.

35. Caroline. Turner, Juan González, and J. Luke Wood, "Faculty of Color in Academe: What 20 Years of Research Tells Us," *Journal of Diversity in Higher Education* 1, no. 3 (2008).

36. K. Chávez and K. Mitchell, "Exploring Bias in Student Evaluations: Gender, Race, and Ethnicity," *PS: Political Science and Politics* 53, no. 2 (2019): 270–74; Therese Houston, "Race and Gender Bias in Higher Education: Could Faculty Course Evaluations Impede Further Progress Towards Parity?" *Seattle Journal for Social Justice* 4, no. 2 (2006): 590–611; Edith Samuel, and N. Wane, "'Unsettling Relations': Racism and Sexism Experienced by Faculty of Color in a Predominantly White Canadian University," *The Journal of Negro Education* 74, no. 1 (2005): 76–87.

37. Rebecca Rogers et al., "Critical Discourse Analysis in Education: A Review of the Literature," *Review of Educational Research* 75, no. 3 (2005): 366. See for instance: Pierre Bourdieu, *Distinction: A Social Critique of the Judgment of Taste*, trans. R. Nice (London: Routledge, 1984); Samuel Bowles and Herber Gintis, *Schooling in Capitalist Society: Educational Reform and the Contradictions of Economic Life* (New York, NY: Basic Books, 1976); G. Ladson-Billings and W. Tate, "Towards a Critical Race Theory of Education," *Teachers College Record* 97, no. 1 (1995): 47–68; Willis, *Learning to Labor.*

38. See for instance: Jacques Derrida, *Of Grammatology* (Baltimore, MD: Johns Hopkins University Press, 1974); Norman Fairclough and Ruth Wodak, "Critical Discourse Analysis," in *Discourse as Social Interaction*, ed. T. van Dijk (London: Sage, 1997), 258–84; Michel Foucault, *Discipline and Punish: The Birth of the Prison* (Harmondsworth, UK: Penguin Books, 1979); Roger Fowler et al., *Language and Control* (London: Routledge, 1979); Robert Hodge and G. Kress, *Social Semiotics* (Cambridge, UK: Polity Press, 1988); Rogers et al., "Critical Discourse Analysis in Education."

REFERENCES

Adams, John V. "Student Evaluations: The Ratings Game." *Inquiry* 1, no. 2 (1997): 10–16.

Allen, Garland E. "Eugenics and Modern Biology: Critiques of Eugenics 1910-1945." *Annals of Human Genetics* 75, no. 3 (2011): 314–22. doi:10.1111/j.1469-1809.2011.00649.x.

Ansley, Francess L. "Stirring the Ashes: Race Class and the Future of Civil Rights Scholarship." *Cornell Law Review* 74 (1988): 993–1077.

Aruguete, Mara S., J. Slater, Joshua S. R. Mwaikindaekella. "The Effects of Professors' Race and Clothing Style on Student Evaluations." *The Journal of Negro Education* 86, no. 4 (2017): 494–502.

Assensoh, A. B. "Trouble in the Promised Land: African American Studies Programs and the Challenges of Incorporation." *Journal of Black Studies* 34, no. 4(2003): 52–62.

Behari-Leak, Kasturi and Nataliele Roux. "Between a Rock and a Hard Place, Third Space Practitioners Exercise Agency." *Perspectives in Education* 36, no. 1 (2018): 30–43.

Bhabha, Homi K. "The Third Space: Interview with Homi Bhabha." In *Identity: Community, Culture and Difference*, edited by J. Rutherford. London: Lawrence and Wishart, 1990.

Bhabha, Homi K. *The Location of Culture*. London: Routledge, 1994.

Bourdieu, Pierre. *Outline of a Theory of Practice*. Cambridge, UK: Cambridge University Press, 1977.

Bourdieu, Pierreierre. *Distinction: A Social Critique of the Judgment of Taste*, translated by R. Nice. London: Routledge, 1984.

Bowles, Samuel and Herber Gintis. *Schooling in Capitalist Society: Educational Reform and the Contradictions of Economic Life*. New York, NY: Basic Books, 1976.

Brown v. Board of Education, 347 U.S. 483. 1953. https://www.loc.gov/item/usrep347483/.

Bunar, Nihad and Anna Ambrose. "Schools, Choice and Reputation: Local Markets and the Distribution of Symbolic Capital in Segregated Cities." *Research in Comparative & International Education* 11, no. 1 (2016): 34–51.

Campbell, E. "The Ethics of Teaching as a Moral Profession." *Journal of Curriculum Inquiry* 38, no. 4 (2008): 357–85.

Casad, Bettina, and William. Bryant. "Addressing Stereotype Threat is Critical to Diversity and Inclusion in Organizational psychology. *Frontiers in Psychology* 7, no. (2016): 1–18.

Chávez, Kerry and Kristina Mitchell. "Exploring Bias in Student Evaluations: Gender, Race, and Ethnicity." *PS: Political Science and Politics* 53, no. 2 (2019): 270–74. https://www.cambridge.org/core/journals/ps-political-science-and-politics/article/exploring-bias-in-student-evaluations-gender-race-and-ethnicity/91670F6003965C5646680D314CF02FA4.

Chitty, C. *Eugenics, Race and Intelligence in Education*. London: Continuum, 2007.

Cooper, Anna J. *A Voice from the South*. Place of Original Publication: Original Publisher, 1892; Place of Online Publication, Online Publisher, 2000. https://docsouth.unc.edu/church/cooper/cooper.html.

Dade, Karen, Carlie Tartakov, Connie Hargrave, and Patricia Leigh. "Assessing the Impact of Racism on Black Faculty in White Academe: A Collective Case Study of African American Female Faculty." *The Western Journal of Black Studies* 39, no. 2 (2015): 134–46.

Darling-Hammond, Linda. *The Fiat World and Education: How America's Commitment to Equity Will Determine Our Future*. New York, NY: Teachers College Press, 2010.

Davis, Shametrice. and Kelly. Brown. "Automatically Discounted: Using Black Feminist Theory to Critically Analyze the Experiences of Black Female Faculty."

International Journal of Educational Leadership Preparation 12, no. 1 (2017). https://files.eric.ed.gov/fulltext/EJ1145466.pdf.

Delpit, Lisa. *Multiplication is for White People: Raising Expectations for Other People's Children*. New York, NY: The New Press, 2012.

Derrida, Jacques. *Of Grammatology*. Baltimore, MD: Johns Hopkins University Press, 1974.

DuBois, W. E. B. "The Souls of Black Folk." In *The Oxford W. E. B. Dubois Reader*, edited by E. J. Sundquist, 97–240. Oxford, UK: Oxford University Press, 1903.

Elfman, Lois. "Two History Professors Chronicle the Lives of the First Black Scholars Hired at PWIs." *Diverse Education*. February 13, 2020. https://diverseeducation.com/article/166436/.

Fairclough, Norman, and Ruth. Wodak. "Critical Discourse Analysis." In *Discourse as Social Interaction*, edited by T. van Dijk, 258–84. London: Sage, 1997.

Feldman, Kenneth. A. "Effective College Teaching from the Students' and Faculty's' View: Matched or Mismatched Priorities." *Research in Higher Education* 28, no. 4 (1988): 291–344.

Foucault, Michel. *Discipline and Punish: The Birth of the Prison*. Harmondsworth, UK: Penguin Books, 1979.

Fowler, Roger, Bob Hodge, Gunther Kress, and Tony Trew. *Language and Control*. London: Routledge, 1979.

Goffman, Erving. *Stigma: Notes on the Management of Spoiled Identity*. New York, NY: Simon & Schuster, 1963.

Grenon, Ingrid, and Joave Merrick. "Intellectual and Developmental Disabilities: Eugenics." *Frontiers in Public Health* 2 (2014). https://www.frontiersin.org/articles/10.3389/fpubh.2014.00201/full.

Hall, Karyn. "Create a Sense of Belonging: Finding Ways to Belong Can Help Ease the Pain of Loneliness." *Psychology Today*. March 24, 2014. https://www.psychologytoday.com/us/blog/pieces-mind/201403/create-sense-belonging.

Hativa, Nira. "University Instructors' Ratings Profiles: Stability Over Time, and Disciplinary Differences." *Research in Higher Education* 37, no. 3 (1996): 341–65.

Hendrix, Katherine G. "Student Perceptions of The Influence of Race on Professor Credibility." *Journal of Black Studies* 28, no. 6 (1998): 738–63.

Hernstein, Richard J., and Charles Murray. *The Bell Curve: Intelligence and Class Structure in American Life*. New York, NY: Free Press Paperbacks, 1994.

Hill-Brisbane, Djanna. "Black Women Teacher Educators, Race, Uplift, and the Academic Other-Mother Identity." *Advancing Women in Leadership* 19, (2005): 1–13.

Ho, A. K., Lotte Thomsen, and J. Sidaniusim. "Perceived Academic Competence and Overall Job Evaluations: Students' Evaluations of African American and European American Professors." *Journal of Applied Social Psychology* 39, no. 2 (2009): 389–406.

Hode, Marlo G., and Rebecca J. Meisenbach, Rr. "Reproducing Whiteness Through Diversity: A Critical Discourse Analysis of the Pro-Affirmative Action Amicus Briefs in the *Fisher* Case." *Journal of Diversity in Higher Education* 10, no. 2 (2017): 162–80.

Hodge, Robert and Gunther Kress. *Social Semiotics*. Cambridge, UK: Polity Press, 1988.

———. *Language as Ideology*. 2nd ed. London: Routledge, 1979/1993.
hooks, bell. *Teaching Community: A Pedagogy of Hope*. New York, NY: Routledge, 2003.
Hornstein, Henry. A. "Student Evaluations of Teaching Are an Inadequate Assessment Tool for Evaluating Faculty Performance." *Cogent Education* 4 (2017): 1–8.
Houston, Therese. "Race and Gender Bias in Higher Education: Could Faculty Course Evaluations Impede Further Progress Towards Parity?" *Seattle Journal for Social Justice* 4, no. 2 (2006): 590–611.
Key, Ellen M. and Phillip J. Ardoin. "Students Rate Male Instructors More Highly Than Female Instructors. We Tried to Counter That Hidden Bias." *The Washington Post*. August 20, 2019. https://www.washingtonpost.com/politics/2019/08/20/students-rate-male-instructors-more-highly-than-female-instructors-we-tried-counter-that-hidden-bias/.
Ladson-Billings, Gloria and W. Tate. "Towards a Critical Race Theory of Education." *Teachers College Record* 97, no. 1 (1995): 47–68.
MacNell, Lillian, Adam Driscoll, and Andrea N. Hunt. "What's in a Name: Exposing Gender Bias in Student Ratings of Teaching." *Innovative Higher Education* 40 (2014): 291–303.
Marsh, Herbert W. "Students' Evaluations of University Teaching: Research Findings, Methodological Issues, and Directions for Further Research." *International Journal of Educational Research* 11 (1987): 253–388.
Mccune, Timothy. "Dewey's Dilemma: Eugenics, Education, and the Art of Living." *The Pluralist* 7, no. 3 (2012): 96–106.
Mengel, Friederike, Jan Sauremann, Ulf Zölitz. Gender Bias in Teaching Evaluations. Discussion Paper Series. *Institute of Labor Economics*, 2017. Retrieved from file:///C:/Users/roseborod/Downloads/dp11000.pdf.
Moldenado-Torres, Nelson. "On the Coloniality of Human Rights." *Revista Crítica de Ciências Sociais* 114 (2016): 117–136.
National Center for Education Statistics (2019). Retrieved from https://nces.ed.gov/programs/digest/2018menu_tables.asp.
Orfield, Gary, and Erika Frankenberg. "Increasingly Segregated and Unequal Schools as Courts Reverse Policy." *Education & Administration Quarterly* 50, no. 5 (2014): 718–34.
Palmer, Parker. (1997). "The heart of a teacher: Identify and integrity in teaching." https://biochem.wisc.edu/sites/default/files/labs/attie/publications/Heart_of_a_Teacher.pdf.
Parsons, Eileen, Domonique Bulls, Tonjua Freeman, and Malcolm. Butler. & Mary M. Atwater "General Experiences + Race + Racism = Work Lives of Black Faculty in Postsecondary Science Education." *Cultural Studies of Science Education* 13 (2018): 371–94.
Phelan, Jo. C., Bruce G. Link, and Naumi. M. Feldman. "The Genomic Revolution and Beliefs About Essential Racial Differences: A Backdoor to Eugenics?" *American Sociological Review* 78, no. 2 (2013): 167–91.
Reid, Landon. D. "The Role of Perceived Race and Gender in the Evaluation of College Teaching on RateMyProfessors.Com." *Journal of Diversity in Higher Education* 3, no. 3 (2010): 137–52.

Regalado, Antonio. "Eugenics 2.0: We're at the Dawn of Choosing Ebryos by Health, Height, and More." *MIT Technology Review*, November 1, 2017. https://www.technologyreview.com/2017/11/01/105176/eugenics-20-were-at-the-dawn-of-choosing-embryos-by-health-height-and-more/.

Rodriguez, Josê E., Kendall M. Campbell, Linda H. Pololi. "Addressing Disparities in Academic Medicine: What of the Minority Tax?" *BMC Medical Education* 15, no. 6 (2015): 1–5.

Rogers, Rebecca, Elizabeth Malaucharuvil-Berkes, Melissa Mosley, Diane Hui, and G. Joseph. "Critical Discourse Analysis in Education: A Review of the Literature." *Review of Educational Research* 75, no. 3 (2005): 365–416.

Roseboro, Donyell, and Candace Thompson. "To Virgo or not to Virgo:" Examining the Closure and Reopening of a Neighborhood School in a Predominantly African American Community." *Equity & Excellence in Education* 47, no. 2 (2014): 187–207.

Samuel, Edith and N. Wanejoki. "'Unsettling Relations:' Racism and Sexism Experienced by Faculty of Color in a Predominantly White Canadian University." *The Journal of Negro Education* 74, no. 1 (2005): 76–87.

Scharff, Darcell, Katherine Mathews, Pamela Jackson, Jonathan Hoffsuemmer, Emeobong Martin, and Dorothy Edwards. "More than Tuskegee: Understanding Mistrust about Participation." *Journal of Health Care for the Poor and Underserved* 21 (2010): 879–97.

Settles, Isis H. "When Multiple Identities Interfere: The Role of Identity Centrality." *Personality & Social Psychology Bulletin* 30, no. 4 (2004): 487–500.

Settles, Isis H., Robert M. Sellers, and Alphonse Damas Jr. "One Role or Two? The Function of Psychological Separation in Role Conflict." *Journal of Applied Psychology* 87, no. 3 (2002): 574–82.

Stein, Marc L. "Public School Choice and Racial Sorting. An Examination of Charter Schools in Indianapolis." *American Journal of Education* 121, (2015): 597–627.

Sweitzer, Kyle and Fredericks J. Volkwein. "Prestige Among Graduate and Professional Schools: Comparing the U.S. News' Graduate School Reputation Ratings Between Disciplines." *Research in Higher Education* 50, no. 8 (2009): 812–36.

Turner, Caroline, Juan González, and J. Luke Wood. "Faculty of Color in Academe: What 20 Years of Research Tells Us." *Journal of Diversity in Higher Education* 1, no. 3 (2008): 139–68.

U.S. Department of Education, National Center for Education Statistics. *The Condition of Education 2019* (NCES 2019-144), Characteristics of Postsecondary Faculty, 2019.

Walton, Gregory M., Geoffrey L. Cohen, David Cwir, and Steven J. Spencer. "Mere Belonging: The Power of Social Connections." *Journal of Personality and Social Psychology* 102, no. 3 (2011): 513–32.

Wing, Adrien K. Wing. Brief Reflections Toward a Multiplicative Theory and Praxis of Being. In *Critical Race Feminism: A Reader*, edited by Adrien Katherine Wing (Editor), 27–34. New York: New York University Press, 1997.

Woodson, Carter G. *The Mis-Education of the Negro*. Location of Original Publication, 1933; History is a Weapon, Year of Online Publication. http://history-isaweapon.com/defcon1/misedne.html.

Vizcrrondo, Felipe. "Human Enhancement: The New Eugenics." *The Linacre Quarterly* 81, no. 3 (2014): 239–43.

Willis, Paul. *Learning to Labor: How Working-Class Kids Get Working Class Jobs*. New York: Columbia University Press, 1977.

Wilkinson, Stephen. "'Eugenics Talk' and the Language of Bioethics." *Journal of Medical Ethics* 34 (2008): 467–71.

Young, Suzanne, Leslie Rush, and Dave Shaw. "Evaluating Gender Bias in Rating of University Instructors' Teaching Effectiveness." *International Journal for the Scholarship of Teaching and Learning* 3, no. 2 (2009): 1–14.

Yudkevich, Maria, Philip Altbach, and Laura Rumbley. "Global University Rankings: The "Olympic Games" of Higher Education." *Prospects* 45 (2015): 411–19.

Chapter 3

Be(Rate) My Professors Dot Com

Cautionary Tales from the Curious World of Student Evaluations

Hilton Kelly, Eleanor Branch, and Stacey Coleman

> Dr. Kelly is very smart and knowledgeable about his field. He's funny and his classes are engaging. Nevertheless, the rumors you've heard are true. I didn't find nightly readings to be overwhelming, but his take homes were brutal. I'm talking writing 14 pages closed note in two to three days. It was a great class, but proceed at your own risk.
> —Anonymous Student Evaluator, RateMyProfessors.com

> Doesn't like upper/middle class White people, I never felt like she was taking me seriously. I agree with the previous poster, she can be catty. Everything had to do with race in her class, it got old, fast. There's other literature to read other than stuff on race!
> —Anonymous Student Evaluator, RateMyProfessors.com

> Best teacher ever. Dr. Coleman is so funny and helps her students really understand sociology in a fun and unique way! One of my favorite professors at WSU, would take her again in a heartbeat!!
> —Anonymous Student Evaluator, RateMyProfessors.com

Across colleges and universities throughout the nation, student evaluations loom large in the lives and careers of professors when they are used to make personnel decisions (Kitsuse 2009; Trout 2000). While the influence of student evaluations may differ across institutions, student opinions can impact a career in higher education both positively and negatively in terms of tenure, promotion, and merit pay. Some professors view student evaluations as positive or as an opportunity for students to give feedback about their learning experiences in the classroom. Others, however, view such evaluations less favorably; they argue that such student evaluations often tell us little about good teaching because students know very little about pedagogy. Most can agree that students are self-interested consumers who often rate or berate professors based upon what they desire in a course. Although student opinions can inform teaching and learning, the downside of student evaluations continues to warrant close examination.

Current research suggests that elective courses with small enrollments often result in better evaluations for faculty and, in both elective and core courses, where students are doing well, faculty evaluations tend to be more positive (Miles and House 2015). Other trends exist as well. Quantitative courses are not evaluated as positively as qualitative courses (Uttl, Cnudde, and White 2019). Professors teaching in the social sciences do not fare as well on evaluations as those teaching humanities courses, and faculty teaching in the sciences do worst of all (Feldman 2007). Additional research has shown that many factors, such as race, class, gender, politics, and attractiveness or sexiness of the professor, play a role in student evaluations (Aruguete, Slater, and Mwaikinda 2017; Baker and Copp 1997; Bavishi, Madera, and Hebl 2010; Campbell, Gerdes, and Steiner 2005; Lazos 2012; Mendez and Mendez 2016; Mitchell and Martin 2018; Williams 2007). Given what we know about patterns of bias and prejudice in student evaluations, it is not surprising that growing numbers of faculty on campuses nationwide are skeptical of student evaluations in general.

Nevertheless, the academy structures student evaluations as a reliable, even necessary, measure of a professor's teaching effectiveness and/or use in informing promotion and tenure decisions. While the task of asking students to evaluate a course assumes that their comments will routinely be constructive, honest, and well-meaning, the reality is that student evaluations are complicated—reflecting the kind of implicit and explicit biases that exist in all human beings and how students wish a class should have been taught or managed. In the end, self-interest often dictates how a student evaluates a course—its form, content, and professor.

In this paper, we draw upon interpretive autoethnography to contribute to an enduring conversation about student evaluations. As a research methodology, according to Denzin (2014, x), interpretive autoethnography is "a practice that begins with the biography of the writer and moves outward to culture, discourse, history and ideology." Working within this framework, we each selected one RateMyProfessors.com comment that we found problematic for various reasons that we discuss throughout the paper. We sought to bring our perspectives, culture, discourses, experiences, and ideologies back into scholarly conversations about student evaluations. Usually, official student evaluations are read and reviewed by us and a department chair or academic dean with little to no opportunity for faculty to "have our say."

Often, students' perspectives are taken at face value with no opportunity for faculty members to write a rebuttal. We approached our lives as social texts to be outlined, analyzed, and challenged (Denzin 2014).

Since we had very different student evaluation metrics from multiple institutions, we decided to use RateMyProfessors.com for its unofficial, public, and anonymous characteristics or conditions (see Brown, Baillie, and Fraser 2009). We were intentional in writing retrospectively—sharing our thoughts and feelings about one of the RateMyProfessors.com postings that we have received. In addition, employing a key part of the interpretive autoethnographic process, we read each other's autobiographical account and discussed emergent themes. Our aim was "to go beyond the purely autobiographical to investigate the meaning of individual experiences," as Jeanette Schmid (2019, 266) aptly stated. After a rigorous writing, thinking, sharing, and re-writing process, we co-constructed a problematic and a question that this paper addresses: *Colleges and universities are going to continue using student evaluations, despite all the negative aspects and consequences from scholarly research. How, then, can our lives and perspectives inform the thinking and decision-making of educational authorities?* Ultimately, we offer cautionary tales that educational authorities must consider if, and when, they either reform the student evaluation process or change it altogether.

BE(RATE) MY PROFESSORS AND THE ANONYMOUS STUDENT EVALUATOR

Kelly

My first encounter with student evaluations occurred as a graduate student at a large, predominantly White state university in New England where I was a token African American gay male in an overwhelmingly White progressive academic department. I begin my account in this way, instead of immediately addressing the second opening RateMyProfessors.com evaluation, because what is obviously a good evaluative comment is actually the result of many years of learning how to get good or excellent evaluations despite my targeted social identities. And I do not mean bringing cupcakes to class on evaluation day or giving easy assignments and tests to ensure student success. I learned how to dissemble and over-perform as a way to compel students to write excellent evaluations of my teaching and classroom rapport.[1]

As a graduate student, I faced harassment because of my sexuality and hostility because of my race. After one incident in which a student expressed discomfort after I disclosed my sexuality in class, a professor explained to me that as a "Black gay male" I could not enjoy certain openness and freedoms in the classroom and that I had to use my eyes and ears to assess students' reactions to me. At the time, I did not appreciate what I understood to be a requirement to behave in ways that depersonalized me in the classroom. I had read bell hooks, and I was tempted to fight the issue and teach to transgress (hooks 1994). Ultimately, I took the professor's advice and pledged to never reveal personal information about myself in the classroom.

The first opening RateMyProfessors.com evaluative comment should be read as the successful outcome of learning how to dissemble and how to read my students. Over time, I began to reveal my sexuality when appropriate although rarely. One of the benefits of teaching at a college or university for more than a decade is the realization that it takes only one time to announce "I'm gay." News travels fast, and students either enroll in your courses or not because of your sexuality (and, I might add, race, gender, or disability). To be clear, my early decision not to disclose my sexuality in the classroom had little to do with staying in the proverbial closet; rather, I needed to pay more attention to students and their verbal and nonverbal cues. How might they be reading me—the professor's body? As I became more self-aware, I began to notice how students reacted or related to me based upon my social identities which then had implications for student evaluations (for a critical discussion of the teacher's body, see Freedman and Holmes 2003).

As I stated earlier, the RateMyProfessors.com evaluative comment is the result of my being able to successfully read my students at a private elite liberal arts college in the South. Recall that the anonymous student wrote:

> Dr. Kelly is very *smart* and *knowledgeable* about his field. He's *funny* and his classes are *engaging*. Nevertheless, *the rumors you've heard are true*. I didn't find nightly readings to be overwhelming, but his take homes were brutal. I'm talking writing 14 pages closed note in two to three days. It was a great class, but proceed at your own risk. (emphasis mine)

Every good professor ought to desire these words in student evaluations: smart, knowledgeable, funny, and engaging. Likewise, I was elated that a former student thought so highly of my teaching—until I thought about what I had to do in order to get such rave reviews. The very first time I read the comment online, I had a flashbulb memory to this sentence: "The rumors you've heard are true." When I first read this particular anonymous posting, I connected this comment to the one semester in graduate school dealing with a homophobic student. I zoomed in on the "rumors" part sadly, instead of focusing on the positive attributes that the anonymous student attributed to me.

Having achieved tenure and a deanship more than a decade later, I can recall the performance of being gay, but not too gay, as a distant memory. Concomitant with the comments I have made about social identities and student evaluations, I must point out another aspect of student evaluations that can be seen in the following comment: "His take homes were brutal. I'm talking writing 14 pages closed note[s] in two to three days." I have begun also to lament all the nights, weekends, and holidays that I endured grading from sunup to sundown so that I could return papers to my students quickly. As one of two African American male faculty members on campus, I never wanted students to write in an evaluation that I was lazy, lackadaisical, or disorganized. A few of my colleagues did receive such brutal feedback. Very early in my training as a professor and as a scholar, I surmised that faculty of color needed to be extraordinary—never appear lazy, always perform well, and be perfectly clear about everything—while White faculty could be ordinary and still earn tenure. Being ordinary for faculty of color could mean not getting tenure or having to fight for it—especially if, and when, "the best and the brightest" students wrote in evaluations that you were not quite measuring up to their expectations.

While it is true that I received exceptional student evaluations during my time as a faculty member at a predominantly White private elite institution, there was indeed a cost. The performance pressures were many, and I had to make it all seem effortless. I learned as a graduate student that, ultimately, students have a great deal of power in the classroom, and I needed to observe and understand it in order to survive. Of course, this did not mean that I lacked power; indeed, power was everywhere and being an excellent teacher in this particular institution required me to notice power relations that were always already based upon social group memberships (Foucault 1998; Schmid 2019). To put it plainly, faculty who receive awesome, excellent, spectacular, or outstanding evaluative comments from students often do so at a price. Sometimes, we must conceal important aspects of who we are, or we have to over-perform to be accepted and evaluated positively.

Branch

The second anonymous posting comes from a Freshman Composition course in an adult and evening program located at a small predominantly White liberal arts college in the South. While teaching there, the college made a public commitment to address and to eradicate institutional racism. As part of that initiative, many faculty and staff underwent anti-racism training, and the institution initiated an anti-racism team, which I chaired. At the time, I took my obligation to advance the college's aims of anti-racist pedagogy and practices very seriously. The institution's seemingly commitment to change blinded me to the more nefarious operations of race and racism in the classroom. And the student evaluation, whether official or unofficial, is one of the places where racism can and did show up.

When I received that incredibly negative evaluation on RateMyProfessors.com, I had been teaching for nearly a decade, mostly in the North, and to populations of traditionally aged White college students. No matter how hard I have tried to dismiss that student's comments over the years, I have not been able to do so. The student evaluation, however, has compelled me to interrogate my pedagogical approach. What had I done or not done in the classroom to make this student feel unwelcome and undervalued? Yet, given the student protests that occurred after I was denied tenure at that same institution, there existed some evidence that many students thought highly of my teaching. Careful reflection, however, has led me to more questions than answers.

My chief responsibility as an instructor has always been to engage students in critical thinking, and this may have contributed to the problem. I am a Socratic questioner in the classroom. I push students to think more deeply, to go beyond their first answers, and to ask why, then why, and why again? Had this behavior come across as catty? Did the anonymous student evaluator see me as just another angry, aggressive, or ill-tempered Black woman—the embodiment of a long-held but pervasive cultural stereotype? Or was I catty because, as a Black woman, I had the audacity to challenge the Southern White woman, who had never experienced such Socratic challenges or interrogations in the classroom? These questions and more, fair or not, have popped into my head over the years.

In that class of fifteen students there were no White men, three White women, and twelve Black students; using context clues and my recall of the course, I have assumed that the student evaluator was one of the three White women. With this in mind, one question has lingered: Could it be that the anonymous student evaluator never had to think about Whiteness and White privilege, especially how both might impact me? Indeed, the student's response to my course on race was clear: "Everything had to do with race in her class, it got old, fast. There's other literature to read other than stuff on race!" The student dismissed race as a negative and dominant academic discourse so casually, but I suspected that the problem with the course did not rest solely in my teaching. Such blatant dismissals of race and racial content in literature arguably demonstrated the student's uncomfortable relationship to the material and to me as the dreadlocks wearing Black literature professor.

When the anonymous student opened the evaluative comments with the observation that I "[don't] like upper/middle class White people, I never felt like she was taking me seriously," the student seemed to telegraph a sense of displacement and disempowerment as a function of both race and class. In other words, once both those social identities were no longer the center of the academic discussion, the student was not able to be a privileged actor in a classroom that centered the Black experience. This is not surprising. Conversations about race are difficult to have in many situations, and students often report feeling uncomfortable, challenged, or even perplexed. In this case, the student seemed understandably angry.

Ultimately, the comments seemed quite personal. Interestingly enough, she did not state that I do not like White people. Rather, the posting suggested, there are particular kinds of White people that I do not like: upper- and middle-class Whites. Ironically, she did not, or perhaps could not, see my own middle-class status. Refusing to find common ground, she endured the class and chose to recoup her power through a very public and anonymous review on RateMyProfessors.com. Hers is the last word, and I am left to ponder not only what I did wrong but, perhaps more importantly, what I could have done right. In spite of years of wonderfully positive and instructive official and unofficial student evaluations of my teaching, it is quite amazing that this posting on RateMyProfessors.com is the one that continues to haunt me.

Coleman

I entered the world of student evaluations unaware of the unwritten rules or informal responsibilities of college teaching. As a novice college sociology instructor, I looked forward to what I imagined would be a positive exchange of ideas between my students and me. I wanted to deliver lectures full of new and exciting content that would intrigue students, spark critical discussions, facilitate thoughtful writing assignments, and fuel students' desire to learn more about human behavior. I had envisioned students who would recognize all these qualities. After one semester, however, I discovered students who did not always see and understand my work in the way I intended. Consequently, I had to learn some hard lessons fast about students and student evaluations in the classroom. These lessons made me aware that, in higher education, student evaluations of me seemed more important than my evaluation of them.

My graduate school mentor helped to shape my ideas, attitudes, and behavior as a developing college sociology instructor. He outlined two fundamental principles of college teaching that he deemed crucial to my success: (1) Identify your social place in the classroom, and (2) Have extensive knowledge of your subject matter. The first principle, or the idea that I might find my social place, means that I needed to "fit in" or always present myself as nonthreatening in predominantly White spaces. My mentor consistently emphasized that students are not focused merely on the content of the lectures, the course materials, or the assignments; rather, a great deal of their time in the classroom would be spent judging and inspecting me. Specifically, he pointed out, students tend to judge the instructor's external characteristics, including body language. Further, he said, as an African American woman instructor I had to become aware of students and my social place—grappling with stereotypes relative to both my race and my gender.

My mentor emphasized that physical appearance would be a primary evaluation tool initially, so it was necessary to dress in a manner not perceived as eye-catching, controversial, or Afrocentric. This would automatically be viewed as radical behavior that would turn off students, in particular White students. He advised me not to place myself in a position where students could reference a television sitcom when describing me. After many years, I am wondering to what extent excellent evaluations of my teaching are the result of finding my social place in the college classroom. Indeed, I consciously toned down my appearance, eliminating items that might be viewed as "loud" or overly eye-catching, and I began to employ what could only be perceived as professional attire.

The second principle was a warning to have extensive knowledge of my subject matter. He underscored this principle. I was never to reference myself or my opinion. "You are the instructor and they are the students," he would say. "They are not your friends, and that should never be the case." In hindsight, his advice prepared me for an unexpected classroom encounter with two students who sought to challenge me during an introductory sociology lecture. While lecturing on the development of the feminist movement in the United States, I was interrupted by two White students who always sat together in the back of the classroom. These students never participated in lectures and always engaged in conversations between themselves. "Don't you think we've come a long way?" asked the young White woman. "Yea, we do allow Blacks to teach in our classrooms, read our books, and we even share the same public restrooms," the young White man added. The classroom went silent. I realized in this moment that I was on stage with pressure to remain calm, manage the classroom, respond to their comments, and/or redirect the lecture.

Choosing to focus on the subject matter, not the attitudes, I calmly informed the class that our current focus was the feminist movement and that we would look more closely at race and race relations in future lectures. This statement was clearly unsatisfying for the two students attempting to command the class' attention. The other students seemed obviously relieved by my ability to disarm as well as reroute these students' statements. More than engaging in a conversation about feminism, they wanted to say something about race. Only people who had been in the class throughout the semester could have detected that "come a long way" in concert with "we do allow Blacks to" was targeted at me. Several students at the close of the class period commended me on my lecture. Certainly, in this particular course and in this specific encounter, I successfully delivered and survived the pitfalls of responding to deliberately offensive comments designed to solicit an emotionally charged response. I used my subject matter as armor, as had been suggested. I have come to understand that the evaluation of my abilities as a sociology instructor rested not only on my academic skills or expertise, but my ability to present myself in a manner tolerable to my students.

THREE CAUTIONARY TALES: INTERPRETATIONS OF AUTOETHNOGRAPHIC ACCOUNTS

Drawing from all three autobiographical accounts, we have outlined three cautionary tales for educational authorities who seek to change the way both good and bad student evaluations can negatively impact the lives and careers of college professors. We present these cautionary tales as statements because the words and phrases came to us in this way, as we discussed and reflected upon our accounts. In this section, we explore these three cautionary tales employing these premises: (1) Students' reading of the teacher's body can result in positive and negative student evaluation. (2) Students are not disinterested observers—they hold implicit and explicit biases. (3) Students have power. We think that educational authorities cannot move in the direction of equitable, fair, and consistent student evaluations for faculty without acknowledging and learning from some of the nuanced readings of student comments or feedback that we offer here.

Students' Reading of the Teacher's Body Can Result in Positive and Negative Student Evaluations

In the classic 1967 film *To Sir, with Love*, the main character, Mark Thackeray, an Afro-Guyanese engineer unable to find work due to racism, accepts a position as the lone Black teacher in an overwhelmingly White school in London's East End (Braithwaite [1959] 1990; Clavell et al. 1967).[2] Perhaps one of the earliest depictions in film of a group of White children reading the Black teacher's body, this cinematic representation touches upon key social dynamics that nearly half a century later still has consequences for student evaluations. Thackeray symbolized middle-class respectability in the face of verbal and physical violence. The White working-poor high school youth are portrayed as rambunctious, precocious and rude, and one reviewer provides this further observation:

> As the students' antics progress from mere disruptive behavior to distasteful pranks, Thackeray retains his calm manner and resists being baited. A turning point comes, however, when one morning he discovers something (presumably a sanitary pad) burning in the classroom grate. He angrily orders the boys out of the classroom and excoriates the girls for their disgusting, "sluttish" behavior.

Dismayed by his lack of restraint, he retreats to the staff room, upset that he let himself be manipulated by "kids." (*To Sir, with Love*, n.d.)

Although all were marginalized in British society, the color and class-of-Thackeray's body mattered greatly in this school setting. Like most Hollywood films, *To Sir, with Love* delivered a "happily ever after" ending. The students learned to look past his color and class, and the teacher learned to "fit in," which set up a dilemma for him to stay or to leave at the end of the film. What becomes clear throughout the film is that both positive and negative evaluations of Thackeray—and never his teaching—are the result of students reacting to and reassessing his color and class. In fact, one could argue that it was not until the students learned to see beyond both his skin color and middle-class differences that they were willing to "learn from him."

In contemporary American society, not 1960s England, the teacher's body still matters (Freedman and Holmes 2003). Branch's account, for example, focused on an evaluative comment in which a student intimated that the course dealt too much with race. Here, we argue that this evaluation in particular is aligned with the twenty-first-century social phenomenon referred to as "teaching while Black" or the politics and microaggressions experienced by Black or African American teachers in predominantly White schools (Daniel 2019; Henry 2020). One of the consequences of "teaching while Black" is that students will make certain assumptions about the teacher's aesthetics, politics, and character based upon skin color. With her dreadlocks and brown skin, Branch's body stood out not only in the classroom but also in her department and the larger college. Consequently, the student may have simply subscribed to a prevailing notion floating around offices, hallways, classrooms, and the larger campus community that Branch teaches only about race.

Branch, like most scholars of color who teach ethnic or cultural studies courses, may have been well aware that students quibble ad nauseam that African American scholars are always talking about race and retelling historical narratives about slavery and Jim Crow that many Whites, and some African Americans, want to forget. What she did not know initially, but found out over time, is something that faculty of color in overwhelmingly White schools learn eventually: The department and the larger institution will often support negative student evaluations articulated as legitimate concerns that are merely problematic reads of a professor's body.

Branch's student also presumed that she was not upper or middle class. In fact, she stated that Branch "doesn't like upper/middle class White people." Raised in Chicago, not in the South, and attending some of the best predominantly White schools from high school to graduate school, Branch clearly did not fit her student's image of a professor. Invariably, students assume that all college professors are upper or middle class, but not in this particular case.[3]

The student read Branch as someone who was not from money, and may have assumed that, like so many late twentieth- and early twenty-first-century professors of color who commenced the changing demography of the professoriate, her professor probably overcame hardships to earn a PhD and secured a job because of affirmative action. Branch, however, was indeed raised middle class in the Midwest by a psychiatric social worker mother and a public school teacher father—both college-educated middle-class professionals.

As Kelly stated earlier, he had always received glowing student evaluations, but he had to learn how to conceal his subordinate identities. To reiterate, he was not in the proverbial closet and he did not bleach his skin. Rather, he learned how to make his students feel at ease by avoiding certain topics (gay marriage, for example) or using the work of White authors to talk about race and racism (Tim Wise, Peggy McIntosh, Joe Feagin, and others, for instance). He learned to dissemble—remove his thoughts, impressions, and perspectives—so that he would not alienate the students who would be evaluating him in an overwhelmingly White and gay-tolerant institution. While he never sat down to literally plan or strategize how he might negotiate his targeted social identities, he figured out and enacted a logic system: Make White and heterosexual people feel comfortable. His attempt to navigate and negotiate his social identities within his school workplace led to his own erasure in the classroom. He literally tried to "downplay" or hide aspects of his Blackness or gayness.

As a gay Black man in the South, he learned how to "present all sides" in the classroom so that his "radical" views would not offend. He learned to focus less on the South's sins and more on the North's problems, using the excuse that "scholars have failed to look at the North" when he knew that it was easier to critique the North than the South in the Southern classroom. He learned to cite his training or education to send a message to students that he was qualified to teach them. He learned to use every means to send a clear message that he was intelligent, nice, and harmless. In the end, his negotiation of Black and gay identities proved to be a success. Ultimately, he learned how to make his students feel comfortable by strategically planning and plotting ways to make himself everyman in the academy—smart, qualified, and nonthreatening.

Clearly, Black professors must become highly aware of their own thoughts and feelings as raced/gendered/classed/sexualized bodies because conflicts with their students can lead to poor evaluations at best and to termination at worst when the administration sides with the students and, sometimes, their parents. Through evaluations, students can employ the institution to whip into submission those teachers they do not like until and unless they find rapport and common ground with their students. While this may be a burden for all teachers or professors, there is an extra burden for teachers' bodies that are not White, male, middle class, heterosexual, and/or able bodied. Often professors who do not fit in leave—teach for one year and then find a job elsewhere. Those who stay, in spite of the resistance that we endure in our classrooms, must find a way to fit in or get along with our students and colleagues.

In Coleman's account, she introduced us to other variables that could explain why some professors' bodies are accepted or valued in spite of their race, gender, class, sexuality, or disability. Proportional representation also colors professor evaluations. In spite of being a Black woman teaching at a large state university, there were indeed many of her kind at her university and in the surrounding urban center. Thus, proportional representation could have made all the difference in how she was perceived by her students. In an urban university setting, students may have seen more people of color in powerful positions on campus and in the city and, therefore, did not react to her body in the same way that Branch's student did. In addition, Coleman's coming of age in the state where she attended school from kindergarten to graduate school may have made her legible to her students in a way that Branch simply was not. Coleman's account reminds us that the price may not be as high in one setting as it is in another due to a host of variables, from proportional representation to cultural matching.

The moral of the story is that while we may be unaware of how students are reading our bodies, many of the comments in their evaluations betray the fact that they are not always already disinterested and well-meaning. Whether the body is read with a focus on some aspect of disadvantage or privilege, student evaluations can mean the end of a career or a distinguished professorship award. Unfortunately, it all depends on how the professor negotiates race, gender, class, disability, and sexuality dynamics in the social setting where they find themselves. On some level, regardless of our social identities, we are all concealing parts of ourselves from the eyes and ears of our students and colleagues, or over-performing in order to receive great evaluations, because student opinions matter for tenure and promotion, as well as general acceptance in school settings.

Students Are Not Disinterested Observers—
They Hold Implicit and Explicit Biases

Just as Mark Thackeray's students in *To Sir, with Love* did not enter his classroom as blank slates—lacking preconceived notions of Black people in 1960s England—neither do our students. They enter colleges and universities with biases, and they employ them to evaluate their professors (Gooblar 2017a). Imagine the student evaluations that Thackeray would have received had his students been given the opportunity to offer feedback. In this filmic account, and in our real lives, student evaluations are not simply tools to assess effective teaching; rather, they can be evidence of students' implicit and explicit biases. While this point may seem obvious to some scholars, the nexus between personal biases and student evaluations deserves more scholarly attention and explanation.

Implicit bias, also known as implicit social cognition, refers to the attitudes or stereotypes that affect our understanding, actions, and decisions in an unconscious manner (Ajzen and Dasgupta 2015; Greenwald and Krieger 2006; Mitchell 2018; Reinsch, Goltz, and Hietapelto 2020). It is a social dynamic that instructors must grapple with while attempting to engage students. For example, when Branch is described as "catty," we wonder to what degree the student's comments are rooted in unconscious gender discourses about young women professors (Ashley 2014; Childs 2005). Such words are meant to be a form of denigration, but it is entirely possible that the student would never speak of or admit to holding gender biases in her choice of words to describe her male professors (Basow 1994; Boring 2015). In fact, she may not have been aware that "catty" in our society is typically used pejoratively to describe women and gay men.

Less implicit and more explicit, however, is Branch's student's comment "Everything had to do with race in her class, it got old, fast. There's other literature to read other than stuff on race!" In order to avoid such claims from students, Kelly tried to manage both implicit and explicit biases by outthinking them. Recall that he chose deliberately to use the work of White authors to talk about race in an overwhelmingly White environment knowing that he would face less resistance from students (see also Littleford et al. 2010). Returning to Branch's account, however, the student should not have been surprised by the syllabus and the course offered by a professor who specializes in African American literature with a research focus on Toni Morrison's novels. Whether one chooses Branch's student's comical statement "it got old, fast," or Coleman's student's "we do allow Blacks to teach in our classrooms" as examples of implicit or explicit biases, we must become aware that biases can show up over the course of a semester with serious consequences for professors.

Students' implicit and explicit biases betray the notion that they are disinterested observers who are capable of evaluating a professor objectively. While a wonderful ideal to aspire to, it fails in practice. Based upon our experiences, students are not disinterested observers of their professors. When students have no prior interest in a topic, faculty evaluations suffer (Degheri 2017). When students are not interested in participating in the faculty evaluation process, their responses are less likely to tell us anything about the quality of a professor's teaching. Moreover, even when students take faculty evaluation seriously, they tend to complain about course workload (Nast 1999). Quite different from implicit and explicit biases, such discussions about disinterested observers point to sampling bias—those students motivated to fill out faculty evaluations are often those who either love or hate the course (Stark and Freishstat 2014).

Baiocco and DeWaters (1998), the authors of *Successful College Teaching*, contend that there are market forces at play. Colleges, today, distinguish themselves by developing a marketable identity to attract students. This shift to a market orientation is problematic because it promotes thinking about students as consumers (Patton 2015). As Martinez-Saenz and Schoonover (2014, 13) convincingly stated, "The dominance of the market model in universities is the dominance of the false idea that the consumer alone can adequately speak in the name of education." When we elevate students as the principal arbiters of learning through student evaluations, they become self-interested consumers.

When students are consumers, as we discussed earlier, professors must take on the role of service provider—responsible for and responsive to the concerns of students—pedagogically and otherwise. Given our stories of "fitting in" and "dissembling," as African American faculty in predominantly White classrooms, we often found ourselves operating out of fear: that we must work harder than our White counterparts, that we should not talk too much about race, that we should not grade too harshly, and that we should wait until tenure to be controversial. Recall that Kelly had concerns about how he presented himself as a gay Black man. Coleman had concerns about how she presented herself as a Black woman teaching feminism. And semesters later, after the course, Branch discovered through an anonymous posting that she should have been concerned about how her students read her at the intersections of class, race, and gender. All of these fears, and more, speak to students' interest in or antipathy toward us and arguably affected how they evaluated us.

Pedagogically, moving away from the market for a moment, we cannot assume that students and professors share the same understanding of effective teaching. Unlike professors, students are not subject matter experts. According to Nast (1999, 106), students often frame their comments about a course around six issues beyond workload and writing assignments: "the difficulty of the course; the degree of controversy entertained in the course; the political position of the teacher; the teacher's personality; the raced, sexed and gendered composition of the teacher's image and performance; and the chemistry of a particular class." Likeability is often the measuring stick, which is not the same as learning.

At the same time, it is important to recognize the ways in which professors may also be consumed by the process (Patton 2015). First and foremost, professors worry excessively about how their evaluations will impact considerations of tenure, promotion, and merit pay. Second, professors of color are concerned about how they are being perceived by students and their colleagues. We cannot risk being perceived as lazy or inadequate in our preparation or delivery of course materials, as Kelly's account pointed out. Third, and finally, good professors experience a perpetually nagging sense of regret that they have not published enough, taught well enough, or reached out to powerful students enough to earn tenure and promotion. Despite the desire for "happily ever after" filmic portrayals of teachers' work, the cost of professors' fears and ruminations can be exhausting for college professors and, over time, can lead to burnout.

Students Have Power

Professors are often theorized as having all power in the classroom. Indeed, they have "power of the pen," or the authority to set the classroom agenda, to dole out assignments or exams, and to give students grades. But students have power as well. Whether students are aware of the power dynamics in classrooms or not, their participation and engagement shape what K-12 teachers or professors can and cannot accomplish (Briskin 2001). Ultimately, students may come to feel silenced, marginalized, or disempowered when their expectations of a course and/or the professor are not met. Student evaluations are places within the schooling process where students can "get back at a teacher" or challenge a professor's authority and expertise.

Many decades ago, French and Raven (1959) wrote persuasively about the domains of social power that are often employed in the classroom: legitimate, expert, reward, coercive, and referent. Legitimate power, they argued, lies in the professor's position, which has been sanctioned by the institution to lead the class and to establish appropriate policies and procedures that will guide a course. It is the responsibility of professors to demonstrate their ability to manage the classroom and to impart their expert knowledge. Expert power, then, refers to the professor's command of their subject matter. Most students understand that the teacher's knowledge exceeds their own, but this type of power can be undermined when students do not want to learn or will not learn from us (Kohl 1993). Reward power refers to a professor's ability to reward students with positive and additional benefits, such as good grades and extra credit. Conversely, coercive power is a function of the professor's ability to punish by exacting penalties and to motivate by instilling fear. Finally, referent power refers to students' high regard for and identification with professors. It is a function of the professor's ability to establish a rapport with students, sometimes plainly based upon students' perceptions of a professor as "cool," likeable, nice, pretty, or funny.

In such framing of power, domains of social power rest largely with the teacher and, according to market logic, leave students unhappy consumers.

Yet, Ng (1991, 100) reshapes the terms of this discussion when she points out that there is a difference between power and authority: "Teachers have authority over students as a consequence of their ascribed role in the educational system. But in an interactional setting, this authority can be challenged by those without formal power." In other words, teachers may wield both power and authority in the classroom, but students exercise informal power based in part on all of the social identities they possess: gender, class, race, ability, sexuality, and so on. They use that power to challenge both directly and indirectly their professors, especially those who are women and/or people of color, in a variety of ways. More importantly, students often can depend upon institutions to reinforce their desires and needs simply because they hold master statuses in the larger society.

According to Bohmer and Briggs (1991, 154), "Students from privileged class and race backgrounds are frequently hostile, or at best neutral to presentations on race, class, and gender stratification; often they respond with guilt, anger, or resistance." In Branch's account, for example, the student was undoubtedly angry; her experience as a Black, middle-class woman had been de-centered. Understanding that the institution was more likely to support her claims and reality of the classroom experience, the anonymous reviewer resisted through a posting on RateMyProfessors.com. Beyond resistance, however, we argue that the student fully exercised her power through a very public and anonymous review. In so doing, a White, middle-class womanhood was reaffirmed at the click of a button. Whether a psychic victory, or otherwise, Branch's teaching had been successfully called into question, attacked, and maligned. As Accapadi (2007, 214) points out, "White privilege allows [Whites] to shift the conversation about [them] and [their] feelings and away from the original goal of the conversation." Until now, hers was the last word.

In Coleman's account, the two students collaborated and challenged her experiences as an African American woman as a way to reclaim power. White women students often align themselves with White men in order to reestablish White cultural norms (Briskin 2001). Whatever they heard about feminism that day, they felt the need to control the classroom conversation by employing normative perspectives and by exhibiting racial animus. Such resistance can happen only in classrooms and schools in which the institution, concomitant with dominant narratives and ideologies, will reinforce students' prejudices. This is power writ large from the student's perspective.

In Kelly's account, making students feel at ease by consciously selecting the work of White writers to talk about race, he both affirmed and unsettled his White students. On the one hand, students were introduced to White authors with strong, progressive, and critical perspectives on race and racism. On the other hand, students were not exposed entirely to authors of color who made the very same points—many of whom were cited by White authors. Under the circumstances, early in his career, this was a strategy that actually worked in his favor. Students had "White" models for how to think, live, and walk in the world differently. No longer could his White students think that only African Americans cared about justice, equality, and equity. As he alluded to earlier, he learned to anticipate his students' likes and dislikes, to read his students' bodies, and to foresee power dynamics in the classroom. Ultimately, as an African American gay professor, it was his responsibility to ensure that his students felt comfortable, safe, accepted, and valued at the expense of his body and "self."

CONCLUDING REMARKS

Our accounts and analyses of actual, and sometimes traumatic, experiences with student evaluations, whether through traditional evaluative systems or RateMyProfessors.com, are a warning to students, professors, administrators, and the larger society. Student evaluations are fraught because they are cultural products and byproducts involving prejudice and discrimination, implicit and explicit biases, and power and resistance. Given this understanding, which we have outlined and explained as cautionary tales, we have demonstrated that

1. students' reading of the teacher's body can result in positive and negative student evaluations;
2. students are not disinterested observers—they hold implicit and explicit biases; and
3. students have power.

While much of what we have discussed derives from our autobiographical experiences as educators in college classrooms, some of what we have uncovered comes from our experiences as students. On the one hand, as college professors, we understand that student evaluations are problematic because students are not disinterested consumers but self-interested human beings who bring all of their cultural baggage into the classroom and to the evaluative situation. On the other hand, as former students, we believe that evaluations are one of the few places within school settings where students can use their voices to articulate their experiences of a course and, hopefully, to offer constructive criticism to improve a course.

We feel an obligation now more than ever to offer solutions based upon the issues that we have raised throughout this paper. It is our hope that administrators and policymakers—those with the power to change the way we create, administer, and use student evaluations—will contemplate the nuances that we have pointed out and the cautionary tales that we have told. There are at least four solutions that could bring us closer to more honest, useful, and equitable student evaluations. First, colleges and universities must triangulate evaluative data, so that one measure does not control the narrative about teaching and learning in a course (Flaherty 2018). For example, student feedback should be considered alongside teaching portfolios and classroom observations over time. Second, students need to be alerted to the mountains of research that make a solid case for pervasive bias and prejudice as a part of the student evaluation process. Simply being informed about bias and prejudice might not end racist, sexist, ableist, or homophobic comments in student evaluations, but the idea that students can be primed for helpful, productive, and thoughtful judgment could reasonably lessen the amount and degree of such responses. Third, administrators and other decision-making bodies need to be clear about what good teaching is and provide professional training on how it is evaluated. Most graduate students are not required to complete a course in effective college teaching; instead, they either teach how they were taught or how they learn. Fourth, student evaluations need redesign—less of a focus on Likert scales and more on open-ended responses. Students should be given the opportunity to give their opinions and perspectives with thick description and authorial context.

As more and more institutions, such as the University of California at Berkeley, University of Oregon, University of Massachusetts at Amherst, and University of Southern California, discontinue the use of traditional student evaluations in personnel decisions, it is clear that there is some momentum to change the way that college professors are evaluated (Doerer 2019; Flaherty 2018). Let us be clear: We are not suggesting that college professors should not undergo some type of evaluation of their teaching (see also Gooblar 2017b). Rather, we want to make clear all the ways in which the lives and work of professors are impacted by poorly constructed evaluation systems that ultimately give students the power to control the work that we do and the lives that we lead.

NOTES

1. The term "dissemble" is borrowed from Darlene Clark Hine's culture of dissemblance theory, which she introduced in her path breaking work on rape and the inner lives of African American women in the Reconstruction Era Middle West. Her historical note of Black women concealing violence and the threat of violence in the name of racial uplift left an indelible mark on me. I use the term "dissemble" quite

differently here—as an individual, not a cultural group, and in reference to sexuality, not race. The cost of silence or concealment is what my account and Hine's history have in common. For a full discussion of "culture of dissemblance" theory, see Hine 1989.

2. In 1959, E. R. Braithwaite published *To Sir, with Love*, an autobiographical novel about his post-WWII teaching experience in London's East End. In 1967, Braithwaite's novel was made into a film starring Sidney Poitier and Lulu, and set in the 1960s.

3. Although the student had the last word by posting her negative student evaluation, as Branch stated earlier, it is troubling that we may never know what she meant by her comments.

REFERENCES

Accapadi, Mamta Motwani. 2007. "When White Women Cry." *The College Student Affairs Journal* 26, no. 2 (Spring): 208–15.

Ajzen, Icek, and Nilanjana Dasgupta. 2015. "Explicit and Implicit Beliefs, Attitudes, and Intentions: The Role of Conscious and Unconscious Processes in Human Behavior." In *Human Agency: Functions and Mechanisms*, edited by Patrick Haggard and Baruch Eitam, 115–44. Oxford, UK: Oxford University Press.

Aruguete, Mara S., Joshua Slater, and Sekela R. Mwaikinda. 2017. "The Effects of Professors' Race and Clothing Style on Student Evaluations." *The Journal of Negro Education* 86 (4): 494–502.

Ashley, Wendy. 2014. "The Angry Black Woman: The Impact of Pejorative Stereotypes on Psychotherapy with Black Women." *Social Work & Public Health* 29 (1): 27–34.

Baiocco, Sharon A., and Jamie N. DeWaters. 1998. *Successful College Teaching: Problem-solving Strategies of Distinguished Professors*. Boston, MA: Allyn and Bacon.

Baker, Phyllis, and Martha Copp. 1997. "Gender Matters Most: The Interaction of Gendered Expectations, Feminist Course Content, and Pregnancy in Student Course Evaluations." *Teaching Sociology* 25 (1): 29–43.

Basow, Susan. 1994. "Student Ratings of Professors Are Not Gender Blind." *Women and CAUT News* (8): 9–11.

Bavishi, Anish, Juan M. Madera, and Michelle R. Hebl. 2010. "The Effect of Professor Ethnicity and Gender on Student Evaluations: Judged Before Met." *Journal of Diversity in Higher Education* 3, no. 4 (November): 245–56.

Bohmer, Susanne, and Joyce L. Briggs. 1991. "Teaching Privileged Students about Gender, Race, and Class Oppression." *Teaching Sociology* 19 (April): 154–63.

Boring, Anne. 2015. "Gender Biases in Student Evaluations of Teachers." April 22, 2015. https://www.ofce.fr/pdf/dtravail/wp2015-13.pdf.

Braithwaite, Eustace Edward Ricardo [1959] 1990. *To Sir, with Love*. New York: Jove Press.

Briskin, Linda. 2001. "Power in the Classroom." In *Voices from the Classroom: Reflections on Teaching and Learning in Higher Education*, edited by Janice Newton, Jerry Ginsburg, Jan Rehner, Pat Rogers, Susan Sbrizzi, and John Spencer, 25–39. Toronto: Centre for the Support of Teaching, York University.

Brown, Michael J., Michelle Baillie, and Shawndel Fraser. 2009. "Rating Ratemyprofessors.com: A Comparison of Online and Official Student Evaluations of Teaching." *College Teaching* 57 (2): 89–92.

Campbell, Heather E., Karen Gerdes, and Sue Steiner. 2005. "What's Looks Got to Do with It? Instructor Appearance and Student Evaluations of Teaching." *Journal of Policy Analysis and Management* 24 (3): 611–20.

Childs, Erica Chito. 2005. "Looking Behind the Stereotypes of the 'Angry Black Woman': An Exploration of Black Women's Responses to Interracial Relationships." *Gender & Society* 19 (4): 544–61.

Daniel, Beverly-Jean. 2019. "Teaching while Black: Racial Dynamics, Evaluations, and the Role of White Females in the Canadian Academy in Carrying the Racism Torch." *Race Ethnicity and Education* 22 (1): 21–37.

Degheri, Travis J. 2017. "An Empirical Look at the Impact of Course and Faculty Characteristics on Student Evaluations." PhD diss., University of San Diego.

Denzin, Norman K. 2014. *Interpretive Autoethnography*. 2nd edition. Washington, DC: SAGE Publications.

Doerer, Kristen. 2019. "Colleges are Getting Smarter about Student Evaluations. Here's How." January 13, 2019. *Chronicle of Higher Education*. https://provost.uoregon.edu/files/chronicle_article.jan_.19.colleges_are_getting_smarter_about_student_evaluations._heres_how._-_the_chronicle_of_higher_education.pdf.

Feldman, Kenneth A. 2007. "Identifying Exemplary Teachers and Teaching: Evidence from Student Ratings." In *The Scholarship of Teaching and Learning in Higher Education: An Evidence-Based Perspective*, edited by Raymond P. Perry and John C. Smart, 93–143. New York: Springer.

Flaherty, Colleen. 2018. "Most Institutions Say They Value Teaching but How They Assess It Tells a Different Story." May 22, 2018. *Insider Higher Ed*. https://www.insidehighered.com/print/news/2018/05/22/most-institutions-say-they-value-teaching-how-they-assess-it-tells-different-story.

Foucault, Michel. 1998. *The History of Sexuality: The Will to Knowledge*. Translated by Robert Hurley. London, UK: Penguin.

Freedman, Diane P., and Martha Stoddard Holmes (Eds). 2003. *The Teacher's Body: Empowerment, Authority and Identity in the Academy*. Albany, NY: SUNY Press.

French, Jr., John R. P., and Bertram Raven. 1959. "The Bases of Social Power." In *Studies in Social Power*, edited by Dorwin Cartwright, 150–67. Ann Arbor, MI: Institute for Social Research.

Gooblar, David. 2017a. "Yes, You Have Implicit Biases, Too." November 20, 2017. *Chronicle of Higher Education*. https://hrs.wsu.edu/wp-content/uploads/2019/06/yes-you-have-implicit-biases-too-the-chronicle-of-higher-education.pdf.

Gooblar, David. 2017b. "No, Student Evaluations Are Not Worthless." May 31, 2017. *ChronicleVitae*. https://chroniclevitae.com/news/1814-no-student-evaluations-aren-t-worthless.

Greenwald, Anthony G., and Linda Krieger. 2006. "Implicit Bias: Scientific Foundations." *California Law Review* 94 (4): 945–67.
Henry, Matthew E. 2020. *Teaching While Black*. Charlotte, NC: Main Street Rag Publishing.
Hine, Darlene Clark. 1989. "Rape and the Inner Lives of Black Women in the Middle West: Preliminary Thoughts on the Culture of Dissemblance." *Signs: Journal of Women in Culture and Society* 14 (4): 912–20.
hooks, bell. 1994. *Teaching to Transgress: Education as the Practice of Freedom*. New York: Routledge.
Kitsuse, John I. 2009. "Talk about Teaching: Reflections on the Problems of Teaching Evaluation." *The American Sociologist* 40: 3–14.
Kohl, Herbert. 1993. *I Will Not Learn from You: The Role of Assent in Learning*. Minneapolis, MN: Milkweed Editions.
Lazos, Sylvia. 2012. "Are Student Teaching Evaluations Holding Back Women and Minorities?: The Perils of 'Doing' Gender and Race in the Classroom." In *Presumed Incompetent: The Intersections of Race and Class for Women in Academia*, edited by Gabriela Gutiérrez y Muhs, Yolanda Flores Niemann, Carmen G. González, and Angela P. Harris, 164–85. Boulder, CO: University Press of Colorado.
Littleford, Linh Nguyen, Katherine S. Ong, Andy Tseng, Jennifer C. Milliken, and Sonya L. Humy. 2010. "Perceptions of European American and African American Instructors Teaching Race-focused Courses." *Journal of Diversity in Higher Education* 3 (4): 230–44.
Martinez-Saenz, Miguel, and Steven Schoonover. 2014. November-December, 2014. "Resisting the 'Student as Consumer' Metaphor." *Academe*. https://www.aaup.org/article/resisting-student-consumer-metaphor#.xjha54homcm.
Mendez, Jeanette Morehouse, and Jesse Perez Mendez. 2016. "Student Inferences Based on Facial Appearance." *Higher Education* 71 (1): 1–19.
Miles, Patti, and Deanna House. 2015. "The Tail Wagging the Dog: An Overdue Examination of Student Teaching Evaluations." *International Journal of Higher Education* 4 (2): 116–26.
Mitchell, Gregory. 2018. "An Implicit Bias Primer." *Virginia Journal of Social Policy & the Law* 25, no. 1 (January): 27–57.
Mitchell, Kristina M. W., and Jonathan Martin. 2018. "Gender Bias in Student Evaluations." *PS: Political Science & Politics* 51, no. 3 (July): 648–52.
Nast, Heidi J. 1999. "Sex, Race, and Multiculturalism: Critical Consumption and the Politics of Student Evaluations." *Journal of Geography in Higher Education* 23 (1): 102–15.
Ng, Roxana. 1991. "Teaching Against the Grain: Contradictions for Minority Teachers." In *Women and Education*, 2nd ed., edited by Jane Gaskell and Arlene McLaren, 99–115. Calgary: Detselig Enterprises.
Patton, Stacey. 2015. May 19, 2015. "Student Evaluations: Feared, Loathed, and Not Going Anywhere." *ChronicleVitae*. https://chroniclevitae.com/news/1011-student-evaluations-feared-loathed-and-not-going-anywhere.

Reinsch, Roger W., Sonya M. Goltz, and Amy B. Hietapelto. 2020. "Student Evaluations and the Problem of Implicit Bias." *Journal of College and University Law* 45 (1): 114–39.

Shmid, Jeanette. 2019. "Autoethnography: Locating the Self as Standpoint in Post-Apartheid South Africa." In *Transforming Research Methods in the Social Sciences: Case Studies from South Africa*, edited by Sumaya Laher, Angelo Flynn, and Sherianne Kramer. Johannesburg, South Africa: Wits University Press.

To Sir, with Love. n.d. Plot summary of *To Sir, with Love*. IMDb. https://www.imdb.com/title/tt0062376/plotsummary?ref_=tt_stry_pl.

Stark, Philip B., and Richard Freishtat. 2014. September 16, 2014. "An Evaluation of Course Evaluations." *ScienceOpen*. https://www.stat.berkeley.edu/~stark/Preprints/evaluations14.pdf.

Trout, Paul A. 2000. "Flunking the Test: The Dismal Record of Student Evaluations." *Academe* 86, no. 4 (July/August): 58–61.

Uttl, Bob, Kelsey Cnudde, and Carmela A. White. 2019. "Conflict of Interest Explains the Size of Student Evaluation of Teaching and Learning Correlations in Multisection Studies: A Meta-analysis." *PeerJ* 7: e7225.

Williams, Damon A. 2007. "Examining the Relation Between Race and Student Evaluations of Faculty Members: A Literature Review." *Profession* 168–173.

Chapter 4

Wonderful Evaluations in the Face of Teaching Anti-Racism and Multicultural Education

Ramon Vasquez

Dr. Vasquez is very intelligent on a wide variety of topics. Great professor that truly cares about his students and their well-being. He made coming to campus worth it. I think if there was a more concrete structure to the class with readings and an emphasis on sticking with the curriculum that is important to learn, I would feel as though this class was beneficial to take.

—Teaching evaluation comment by anonymous student (2019)

INTRODUCTION

The impetus for this *testimonio* grew out of a desire to name and theorize incongruities found within the boundaries of optional comments in my student evaluations of teaching (SETs).[1] Locating and theorizing these contradictions in comments such as "wonderful, but talks a little too much about race," matters for anti-oppressive teaching, as well as for disrupting the dichotomy between positive and negative evaluations.[2] In many ways, these contradictions hold implications for insurgent anti-racist pedagogical approaches that BIPOC[3] faculty might deploy to confront and unsettle the cultural structures of white supremacy in teacher education. These types of comments also have implications for emergent struggles against the primacy of Euro-centered epistemologies that universalize a single fabrication of the "common good" as the only endpoint in teacher education.[4] The logic of the "common good" rests on the belief that working for the "community" always results in the greatest good for all.[5] Who counts as a member of the community, however, or whose knowledge has value and "is important to learn," as mentioned in the student comment with which I open this chapter, remains closely attached to conceptualizations of Whiteness and BIPOC accommodation or subjugation.[6]

OVERVIEW

I organize this chapter as follows: first, after providing relevant context and naming my positionality, I situate my insurgent pedagogical approach within a framework of epistemic disobedience. The aim of this section is to use nuanced specificity to explore why, despite receiving high scores for technical categories, such as "presented the subject matter clearly" or "the instructor was organized," students still included noxious phrases in the optional comments section. The disparaging of my teaching and marginalization of BIPOC knowledge was manifested in comments such as "did not cover the content I wanted to learn."

I understand these comments as ways of punishing me for disobeying the hegemony of the "common good," as well as for pointing out the theoretical and ethical limits of dominant knowledge for "diversity and inclusion" work.[7] Many scholars, including some in this text, have already discussed negative SET comments; thus, I have chosen not to summarize that knowledge in this chapter.[8] What I seek to disentangle and illuminate in my work involves the corrosive invalidations embedded within superficially "nice" comments. Within a discussion of the hegemony of teacher education, I make visible how malicious fragments within partially positive comments function as forms of violence intended to injure BIPOC faculty. Students include these negative markers as a means of reasserting Whiteness as property and recentering the legitimacy of White methods and Euro-centered dominant epistemologies in teacher education.[9]

In the first part of this chapter, I also explore the process of upsetting and transgressing students' attachments to superficial, painless, and defanged forms of "diversity and inclusion," which they policed and protected through discourses of "wanting a normal content." The generic diversity "content" students defended during class conversations, such as "we need teaching strategies to help the disadvantaged," operates as a bridge to macro-narratives that glorify the inevitability of Euro-centered epistemologies.[10] I also trace the way teacher education compels marginalized faculty to educate White students about the nature of "social justice" without, however, displacing the racist "content" or *White knowledge* that students demand.[11] I conclude by considering how epistemic disobedience—intentionally disobeying and unlinking from the logics of Western epistemologies, including hierarchies of knowledge production and "best practices" that sustain Whiteness—may provide a possible path for moving away from assimilationist multicultural "savior" doctrines that reify existing power structures and protect multiple layers of white supremacy in teacher education.[12]

RESEARCHER POSITIONALITY

This *testimonio* documents my efforts at resisting white supremacy through insurgent teaching. As a Brown BIPOC man and first-generation college graduate who self-identifies as Chicano, I recognize that my positionality has implications for any conceptual work, particularly for a *testimonio* where I narrate the different ways I am subjected to punishment for my desire to disrupt the White narcissism implicit in affirmations of the common good.[13] It is my hope that acknowledging my social location might contribute to a different understanding of my teaching experiences and evaluations discussed in this chapter.

As a marginalized scholar in teacher education, my presence in a White and gendered space, hypervisible, yet at the same time invisible, presents multiple anomalies and tensions related to the intersections of race, gender, class, and commitments to different possibilities. What unfolds in this chapter does not include an analysis of the damage done to BIPOC faculty by the "social justice" performativity of promotion and tenure committees.[14] This chapter also does not propose a solution to the invalidations and racialized violence of student comments on SETs. Moreover, it does not seek to demonstrate how "empirical" measures of teaching effectiveness fail to capture the fluidity, complexity, and joyfulness of anti-racist teaching. A considerable amount of scholarly literature already addresses the problems of objectivity, reliability, and validity in SETs, particularly when White students evaluate BIPOC faculty.[15] Instead, I offer this *testimonio* as a counter-story to dominant narratives of diversity, social justice, incremental change, and progress in teacher education.

WHOSE COMMON GOOD?

This chapter focuses on the entanglements of Whiteness with the "common good" to show how students draw on a repertoire of White discursive practices to rearticulate a condition of normalized Euro-centered "known" teaching content in teacher education. In the space opened by theorizing SETs in this *testimonio*, which I realize makes me vulnerable as an untenured Brown man, I pursue the idea that many superficially "positive" comments, even when attached to high numerical scores, constitute an undertheorized weapon used by students to strategically defend their Whiteness and reassert their epistemic arrogance.[16]

It was while teaching diversity and inclusion courses at a "traditional," conservative, historically White university (HWU)[17] that I first observed and located certain entanglements within the complex tensions of my anti-racist teaching. An exploration of these entanglements, while essentially theoretical but also testimonial, provides a launching point for a discussion of anti-racist teaching opportunities and risks for BIPOC faculty. For example, comments such as "I believe he did a great job, but the course is not set up for students to properly succeed and learn content," includes a banal complement of sorts—"great job"—within a deadly invalidation of the knowledge examined in the course. This comment exemplifies the type of hostility found in my SETs, which also mirrors the oppressive racist environment in the program.

CONTEXT AND RESEARCH SITE

Situated in a segregated post-industrial city in the Midwest, a place with a long history of displacing Black people by forcing them to live in neglected and underserved neighborhoods, the University discussed in this chapter recently embarked on a new mission to produce what they refer to as "culturally relevant" candidates prepared for urban teaching.[18] The K-12 public schools located in these segregated areas of the city, euphemistically referred to by students as "areas with challenges," suffer from intentional underfunding and consistently struggle to avoid succumbing to the yearly threat of state receivership.[19]

This University, a regionally celebrated private institution with a high-priced tuition, conservative orientation, and self-described "sheltered" student body, was commonly referred to by most teacher education students in my courses, as well by some professional colleagues, as a "bubble." This conceptualization of the University, an obvious attempt to differentiate itself from the rest of this "scrappy" city, also positioned the institution as a type of "last great hope" for the common good. In short, the University occupies a space separate from "the place where the hopeless people live," as described by one student during a conversation after class. The idea of providing hope to the hopeless as the only possible trajectory for their individual "progress and uplift" was hardly isolated. On the contrary, this logic actually forms a recurring theme among students, as did the unrelenting enterprise of "helping" Black children assimilate by imposing the *right* content or *normal* curriculum on them. This underlying logic also shaped White ideas and expectations about the program, including what "content" they "wanted" from my diversity and inclusion class.[20]

INSURGENT PEDAGOGY

In my teaching, I define insurgent pedagogy as a decolonizing process that educators can use to unsettle fixed notions of knowledge linked to Whiteness. It was during a spontaneous hallway conversation after class with a White teacher education student, concerning what she described as her desire to "really learn how to uplift multicultural students for the common good," rather than always discussing "the negative stuff like racism," that I first grasped the need to address the unspoken arrangements that link Whiteness, capitalism, racialized oppression, and Euro-centered epistemologies. I embarked on this path with some trepidation, especially given my status as a recent "diversity cluster hire" faculty member.

I was uncomfortable with the discourse of the common good after only a few weeks, especially as it was linked to individualism and conflated White knowledge with merit and "everything good in the world."[21] After that conversation with the student, this discourse became disconcerting, and was especially unbearable and painful for me as someone who attended urban schools in Los Angeles. Earlier that week, in one of my other courses required for elementary teacher certification, another White student, also a woman, articulated a similar thought by saying that "part of our job as teachers is to give hope to kids in the bad parts." Another White student at this point added, "yup, we need to provide bridges to success." This comment elicited head nodding from the majority of the class, mostly women. When I problematized the idea of hope by suggesting that some children and parents might interpret this as condescending, students responded with skepticism that anyone would criticize what "obviously" involves a common good for all, but especially for the disadvantaged.

From that starting point, I decided that I must intervene somehow in order to disrupt the belief among students, which they shared in class often, that the common good always consists of "neutral" teaching. Students in class referred to this "unbiased approach" as "commonsense teaching" rather than "crazy stuff." In this case, "crazy stuff" refers to any content or pedagogical approach, including forms of decolonial knowledge, that departs from familiar notions of the "content" necessary for the "right" way to teach.[22] This "right" way reflects teaching produced through a grid of best practices whose attachments to dominant epistemologies and Whiteness constitute a necessary "common good" for "uplift" and "normal" individual progress in society. Interestingly, during class discussions concerning the permeance of systemic racism, a topic of my insurgent pedagogy, many students articulated a version of "they have to *want* to succeed as well," as a way of shifting attention away from "crazy" concepts such as the brutality of racialized capitalism. This recentering of Whiteness made me worry about the harm these preservice teachers were likely to inflict on BIPOC children once entrenched in their own classrooms.

Another stream of in-class comments posited that "we need to help students develop the *right* values so they can succeed." I was rebuffed for suggesting that "blaming the children" reifies notions of society composed of atomized individuals or deracinated self-entrepreneurs rather than communities with long traditions of experiencing and opposing racism. When my teaching troubled the social processes and ideologies that underpin teacher education, including notions of neutrality, merit, and entitlement, many students expressed dissatisfaction with the "content covered" or the "controversial stuff." Hesitant to openly disparage the situated knowledge of BIPOC people who have been historically oppressed, students in class still found a way to express their anger and privilege. For instance, students penalized me for teaching "crazy stuff" by inserting superficially "positive criticism" in comments such as "the syllabus did not have all of the rubrics" or "class needs more on HOW to teach the subject."

My attempts to show students that teaching never involves neutral knowledge were met with constant opposition.[23] The use of the term *crazy* by students highlights the extent to which they felt my teaching, which unsettled everyday "normal" beliefs, was attacking the common good by diverging from the normal content students demanded. As one student commented in my SET: "I felt that the class did not cover much of the material that was supposed to be covered in class." As I shared with my class, my principal teaching commitment involves opening new possibilities for unsettling the White epistemic arrogance that invalidities and silences BIPOC knowledge of everyday racism in schools.[24] Student incredulity took the form of grotesque arrogance, which they attempted to use as a bludgeon to discipline me through a privileging of self-serving definitions of "properly teaching" as highlighted in my evaluations.

Through the unrelenting and intimidating surveillance of the White gaze, which foreshadowed the regulating of my teaching in SET comments, I was also reminded that I was expected to deliver White content "properly." Of course, in this case, properly refers to what students believed was *right* for them, not BIPOC children. Interestingly, my scores for categories such as "provides feedback" averaged 4.8 on a scale of 1 to 5. This phenomenon highlights one of the tensions of anti-racist teaching—the contradictory nature and purpose of SETs. For example, even when I exceeded all of the technical demands of the bureaucratic university as described in the SET, which satisfies promotion and tenure requirements, students still found ways to exert their Whiteness and strategic ignorance by resisting the anti-racist learning in the course. This experience taught me that academic freedom does not apply to BIPOC faculty in HWUs.

STUDENT EVALUATIONS AS PUNISHMENT

In terms of SETs, this displeasure with other knowledge was manifested by comments such as "the textbook was one-sided and harsh toward conservatives. We are ALL entitled to believe what we want and to think our own individual thoughts." Other comments along the same lines included "I took personal offense to some of the authors [sic] opinions in the book. I will most likely be sharing this book with my fire pit." Remarkably, and perhaps in recognition of my teaching proficiency, the same student also wrote in the SET "this is my favorite class to attend." The positioning of different epistemologies as merely opinions, rather than knowledge, provides a way for students to reassert their rights and entitlements, while also avoiding a direct attack on me, perhaps out of fear that SETs could be traced back to them.

The use of "personal offense" and "individual thoughts" in the comments highlights the way students in this course remained faithful to the hegemony of Whiteness as a form of property, which grants them certain rights over me. Asserting that they know what counts as knowledge, as well as what is even worth knowing, reflects one of the hallmarks of Whiteness. Interestingly, the term "anti-racist" appears in none of the student evaluations of my teaching. Instead, they repeatedly mention that "the content" was not covered through the discourse of "I don't *know* what I learned." These comments also operate as a type of White strategic ignorance that dictates knowledge by establishing boundaries around what counts as worth knowing.[25]

THE VIOLENCE OF STUDENT EVALUATIONS

Teacher education curriculum remains Euro-centered and continues to reinforce dominant epistemologies and White privilege. Positioning my challenges to the status quo as "not teaching the content" exemplifies that violence. For instance, student comments such as "a little biased, really pushed for cultural content" may appear ambiguous on the surface. This discursive move, however, of embedding comments in evaluations about biased content, allows students to use evaluations as a tool to damage faculty by positioning them as unwilling to help students learn the normal "content." While they avoid mentioning anti-racist teaching in favor of the generic-sounding term "cultural content," these student comments constitute a coded form of violence meant to suppress, intimidate, and undermine faculty who defy or transgress the limits of commonsense. Since students receive multiple reminders from administration that SETs serve the common good, they know the audience for these comments includes more than just faculty members.[26]

This violence holds implications for BIPOC faculty who seek to teach for a lasting anti-racist transformation of society rather than merely for liberal reform.[27] Since students at this particular university receive emails with guidelines for remaining completely "objective" while writing only "constructive criticism," they likely feel that overtly denigrating me in their evaluations, or criticizing my anti-racist teaching, might lead to repercussions for them for making "inappropriate comments."[28] The university policy of "not tolerating" harassing speech, as well as student self-interest, could play a role in explaining why students avoid directly naming anti-racism in their disapproval of my teaching.

RISKY TEACHING

What I call risky teaching in this *testimonio* involves initiating possibilities for students to travel across boundaries of knowledge in ways that may activate new thinking. The risk of intervening in the everyday exaltation of a universal macro-narrative of a "common good" involves jeopardizing progress toward merit raises, promotion, and contract renewal. Even mildly negative SETs involve a range of different forms of punishment for BIPOC faculty, including criticisms and invalidations from peers who serve as mentors and administrators.[29] Opportunities for anti-racist teaching, however, particularly for unraveling and subverting the matrix of meanings associated with the "common good," can exist even within the most oppressive spaces in teacher education. Many comments on my SETs were positive, including, "he made me consider aspects of teaching I had not considered before," but these were less typical. These types of comments produced the necessary bureaucratic validation that the chair of my department required for my contract renewal, but still triggered suggestions for improving my practice. For instance, I was given a list of "good practices" including "ask a peer for help."

Quantifying learning in teacher education, or in any educational setting for that matter, remains an elusive and problematic goal, especially when BIPOC faculty disobey logics that continue to situate Western systems of reason at the uppermost level of knowledge hierarchies. Even alternative measures of learning touted by universities as efficient and objective, such as faculty-designed mid-semester survey instruments, still rely on student self-reporting that reveals little about the unlearning or unsettling of racist dominant narratives. All student surveys rest on positivist logics that remain inadequate for evaluating the depth, breadth, and power of disruptive teaching by BIPOC faculty.[30] The continued use of these instruments raises serious questions about the commitment of HWUs to retain BIPOC faculty in teacher education. Not surprisingly, I no longer teach at this university having found the experience intellectually draining and emotionally depleting.

THE "COOKBOOK" CLASS

Forced to work with a syllabus aligned to external goals related to state accreditation poses a distinct set of pedagogical challenges to anti-racist teaching. For instance, in this course, one week was dedicated to Black students while another to LGBTQ students and so forth. Much like the changing specials in a menu, which is how I critiqued the syllabus in class, each week was dedicated to one special group. Within a few weeks of teaching this course, I realized I would need to use an approach that challenged the "Othering" of people from non-dominant groups. My approach was to unsettle these future teachers by moving away from the myths associated with the common good that they so cherished. Above all my goal was to teach independent thinking about race, racism, and knowledge. This method led to a range of comments on my SETs along the lines of "he changed the syllabus and talked about other stuff." Thus, broaching the subject of knowledge and its relationship to Whiteness and oppression in a mandated "cookbook style" diversity course involves tensions.

DANGEROUS TEACHING

Work that draws attention to the racist underpinnings of commonsense Eurocentered knowledge constitutes dangerous teaching. For instance, this teacher education preparation (TEP) promotes the "commonsense" idea that racism no longer constitutes a threat to the existence of BIPOC people. In other words, teachers simply need to "find a way to reach non-White students."[31] To counteract this myth, I decided to embark on a dangerous path. Instead of simply adding the topic of epistemology to the bland domesticated cookbook, or merely reproducing the diversity and inclusion rhetoric that elementary teachers should only celebrate multicultural or "diversity traditions," I sought to probe and upset notions of post-racial progress. Several students referred to my approach as "the crazy stuff" in recognition of my delinking from the logics and "neutral" methods of Western epistemologies, including systems of reason that uncritically celebrate schools as the only knowledge bases that produce anything worthy of "merit and achievement."[32]

This approach required examining the structures of domination manifested through notions of a common good, such as meritocracy, as well as circumventing the banking model of learning still privileged as real teaching. While anti-racist teaching can resemble other types of teaching, it remains grounded in ethnic studies or abolitionist approaches, which constitute forms of fugitive practice.[33] The risk of this teaching to BIPOC faculty involves the always looming threat of negative SET scores and their consequences for tenure. The power of promotion and tenure committees to harm pre-tenure BIPOC faculty by imposing restrictive "teaching goals" and "friendly" mentoring that demands fidelity to standards and frameworks based on best practices has already been well described in related research.[34]

WHITE COUNTER-RESISTANCE

A considerable amount of scholarly literature has been published on the subject of Whiteness and related concepts such as White privilege, White fragility, and White innocence.[35] In much of this literature, the different ways that Whiteness operates in teacher education, and how it affects students and faculty, has been subject to considerable discussion among scholars. For that reason, I do not summarize that literature in this chapter.

As a means of framing White counter-resistance, I draw on the critical race theory (CRT) principle of Whiteness as property as a useful heuristic for highlighting how Whiteness in teacher education is constructed as a form of private property, a Western logic and epistemology, which grants Whites additional rights over BIPOC people, including the right to control faculty.[36] Moreover, rights also refer to the right to control what counts as knowledge and who can be someone with worthwhile knowledge. This thinking elevates White students to the status of knowers who can demand the exact type of content they want from BIPOC faculty.

In this case, student-desired knowledge, that is, what I refer to as *White knowledge*, does not include anything, in terms of anti-racist content, that unsettles the logics of Western epistemologies, including individualism, meritocracy, and the inevitability of our current social arrangements. An example of the ingrained White knowledge includes the idea that learning to teach elementary school means gaining the technical skills and dispositions necessary for saving or "uplifting the less fortunate people." It never means questioning the underlying logics of teacher education and White knowledge or what forms of systemic racism remain embedded within schools and in commonsense teaching.

Understanding and examining this dimension of Whiteness as a form of property provides a useful tool for theorizing the underlying purpose of excluding BIPOC and other non-Western perspectives from teacher education. While much literature exists on different aspects of Whiteness, including from fields such as critical Whiteness studies, the focus of this chapter is on the way Whiteness operates as a tool to protect White cultural hegemony in schools by displacing all other epistemologies through a form of normalized epistemicide or displacement of other ways of knowing and making meaning of the world.[37]

For instance, Whiteness as property explains the privileged position of Euro-centered epistemologies by making visible the link between property rights and the right of White students to exercise their control over BIPOC faculty. SETs constitute an important tool for exercising power in ways that invalidate knowledge that does not conform to White dominant knowledge. In short, Whiteness as property shows how Whites believe they are entitled to define what counts as the common good, as well as what is worth knowing, by virtue of owning the land and everyone on it, including BIPOC faculty. BIPOC people, including faculty, who have no such entitlement, have, therefore, no right to make claims in schools about what counts as knowledge. Interestingly, student comments such as "I learned a lot that I was not exposed to before, but I wish that time had been spent focusing on specific ideas and lessons a teacher could implement" uses the passive voice "time had been spent" to avoid naming me. What content the student was exposed to remains a mystery as anti-racism appears nowhere in the SET.

EPISTEMIC DISOBEDIENCE: INSURGENT TEACHING

To date, little research exists on the necessity for epistemic disobedience as a mode for BIPOC flourishing or as a way of sustaining the integrity of non-Western epistemologies in TEPs.[38] This chapter addresses this gap in the existing research and produces new knowledge about the continued violence against BIPOC faculty who draw on non-Western epistemologies in teacher education in anti-racist teaching.[39] For instance, insurgent teaching refers to pedagogical actions grounded in a vision of disobedience that aims to unsettle commonsense cultural assumptions and discourses of the "common good" among White teacher education students. By questioning the logics of Western epistemologies that reproduce and uphold notions of White superiority, including ideas related to the achievement gap, White teachers as saviors, and the inherent inferiority of BIPOC peoples, I unsettled some of the commonsense "truths" of urban teaching. While conceptualizations of the "common good" may vary across HWUs, one commonality includes the idea of White teachers as overseers or curators of the community.

TEACHING OPPORTUNITIES AND RISKS

Regardless of the context, whether inside the classroom or in the hallway between classes, as a teacher educator I always work to help loosen student thinking from Western logics. For instance, by engaging in and modeling independent and decolonial thinking, I show students the boundaries and contours of the colonial matrix of domination in which we all live.[40] This disobedience of "normal" thinking sometimes leads students to verbally question notions of certainty or regimes of truth in teacher education.[41] The space created by disobeying constitutes an opportunity for BIPOC faculty to intervene in the reproduction of systemic racism in teacher education. For example, during a small group activity discussing the *killability* of Black people by police, a difficult concept, a student in my diversity course exclaimed, "You don't just do an information dump, you actually let us think!" This comment serves as an acknowledgment of the success of my approach of encouraging student intellectual growth and independent thinking. It also addresses a tension in teacher education that another student mentioned earlier in the year: "I'm frustrated that we're basically a vocational program."

For most students, however, this attachment to the vocational allows them to enact their Whiteness in ways that punish me for not celebrating their White professional "neutrality." For instance, one of my SET comments included, "wonderful professor, but he always makes it seem like White people are to blame for everything." Similarly, a different student wrote, "he uses lots of videos and articles that are cool, but they are always about race and racism." Anti-racist teaching, when enacted in ways that problematize liberal multicultural education, can unsettle macro-narratives by creating an opportunity for insurgent actions and abolitionist teaching informed by desires for a different world.[42] While I saw my teaching as moving beyond the conventional themes and taken for granted assumptions of the common good, students interpreted as "he made me think about things[;] however, some videos and stuff may have hinted that all White people have done horrible things which isn't true."[43]

"FAULTY" FACULTY AND DOMINANT EPISTEMOLOGIES

The risks that BIPOC faculty face for disobeying this logic involves more than rebuke from department chairs and administrators. The risk involves unintentionally reifying the very logics that demand questioning and unsettling. In this case, what my SETs reify involves the stereotype that BIPOC faculty cannot teach "regular" content. For students in my classes, compartmentalizing what they see as different elements of "radical" always means remaining faithful to the content. As one student said to me in class: "We like your radical way of teaching, it's just the stuff is sometimes too much." While provoking uneasiness can create openings for discussion, students who remain most invested in defending Whiteness will make their displeasure known through optional comments on SETs.

Recognizing this tension, I trouble the loyalty of my students "to uplifting the less advantaged." By introducing students in my courses to different frameworks for understanding how education rests on Western logics and epistemologies, and actually produces and protects inequalities instead of contributing to human flourishing, I create productive tension. Epistemic disobedience, among other related concepts, constitutes one of the approaches I share with students in order for them to start recognizing that their beliefs, based on their social location, do not constitute a universal truth. Engaging students in the study of knowledge systems and approaches such as abolitionist teaching requires that I structure my teaching methods around the principles of dialogic learning that move away from rubrics and hierarchies used to quantify every aspect of classroom interaction. I also share my own social location as a member of an oppressed group and describe how that affects my perspectives on knowledge.

Rather than treating knowledge as static or immutable, which many students still believe forms the only type of teaching that counts, particularly in this conservative school, I create a space in my classes where students start considering why acquiring new knowledge always requires engaging intellectually and ethically with a range of diverse perspectives, narratives, and traditions. Again, the paradox, in this case, centers on the fact that students recognize and acknowledge the use of "critical thinking" while disavowing the actual content, which focuses on illuminating the White racism in schools obscured by the logic of working for the common good.

Another way I deploy insurgent pedagogies in an attempt to help students as they develop a disequilibrium, as well as a drive to continue learning about and recognizing different types of epistemologies and systems of reason, has been by encouraging them to examine and question the conventions, content, and pedagogy of their own educational experiences. By analyzing and challenging their own previous educational experiences, students in my courses begin to engage in the process of developing an understanding of teachers as active intellectuals, rather than merely passive transmitters of "neutral" content. Of course, part of the tension in this case involves the idea that criticality itself involves adherence to certain Western logics.[44] Therein lies another unresolved tension that comingles with opportunity and complicates what counts as knowledge. By discussing relevant case studies, participating in role-playing activities, and observing everyday interactions in schools from new vantage points, I immerse my students in unfamiliar situations that I hope will extend their thinking and contribute to different learning. While it remains possible that this learning contributes to a reimagining of knowledge and hope, this learning also influences comments on SETs, such as "an over emphasis on racism."

PROBLEMATIZING LEARNING

Although the terms social justice and White privilege have taken on an element of public confessional, it remains difficult to pinpoint what they actually refer to in the context of everyday K-12 schooling. For this reason, I encourage my students to engage in discussions concerning the intersections of race, social class, religion, gender, ability, and sexual orientation in U.S. public schools. To these discussions, I work to cultivate relationships of mutual trust and respect with my students, which some do recognize. At every opportunity, formal and informal, I attempt to nurture an enthusiasm for intellectual discourse and reflection that moves away from self-reflection as mere White confessional.[45] I do this by showing my own enthusiasm for rethinking dominant oppressive paradigms. For example, I impart to students that thinking in new ways requires knowing different people and understanding other ways of being in the world. Such thinking could help students question the logic of universalism.

Through my work with these core principles and by problematizing superficial teacher positivity and niceness, I did sometimes observe students during small group activities demonstrate evidence of the divergent thinking necessary for engaging with complex concepts and theories. What all this created however, to my dismay, was high SET numerical scores for technical categories such as "excellent in organizing and presenting materials," while still maligning me for not teaching the content that positions children as atomized individuals. To counteract individualism, I also required that students support and mentor one another in an effort to show them the value of non-Western systems of collective action, community, and accountability to each other.[46] For this reason, my teaching repertoire included informal sessions, group projects, and collaborative presentations minus the usual rubrics or "model" assignments. Surprisingly, despite all my work of decentering or problematizing individualism, comments still included multiple references to "treats us like individuals."

All students in my courses learn about the importance of mutual respect and genuine collaboration, which I explain to them constitute important values in BIPOC communities. Yet many students still remain unable or unwilling to connect these ideas to different epistemologies or ways being, as evidenced by the SET comments. While it is my hope that students will leave my classroom knowing how to collaborate effectively with people with different knowledge and ways of being, much remains unchanged. While I explained that the ability to collaborate will serve them well in teaching and in life, they still sought to reframe and refashion this learning into a type of tool useful for saving disadvantage students or, worse, as something to highlight in their résumé. When I attempted to go beyond the "anti" in anti-racism to show students that education can stand for something else, for instance cultivating Black joy rather than merely countering Euro-centered epistemologies, students responded with vague SET comments such as "our discussions really helped me think outside the box." While I hope that reverberations of this thinking will remain with students, and perhaps influence how they might interact with their students, I recognize that SETs actually contribute to an undermining and erosion of my work. The use of "objective" tools for quantifying, ranking and comparing faculty actually normalizes mediocre teaching that suppresses and betrays the underlying imperatives of anti-racism.

Finally, while I fostered intellectual change in my students by encouraging them to develop new ethical approaches to open discussion that might help them unlink from dominant epistemologies throughout their lives inside and outside of schools, it may not have had the impact I intended. For instance, in SETs this was positioned as "class discussions sometimes did not have a clear focus." I had high expectations for "radical work" and communicated this to my students. They, in turn, responded sometimes, but that was only when learning did not upset their beliefs about race and anti-racism. While my teaching emphasized a sense of ethics, open-mindedness, and a love of learning free from instrumentalist ideas of "putting it in a toolbox," they defended their values in SET comments. For the most part, SET comments failed to reflect what I assumed or hoped had occurred in my classes, which was an unlearning of dominant paradigms. While BIPOC faculty have the ethical responsibility to clean up the disasters created by White minds, unfortunately, we receive little credit for such work on SETs.

Although my commitment to justice within the context of teacher education pertains to anti-racism in schools, which I openly share with students, a goal of mine includes helping students to simultaneously question and engage with what it means to become insightful, enthusiastic thinkers, and advocates for justice in their own lives. Discussing the logic of teacher education and the common good includes confronting white supremacy, while also highlighting and supporting possible paths toward abolitionist teacher preparation that decenters Whiteness and assimilation as the only measures of success.[47]

RETHINKING STUDENT EVALUATIONS OF TEACHING

In addition to examining a range of dimensions of subjugation and resistance experienced by BIPOC faculty in TEPs, this chapter offers a set of cautions for any faculty member interested in disobeying the Euro-centered logics of teacher education, including dominant notions of who can serve as a teacher educator for White college students. For instance, as a way of revealing how TEPs protect the "authority" and knowledge of the dominant culture by "Othering" BIPOC faculty, this chapter addresses relevant considerations and concerns using vignettes from classroom discussions, conversations with peers, as well as related materials. As mentioned earlier, student comments in my SETs such as "I don't really *know* what I learned" serve as a point of reference for understanding epistemic disobedience.

This rethinking of SETs, and the paradox of how students parse out "radical" or anti-racist teaching from the normal content, also troubles some of the undertheorized dimensions of the daily struggles that BIPOC faculty in teacher education face when they attempt to reframe dominant "commonsense" discourses of racial progress, diversity, and inclusion. An example of this reframing, particularly in my diversity and inclusion courses, includes questioning who and what remains excluded or displaced from liberal conceptions of the common good. By attempting to center struggles for justice that go beyond "commonsense" approaches to education grounded in the inevitability of Euro-centered logics that protect Whiteness and incremental change as "normal," I unsettle students with lessons on epistemology and anti-racism.

In this work, I situate the violence of SETs within an examination of the opportunities and risks for BIPOC faculty who purposefully seek to unsettle White students.[48] For this context, engaging in epistemic disobedience of Whiteness refers not only to simply a metaphor of decolonizing higher education[49] but to actually delinking from attachments to Western ideas of a universal, foreseeable, and inevitable "common good" in education. As it stands now in teacher education, the common good celebrates achievement through assimilation to Euro-centered norms and perspectives while insulating and protecting Whiteness and White students from critique. The comment in my SET "did not talk about units or content standards, large focus on controversial topics in the classroom" exemplifies this protection of Whiteness by highlighting the standards.

Learning did occur in my courses. For instance, students sometimes experienced an unsettling of beliefs and assumptions when learning to engage in the active process of thinking rather than merely memorizing content. Student evaluations, however, left many aspects of that learning—especially dissonance—unexamined, including to students themselves who came to class with myriad assumptions of what diversity and inclusion should mean for teachers. Moreover, since Euro-centered logics remain embedded in all institutional structures, policies, settings, routines, and procedures, it would seem unlikely that student evaluations could ever serve as adequate tools for assessing the performance or competency of BIPOC faculty. The logics of Euro-centered epistemologies, I posit, remain concealed in systems and processes whose forms, such as SETs, merely represent the most superficial dimension.

OTHER CONSIDERATIONS

To achieve teaching that elevates life over individual achievement and solidarity over competition, one must realize that the very foundations of teacher education guarantee the perpetuation of white supremacy and the continuing marginalization of BIPOC faculty. My use of insurgent pedagogies attempted to help students see the violence inflicted on epistemologies that fall outside of the European Enlightenment. Perhaps this was a little too ambitious on my part; however, SETs can never tell the whole story of what happened in my classes. A goal of my teaching involved addressing the harms caused to BIPOC children through the process of making them docile and domesticated subjects who require "saving" by White teachers. But SET habits and routines make it difficult to address this learning. While a core principle of my work centers on challenging the inevitability of humanist notions of progress and Enlightenment conceptualizations of the self, students did not mention this in the optional comments. Instead, they mention content in conventional terms, such as "did not teach content."

Describing me as "not teaching content" constitutes a type violence that seeks to force me to understand myself as an "Other" in the department—an "Other" who does not conform to the traditional values of the established community for the common good. Mapping the contours of this "Othering" can help reveal previously unexamined aspects of White racism in teacher education, especially in relation to mastery of knowledge. This "Othering" also placed an immense burden on me to defend my ontological legitimacy in this particular department. While I expected White counter-resistance to my teaching, and was prepared to address that harm intellectually, it still created toxic everyday experiences. I knew disobeying White knowledge involved some level of risk, but I was still surprised by the maliciousness and pettiness displayed in the optional comments. Enduring this viciousness is a price I am willing to pay to unsettle white supremacy, though it need not be this way if institutions attend to the issues in this chapter and this book.

NOTES

1. These evaluation instruments include open-ended prompts for optional comments.

2. Boatright-Horowitz, Su L., and Sojattra Soeung. "Teaching White privilege to White students can mean saying good-bye to positive student evaluations" (2009): 574.

3. See the BIPOC Project at https://www.thebipocproject.org.

4. Santos, Boaventura de Sousa. *The End of the Cognitive Empire: The Coming of Age of Epistemologies of the South*. Duke University Press, 2018.

5. Hollenbach, S. J., and David Hollenbach. *The Common Good and Christian Ethics*. Vol. 22. Cambridge University Press, 2002.

6. Wynter, Sylvia. "Unsettling the coloniality of being/power/truth/freedom: Towards the human, after man, its overrepresentation—An argument." *CR: The new centennial review*, *3*, no. 3 (2003), 257–337.

7. Smith, Linda Tuhiwai. *Decolonizing Methodologies: Research and Indigenous Peoples*. Zed Books Ltd., 2013.

8. See Lavada Taylor in the text.

9. Harris, Cheryl I. "Whiteness as property." *Harvard law review* (1993): 1707–1791.

10. Santos, Boaventura de Sousa. *The End of the Cognitive Empire*, Duke University Press 2018.

11. Applebaum, Barbara. *Being White, Being Good: White Complicity, White Moral Responsibility, and Social Justice Pedagogy*. Lexington Books, 2010.

12. Matias, Cheryl E. "Why do you make me hate myself?: Re-teaching Whiteness, abuse, and love in urban teacher education." *Teaching Education* 27, no. 2 (2016): 194–211.

13. Hook, Derek. "White privilege, psychoanalytic ethics, and the limitations of political silence." *South African Journal of Philosophy* 30, no. 4 (2011): 494–501.

14. Ahmed, Sara. "The nonperformativity of antiracism." *Meridians* 7, no. 1 (2006): 104–126.

15. Esarey, Justin, and Natalie Valdes. "Unbiased, reliable, and valid student evaluations can still be unfair." *Assessment & Evaluation in Higher Education* (2020): 1–15.

16. Mitchell, Megan. "White people, we need to stop being so damn fragile!: White and Male Fragility as Epistemic Arrogance." In *Pacifism, Politics, and Feminism*, pp. 51–67. Brill Rodopi, 2019.

17. Dancy, T. Elon, Kirsten T. Edwards, and James Earl Davis. "Historically white universities and plantation politics: Anti-Blackness and higher education in the Black Lives Matter era." *Urban Education* 53, no. 2 (2018): 176–195.

18. Ladson-Billings, Gloria. "Toward a theory of culturally relevant pedagogy." *American Educational Research Journal* 32, no. 3 (1995): 465–491.

19. See http://education.ohio.gov/lists_and_rankings for school at risk.

20. Bailey, Alison. "Strategic ignorance." *Race and Epistemologies of Ignorance* (2007): 77–94.

21. Goitom, Mary. "'Legitimate Knowledge': An Auto-Ethnographical Account of an African Writing Past the White Gaze in Academia." *Social Epistemology* 33, no. 3 (2019): 193–204; Levina, Marina. "The Violence of Merit." *Departures in Critical Qualitative Research* 9, no. 1 (2020): 20–24.

22. Battiste, Marie. *Decolonizing Education: Nourishing the Learning Spirit*. UBC Press, 2017.

23. Grande, Sandy. *Red pedagogy: Native American Social and Political Thought*. Rowman & Littlefield, 2015.

24. Grosfoguel, R. Decolonizing post-colonial studies and paradigms of political-economy: Transmodernity, decolonial thinking, and global coloniality. *Transmodernity: Journal of Peripheral Cultural Production of the Luso-Hispanic World* 1, no. 1 (2011).

25. Bailey, Alison. "Strategic ignorance." *Race and epistemologies of ignorance* (2007): 77–94.

26. Students receive email instructions from the university about SETs and community.

27. Castro-Gómez, Santiago. "The missing chapter of empire: Postmodern reorganization of coloniality and post-Fordist capitalism." *Cultural Studies* 21, no. 2–3 (2007): 428–448.

28. Report from the 2016-2017 Advisor to the Provost on Gender Equity and Climate.

29. Bernal, Dolores Delgado, and Octavio Villalpando. "An apartheid of knowledge in academia: The struggle over the "legitimate" knowledge of faculty of color." *Equity & Excellence in Education* 35, no. 2 (2002): 169–180; Castro-Gómez, Santiago, and Desiree A. Martin. "The social sciences, epistemic violence, and the problem of the invention of the other." *Nepantla: Views from South* 3, no. 2 (2002): 269–285.

30. Kolitch, E., & Dean, A. V. "Student ratings of instruction in the USA: Hidden assumptions and missing conceptions about 'good teaching.'" *Studies in Higher Education* 24, no. 1 (1999): 27–42.

31. Dancy, T. Elon, Kirsten T. Edwards, and James Earl Davis. "Historically white universities and plantation politics: Anti-Blackness and higher education in the Black Lives Matter era." *Urban Education* 53, no. 2 (2018): 176–195.

32. Kerr, Jeannie, and Vanessa Andreotti. "Crossing borders in initial teacher education: mapping dispositions to diversity and inequity." *Race Ethnicity and Education* 22, no. 5 (2019): 647–665.

33. Patel, Leigh. "Fugitive practices: Learning in a settler colony." *Educational Studies* 55, no. 3 (2019): 253–261.; Love, Bettina L. *We Want to do More than Survive: Abolitionist Teaching and the Pursuit of Educational Freedom*. Beacon Press, 2019.

34. Hornstein, Henry A. "Student evaluations of teaching are an inadequate assessment tool for evaluating faculty performance." *Cogent Education* 4, no. 1 (2017).

35. Matias, Cheryl E. ""Why do you make me hate myself?": Re-teaching Whiteness, abuse, and love in urban teacher education." *Teaching Education* 27, no. 2

(2016): 194–211; Vasquez, Ramon. "Twenty-Four White Women and Me": Controlling and Managing Men of Color in Teacher Education." *Urban Education* (2019).
   36. Ramon Vasquez. "Twenty-Four White Women and Me."
   37. Paraskeva, João M. *Curriculum Epistemicide: Towards an Itinerant Curriculum Theory*. Routledge, 2016.
   38. Mignolo, Walter. *The Darker Side of Western Modernity: Global Futures, Decolonial Options*. Duke University Press, 2011.
   39. Sefa Dei, George J. "Indigenous knowledge studies and the next generation: Pedagogical possibilities for anti-colonial education." *The Australian Journal of Indigenous Education*, 37, no. Supplementary (2008): 5.
   40. Mignolo, Walter D. "Epistemic disobedience, independent thought and decolonial freedom." *Theory, Culture & Society* 26, no. 7–8 (2009): 159–181.
   41. Lorenzini, Daniele. "Foucault, regimes of truth and the making of the subject." *Foucault and the Making of Subjects* (2016): 63–75.
   42. Mignolo, "Epistemic disobedience."
   43. Lander, Edgardo, and Mariana Past. "Eurocentrism, modern knowledges, and the "natural" order of global capital." *Nepantla: Views from South* 3, no. 2 (2002): 245–268.
   44. Lewis, Tyson E. "Education for potentiality (against instrumentality)." *Policy Futures in Education* (2020); Biesta, Gert JJ. *Beautiful Risk of Education*. Routledge, 2015.
   45. Ahmed, Sara. "The nonperformativity of antiracism." *Meridians* 7, no. 1 (2006): 104–126.
   46. Grande, Sandy. *Red Pedagogy: Native American Social and Political Thought*. Rowman & Littlefield, 2015.
   47. Andreotti, Vanessa. "(re) imagining education as an un-coercive re-arrangement of desires." *Other Education* 5, no. 1 (2016): 79–88; Reed, Joquina M., and Ashley Noel Mack. "Act Right White: Displacing Meritocracy and Recentering Intimacy." *Departures in Critical Qualitative Research* 8, no. 4 (2019): 94–99.
   48. Ohito, Esther O. "Making the emperor's new clothes visible in anti-racist teacher education: Enacting a pedagogy of discomfort with white preservice teachers." *Equity & Excellence in Education* 49, no. 4 (2016): 454–467; Zembylas, Michalinos. "Affect, race, and white discomfort in schooling: Decolonial strategies for 'pedagogies of discomfort.'" *Ethics and Education* 13, no. 1 (2018): 86–104.
   49. Tuck, Eve, and K. Wayne Yang. "Decolonization is not a metaphor." *Decolonization: Indigeneity, Education & Society* 1, no. 1 (2012).

REFERENCES

Ahmed, Sara. "The nonperformativity of antiracism." *Meridians* 7, no. 1 (2006): 104–126.
Andreotti, Vanessa. "(re) imagining education as an un-coercive re-arrangement of desires." *Other Education* 5, no. 1 (2016): 79–88.

Applebaum, Barbara. *Being White, Being Good: White Complicity, White Moral Responsibility, and Social Justice Pedagogy*. Lexington Books, 2010.

Bailey, Alison. "Strategic ignorance." *Race and Epistemologies of Ignorance* (2007): 77–94.

Battiste, Marie. *Decolonizing Education: Nourishing the Learning Spirit*. UBC Press, 2017.

Bernal, Dolores Delgado, and Octavio Villalpando. "An apartheid of knowledge in academia: The struggle over the 'legitimate' knowledge of faculty of color." *Equity & Excellence in Education* 35, no. 2 (2002): 169–180.

Biesta, Gert JJ. *Beautiful Risk of Education*. Routledge, 2015.

Boatright-Horowitz, Su L., and Sojattra Soeung. "Teaching White privilege to White students can mean saying good-bye to positive student evaluations." (2009): 574–575.

Castro-Gómez, Santiago. "The missing chapter of empire: Postmodern reorganization of coloniality and post-Fordist capitalism." *Cultural Studies* 21, no. 2–3 (2007): 428–448.

Castro-Gómez, Santiago, and Desiree A. Martin. "The Social Sciences, Epistemic Violence, and the Problem of the 'Invention of the Other'." *Nepantla: views from South* 3, no. 2 (2002): 269–285.

Dancy, T. Elon, Kirsten T. Edwards, and James Earl Davis. "Historically white universities and plantation politics: Anti-Blackness and higher education in the Black Lives Matter era." *Urban Education* 53, no. 2 (2018): 176–195.

Santos, Boaventura de Sousa. *The End of the Cognitive Empire: The Coming of Age of Epistemologies of the South*. Duke University Press, 2018.

Esarey, Justin, and Natalie Valdes. "Unbiased, reliable, and valid student evaluations can still be unfair." *Assessment & Evaluation in Higher Education* (2020): 1–15.

Kolitch, Elaine, & Dean, Ann V. "Student ratings of instruction in the USA: Hidden assumptions and missing conceptions about 'good' teaching." *Studies in Higher Education* 24, no. 1 (1999): 27–42.

Grande, Sandy. *Red Pedagogy: Native American Social and Political Thought*. Rowman & Littlefield, 2015.

Harris, Cheryl I. "Whiteness as property." *Harvard Law Review* (1993): 1707–1791.

Hornstein, Henry A. "Student evaluations of teaching are an inadequate assessment tool for evaluating faculty performance." *Cogent Education* 4, no. 1 (2017).

Goitom, Mary. "'Legitimate Knowledge': An Auto-Ethnographical Account of an African Writing Past the White Gaze in Academia." *Social Epistemology* 33, no. 3 (2019): 193–204.

Grosfoguel, Ramón. "Decolonizing post-colonial studies and paradigms of political-economy: Transmodernity, decolonial thinking, and global coloniality." *Transmodernity: Journal of Peripheral Cultural Production of the Luso-Hispanic World* 1, no. 1 (2011).

Hook, Derek. "White privilege, psychoanalytic ethics, and the limitations of political silence." *South African Journal of Philosophy* 30, no. 4 (2011): 494–501.

Ladson-Billings, Gloria. "Toward a theory of culturally relevant pedagogy." *American Educational Research Journal* 32, no. 3 (1995): 465–491.

Kerr, Jeannie, and Vanessa Andreotti. "Crossing borders in initial teacher education: mapping dispositions to diversity and inequity." *Race Ethnicity and Education* 22, no. 5 (2019): 647–665.

Lander, Edgardo, and Mariana Past. "Eurocentrism, modern knowledges, and the 'natural' order of global capital." *Nepantla: Views from South* 3, no. 2 (2002): 245–268.

Levina, Marina. "The Violence of Merit." *Departures in Critical Qualitative Research* 9, no. 1 (2020): 20–24.

Lewis, Tyson E. "Education for potentiality (against instrumentality)." *Policy Futures in Education* (2020).

Lorenzini, Daniele. "Foucault, Regimes of Truth and the Making of the Subject." *Foucault and the Making of Subjects* (2016): 63–75.

Love, Bettina L. *We Want To Do More Than Survive: Abolitionist Teaching and the Pursuit of Educational Freedom*. Beacon Press, 2019.

Matias, Cheryl E. "Why do you make me hate myself?": Re-teaching Whiteness, abuse, and love in urban teacher education." *Teaching Education* 27, no. 2 (2016): 194–211.

Mignolo, Walter. *The Darker Side of Western Modernity: Global Futures, Decolonial Options*. Duke University Press, 2011.

Mignolo, Walter D. "Epistemic disobedience, independent thought and decolonial freedom." *Theory, Culture & Society* 26, no. 7–8 (2009): 159–181.

Mitchell, Megan. "White people, we need to stop being so damn fragile!": White and Male Fragility as Epistemic Arrogance." In *Pacifism, Politics, and Feminism*, pp. 51–67. Brill Rodopi, 2019.

Maldonado-Torres, Nelson. *Outline of Ten Theses on Coloniality and Decoloniality*. Paris: Frantz Fanon Foundation, 2016.

Ohito, Esther O. "Making the emperor's new clothes visible in anti-racist teacher education: Enacting a pedagogy of discomfort with white preservice teachers." *Equity & Excellence in Education* 49, no. 4 (2016): 454–467.

Paraskeva, João M. *Curriculum Epistemicide: Towards An Itinerant Curriculum Theory*. Routledge, 2016.

Patel, Leigh. "Fugitive practices: Learning in a settler colony." *Educational Studies* 55, no. 3 (2019): 253–261.

Popkewitz, Thomas S. "The paradoxes of practical research: The good intentions of inclusion that exclude and abject." *European Educational Research Journal* 19, no. 4 (2020): 271–288.

Popkewitz, Thomas. "The sociology of education as the history of the present: Fabrication, difference and abjection." *Discourse: Studies in the Cultural Politics of Education* 34, no. 3 (2013): 439–456.

Reed, Joquina M., and Ashley Noel Mack. "Act Right White: Displacing Meritocracy and Recentering Intimacy." *Departures in Critical Qualitative Research* 8, no. 4 (2019): 94–99.

Sefa Dei, George J. "Indigenous knowledge studies and the next generation: Pedagogical possibilites for anti-colonial education." *Australian Journal of Indigenous Education, The* 37, no. Supplementary (2008): 5.

Smith, Linda Tuhiwai. *Decolonizing Methodologies: Research and Indigenous Peoples*. Zed Books Ltd., 2013.

Vasquez, Ramon. "Twenty-Four White Women and Me": Controlling and Managing Men of Color in Teacher Education." *Urban Education* (2019).

Vlieghe, Joris, and Piotr Zamojski. *Towards an Ontology of Teaching*. Springer International Publishing, 2019.

Wynter, Sylvia. "Unsettling the coloniality of being/power/truth/freedom: Towards the human, after man, its overrepresentation—An argument." *CR: The new centennial review* 3, no. 3 (2003): 257–337.

Tuck, Eve, and K. Wayne Yang. "Decolonization is not a metaphor." *Decolonization: Indigeneity, Education & Society* 1, no. 1 (2012).

Zembylas, Michalinos. "Affect, race, and white discomfort in schooling: Decolonial strategies for 'pedagogies of discomfort.'" *Ethics and Education* 13, no. 1 (2018): 86–104.

Chapter 5

Journey to Critical Whiteness in Higher Education

Yvette Freter

INTRODUCTION

When I was a graduate teaching assistant at a large state university in the southeast of the United States, my supervisor, Dr. Denise Harvey, was a Black woman. She had carved out a niche for herself, promoting diversity at the university. Rather than being tenure track, her line was paid for in part by the central administration and by the Dean's Office.[1] The chancellor at the time was said to have admired her "intelligence, competence, and personality."[2] She was soft spoken, her age inscrutable, and she dealt with me with consummate kindness, professionalism, and politeness, but with firm distance. I was consequently delighted and a bit surprised when she invited me—based on feedback she had received from my students—to speak at a class she was teaching. It was to "get real" in a culture of teaching that fostered in large part "urban white saviors," "there-by-the-grace-of-god-go-I" suburban educators, and the forgotten teachers of the rural poor. This was during America's illusory "post-racial" period when Barack Obama was president[3] and we were trying to explain to a class of preservice teachers how race-neutrality was a myth[4] and destructive.[5] This was ten years before a policeman knelt on the neck of George Floyd,[6] and #BLM,[7] white supremacy/fragility,[8] systemic racism,[9] anti-racism,[10] and critical consciousness brought being "woke"[11] back again to the streets, the 24-hour news cycle, and our social media feeds.

Critical Race Theory scholar Gloria Ladson-Billings has long made the case that race "continues to be a significant factor in determining inequity in the United States."[12] This book, too, argues that race and racism are hugely influential in student evaluations. In my experience, even if white students have good-will toward Black, Indigenous and People of Color (BIPOC) in institutes of higher learning, race remains a stumbling block of awkward reverence and distant politeness blocking free exchange of ideas and appreciation of unique abilities and contributions. As Toni Morrison remarks,

> in matters of race, silence and evasion have historically ruled literary discourse. Evasion has fostered another, substitute language in which the issues are encoded, foreclosing open debate. It is further complicated by the fact that the habit of ignoring race is understood to be a graceful, even generous, liberal gesture.[13]

Dealing with white guilt[14] as a child of *apartheid* South Africa living in east Tennessee, I approached Dr. Harvey with what must have been taxing enthusiasm and deference. While this might seem appealing, my desire to be atoned for my whiteness in relation to her Blackness kept race at the existential center of our interactions.

Then the unspeakable happened. Dr. Harvey died of cancer. Her obituary revealed she was only fifty-seven years old. Just like that, after all the hard work to achieve her position in academia and the love and respect of her students and colleagues, she was gone. I had just been home to South Africa. She had asked me to bring her something. I was sure her parents wondered who that weeping blonde lady was who incoherently gave them a carved elephant in the forever-long receiving line. It has been ten years since that hot summer day of the funeral and I was finally able to properly introduce myself to Dr. Harvey's 95-year-old mother to interview her for this chapter. A decade after my clumsy gift giving, I got a card from Mrs. Edwina Harvey[15] in delicate, fragile cursive, thanking me . . . for the elephant.

In order to consider the complexities of academic interactions between BIPOC and whites in higher education my elephant gift serves as a microcosm—with Dr. Harvey and myself at the center. This is a process of looking at a single example of the intersection of two women engaged in anti-racism. It is an exploration of the discomfort of cultural dissonance that seeks to unpack the greater issues in the macrocosm of Black/white subjectivity and the process of knowing and growing through relationship toward the negation of privilege and the undermining of marginalization in our schools of higher education and beyond.

The elephant in question was, if memory serves, about 15 cm × 15 cm and hand-carved from either Ebony or Ironwood. I bought it at the back of a shopping center in Rondebosch, Cape Town, from a vendor who came in from the townships every day with a large bag full of beaded and carved goods. He had laid them out on the asphalt. There were many such artists like him at that time, men that had travelled down from the Congo or Zambia to sell to the tourists of South Africa. I was in awe of the art and acutely aware of how far my converted dollars could go, so I spent the last of my brightly colored South African Rand bills on buying gifts for those back in the States. I have no idea why I picked the elephant for Dr. Harvey until, ten years later, a bold Black female colleague told me it was time to find out. My research brought me to a copy of Doran Ross's *Elephant: The Animal and Its Ivory in African Culture* (1992) which consequently gave me an analytical framework for my investigation.

ELEPHANT CONSIDERATIONS

Ross's book points out that the colonizing west thinks of things and people associated with Africa as curiosities, infantile, and caricatures. In the case of elephants, we are reminded of Jumbo, Dumbo, and Babar.[16] Ross notes that "elephants are indeed a component of the Western world's invention of Africa. They are also, however, an end product of the same process of invention."[17] As I consider my white subjectivity as it relates to Dr. Harvey's Blackness I wonder how much of what I perceived about her was based on my Eurowestern lens. Did I also make her a caricature, assuming traits based on stereotypes gained from the media or my fractured lens as a South African? Or did I perhaps treat her as a revered exotic in my longing for the familiarity of my African homeland and her people, or engage with her using cautiously curated political correctness?

I have discovered there is much still to be learned by humankind about African elephants.[18] This is also so true of the willfully ignorant or disinterested whites regarding BIPOC. How little I knew about Dr. Harvey at the time I worked with her. How little I knew of the experience of BIPOC in general. In the Ross text the elephant was chosen as the topic as it played a significant role in "shaping the nature of contact with the rest of the world"[19] and Africa due, unfortunately, to the once prolific ivory trade. I chose Dr. Harvey as the subject of my chapter because she left an impression on me at a critical juncture in my growth toward anti-racism.

In another parallel, the elephant is important subject matter because of the "specter of the potential extinction of the elephant through poaching and the illegal trade in ivory."[20] Poignantly, BIPOC in academia are fighting their own battle against poaching and extinction in the general form of "institutional racism, sexism, police brutality, the prison industrial complex, social class exploitation, de jure segregation, eugenics, and political/economical disenfranchisement,"[21] and in particular through lower student evaluations of teaching (SET) scores and their consequent weaponization to control, limit promotion and tenure,[22] and undermine the authority and scholarship of BIPOC.

Ross's consideration of elephants offered me a mental map to consider Dr. Harvey. The west sees the elephant as a peculiarity who suffers misinterpretation, misrepresentation, and exploitation.[23] This is the "illegitimate, difficult/aggressive while gendered kind, servile, and less academic"[24] type-casting which research demonstrates BIPOC frequently experience. As elephants need to be known as their full selves and we need to consider what they represent to us, I wished to know Dr. Harvey and why she was such a symbol to me, even after her death. Of course, the elephant is not the only animal from Africa that needs to be better understood and we should not study it out of context or imagine that its symbolism is static. The same is true for my investigation into the life of Dr. Harvey—she was multidimensional and evolved throughout her lifetime. And most importantly, she is not to be misappropriated as a monolithic exemplar as, in the language of critical race theory, a token of all African American women in academia.

The African depictions of elephants have "as much to say about human society as about the animal itself. Ultimately, historical events, social responsibilities, religious beliefs, and political relationships are the primary subjects of elephant imagery."[25] I want to take some of these broad categories and use them to consider the life (fuller dimensions) and influence (symbolism) of Dr. Harvey. Recollections of family, friends, and colleagues and primary sources associated with Dr. Harvey are combined to build a fuller picture of who she was, to help demonstrate what she brought to our relationship. I will then do the same work to excavate my own white subjectivity with a view to fostering journeys of conscious-raising and white anti-racist allyship.

BLACK SUBJECT(IVITY)

Historical Events

Dr. Harvey was one of three children born to Edwina Harvey and the late Dr. Robert Harvey.[26] A remarkable couple, Dr. and Mrs. Harvey were vitally involved in the life of Knoxville College, a historically Black college, founded in 1875,[27] were married seventy years, and were key members of their church[28] and community. My Dr. Harvey went to Holston High School in Knoxville, Tennessee. Her mother recalls that when Denise was in high school she said she wanted to be like her father and declared, "Mother, I may get married, but I will not change my name. I am going to be Dr. Harvey, like my daddy!"[29]

Mrs. Harvey recollects that her daughter "had nerve—more nerve than I had!"[30] During high school she was an exchange student to the Netherlands. This opportunity was advertised at her Black high school and Mrs. Harvey recalled that she said with her usual aplomb, "Mother, I would love to do that, I will apply, how we gonna pay for it?"[31] Mrs. Harvey answered, "You get a scholarship and we will go with your grandmother to co-sign and we will borrow the money."[32] This powerful combination of three generations of women made it possible for a young Black girl from the south to travel internationally in the early Seventies. Dr. Harvey's international travel did not end there: she later also spent a semester as an undergraduate student at the University of Denmark, Copenhagen. Mrs. Harvey recollects that "she got to stay in an approved private home, not a dormitory. The host family was very happy to have her."[33] In fact, the families became friends—they visited together three times over the years, enjoying each-others hospitality and exploring the sites together.

Dr. Harvey went to Oxford College of Emory University in 1974. After receiving her Associates Degree, she earned a BA from Vanderbilt-Peabody in 1976, she got her degree in Social Welfare, Administration, and Planning from University of Tennessee (1978), obtained an MA from Tulane in Sociology (1991), and an MS and PhD from University of Tennessee in 1996. Mrs. Harvey's reminiscences remind one this was not as easy as it sounds:

> Denise was married and lived in New Orleans. She was working on her doctorate at a private university. She felt they weren't ready for a Black doctor. She had a [white] classmate that was having difficulty and she was hired to tutor him. She continued her courses while she tutored her classmate. That student got his doctorate. She did not pass her oral exams! How could she tutor a passing student and not pass herself? She took the exam again—coming back into town and staying in a hotel and studying again and preparing as best she could. She had fulfilled all requirements. She did not pass again. And, you know, you were only allowed two tries. Denise's marriage broke up and she returned to Knoxville. She lived with us for a year working at school. She got her masters and then a second masters at Tulane and then finally her doctorate at University of Tennessee.[34]

Social Responsibilities

Dr. Harvey's positionality as a woman of color greatly impacted her actions. A cursory investigation shows that she was a member of the Commission for Blacks at University of Tennessee, Knoxville (1984);[35] in her capacity as staff in the Office of Affirmative Action she submitted a report to the university paper condemning sexist language (1985);[36] and she served on the Commission for Women (1985) dealing with salary inequities, underrepresentation of female professors, need for women's academic contributions beyond women's studies courses, job insecurity preventing the teaching of controversial issues or taking an unpopular position, and the need for representation in the university administration.[37]

Completing her dissertation in the summer of 1996, Dr. Harvey's ongoing social commitment to equality was demonstrated again as she tackled inequities in her sphere of influence. She wrote, "As a former affirmative action officer at a large state supported university in the southeastern United States, I witnessed this lack of representation across the fields of study at my university and worked to eradicate it."[38] She went on to state, "I investigated whether barriers referred to in the 1980s as the 'glass ceiling,' which slowed women's progress to the upper ranks of administration, still exist or have been compounded by what I call a 'glass façade.'"[39] And I cannot help by thinking Denise would have been so proud to know that the metaphor of her dissertation, *Beyond the Glass Façade*, was joyfully smashed by another powerful BIPOC woman when Kamala Harris broke through the glass ceiling and became the vice-president of the United States.

Later in her career Dr. Harvey was a member of the University of Tennessee Black Faculty and Staff Association, advisor for UT-Project GRAD Summer Institute (helping under-represented students get a sense of the college experience), and engaged in community service with United Way.[40]

Political Relationships

There is clearly no way for me to speak to how Dr. Harvey navigated her embodied self or how her actions were negotiated as she dealt with Blackness and whiteness. As South Africa anti-*apartheid* activist, Strinivasa (Strini) Moodley wrote about Black representation, "who can speak the heart of the Blackman, who can sing the rhythm of the Blackman, who can paint the suffering of the Blackman and who can act the pain, the desires, the loves and hates of the Black experience?"[41] However, perhaps Dr. Harvey's positionality can be considered through the optics of the personal narrative of another. Damon Young observes in his 2019 book *What Doesn't Kill You Makes You Blacker*: "To be [B]lack in America is to exist in a ceaseless state of absurdity; a perpetual surreality that twists and contorts and transmutes equilibrium and homeostasis the way an extended stay in space alters human DNA."[42] He goes on,

> Of course, there are other places that America takes us, and other places we jaunt to ourselves. It is perfectly sane, for instance, to be Black and to allow outrage to conquer you. . . . How else are you supposed to react when first learning about redlining; when first reading about lynching; when first having gerrymandering and gentrification explained to you; when first studying the myriad and colossal racial disparities in everything from income to education; and when first encouraging a white person intentionally oblivious to how being

white in America is like being free to take an open-book exam on the same lesson materials that we weren't even allowed to study for?[43]

Perhaps Dr. Harvey might have used her renowned wit and intellect as Damon does to consider that being Black is

> sometimes, finding the farce and the humor embedded in the absurd, and allowing yourself to marinate in it long enough to lose your shit in laughter. It is, sometimes, stepping back and interrogating exactly when, why, and how white supremacy and patriarchy converged to construct the feelings you've internalized and the acts sprung from them, and then reckoning with what you need to do to rectify that. It is, sometimes, finding comfort and colony in a colloquial version of a centuries-old word created to destroy. It is, sometimes, just sitting on a futon with your homies at a game night, doing nothing but enjoying a shared moment where your personhoods need no explanations or alibi.[44]

Implications

Seeking to know Dr. Harvey in a more dimensional way gives a cursory insight into the life of a Black teacher in higher education. Dr. Harvey navigated Black/white subjectivity through education, travel, forging diverse relationships, activism, and her warm humanity, and was able to develop the knowledge and relationships necessary to advance the negation of privilege and the undermining of marginalization in her educational context and beyond. At her passing Dr. Harvey was described as: "Teacher, mentor, and colleague."[45] It was noted that "Dr. Harvey had a profound impact on many students, faculty, and staff at UT."[46] We can see that her trajectory caused her to be remembered as "a strong and passionate supporter of diversity and inclusion"[47] and "such an inspiration for academic success amongst young African-American students."[48] An associate noted at the time of her passing: "Denise was such a great support of community engagement and education for all."[49]

Dr. Harvey responded to social justice issues through inclusion and compassion:

> I had the honor of working with Dr. Harvey on an annual Katrina program at UT [University of Tennessee]. She had a gift of bringing people together and giving herself to achieve greater outcomes than any of us could accomplish alone. I remember her talking about how she met a young man who had transferred to UT following the storm who only had a light jacket which was not sufficient for Knoxville's climate. She made sure that he got a coat and felt comfortable for

his stay away from home. I am sure there are a million other instances of her kindness, generosity and thoughtfulness that we will never know.[50]

The lives of Dr. Harvey's colleagues and students, be they Black, white, male, female, privileged, or poor, were impacted as notes written at the time of her death reveal

> her earnest . . . belief in not only my ability to succeed in my educational pursuit of obtaining a PhD, but also the countless other "students of color" she has impacted throughout her tenure.[51]

> . . . she made a real difference in the lives of many people.[52]

> Her loving guidance gave me the reassurance I needed to graduate from UT.[53]

We see too a hope for BIPOC educators when students of all races praise her teaching, her personhood, and her ability to challenge and empower:

> I had the privilege of having her as a teacher . . . and enjoyed every minute of her class. I will miss her smile and words of wisdom. The cultural studies department will not be the same without her.[54]

> Dr. Harvey was one of the most memorable teachers I had during twenty-one years of sitting in classrooms. Her assignments were unusual and thought provoking.[55]

> WOW. Dr. H you meant so much to me in such a short span of time.[56]

> She was a great mentor and inspired me to travel and live through growth and experiences of this world. She was able to believe in me and without that support, I would not have had the success today.[57]

> . . . you always managed to make me feel positive and empowered. I know of sooo many students of whom you impacted.[58]

WHITE SUBJECT(IVITY)

Historical Events

As a historical colonizer I am driven by remembrances of squatter camps and mansions; the milky smell of my Xhosa nanny, Grace, who had left her baby to come and take care of me; signs that let me go to the best beaches; and the moment as a little girl I realized that it didn't feel right for me to go into the door marked *Slegs Blankes* (Whites Only) when I went to the doctor. I cannot be sure of how it came to be that I knew it was wrong. Perhaps was taught to me by my liberal church that secretly helped conscientious objectors who would not join the South African Defense Force as they were routinely deployed to quell Black uprisings;[59] and hid, in our whites-only suburb, hundreds fleeing from the Crossroads Black Township during a government-endorsed fratricide/forced-relocation effort.[60] It might have been the activism of my uncle who sought to use the arts to unify across the races despite the *apartheid* laws of forced racial segregation and the days spent hanging out at multiracial rehearsals. Perhaps I knew racial discrimination was wrong from the times that my mother eschewed convention and let me go to the home of a Muslim friend in a Colored[61] neighborhood to spend the night. It might also have been that my first job was in a shop close to the railway station that catered to Africans, and my boss was a Xhosa man and my co-workers were Colored. Or maybe it was the time my father snuck me into the townships while he was working with his Black colleagues from the television industry and I again saw what most other white children never did, the daily life of BIPOC.

These clandestine crossings of the race-bound barriers in South Africa allowed me to traverse between races, religions, and cultures and showed me the system needed to be dismantled. If I try to recall how I felt, I remember being proudly aware that I was occasionally, with intentionality, defying *apartheid*. However, simultaneously, this was also just the openness of a kid growing up in a seriously messed up system playing and working with the Xhosa and Colored people around me. That's how it is sometimes: riots, bombings, protests, vigils and swimming, getting your first kiss, going to school; life is just still happening. You don't realize yet you're the one that needs to dismantle the system you know is wrong.

That was how it was for us white South African kids who grew up loving their Black nannies and playing with the Colored children of their gardeners or farm laborers, most of us with no awareness of our "awkward forms of privilege."[62] Our cognitive dissonance was generational: my grandmother was an avid supporter of the liberal, anti-*apartheid* Progressive Party and vigorously opposed the nationalist Afrikaans government, but Granny still got mad if she thought her Black weekly cleaner, Princess, stole her Paracetamol or used too much sugar. It is with embarrassment that I recall how, after moving to the United States in my early twenties, I would disavow racial classifications by stating "human" when a form asked what race I was. I earnestly declared impartiality, invoking color-blindness, asserting my class-less outlook, and proclaimed gender-equality. I believed in individual egalitarianism. I embraced the meritocratic ideal that anything is possible if we just are sufficiently motivated and work hard enough. Little did I know my outlook was based on the fact that I could assume a stance of race-, class-, and gender-blindness because of the invisibility of my race, the ubiquity of being middle-class, and lack of awareness of the experience of being a nondominant culture woman.

Social Responsibilities

I came to the United States to add to my South African teaching qualification and, upon graduating from a small private southern college, I immediately sought out a job teaching in the "inner-city." *Mea culpa* meets white savior time as my guilt intersected my privileged belief I could "help" the "less fortunate." As a product of a teacher education program that only offered superficial overviews of the deeper issues of the social foundations of education and little on issues of systemic injustice, I was ill-equipped to deal with the "gaps" I encountered as a white, middle-class woman. I was devastated by my experiences. I was not equipped to help. I was ignorant of the culture, clueless about systemic racism. Hopped up on the "American Dream" and high on education-as-the-panacea, I crashed and burned. White good-will wasn't enough.

My "urban"/Black community teaching experience began a journey for me to investigate the so-called achievement gaps in the United States. I went to graduate school and immersed myself in multicultural education, critical race and feminist theory, and social justice issues. I was offended when I was confronted with what is now known as my white fragility.[63] I was made uncomfortable with the awareness of systemic racism that critical race theory brought to the fore. Then I started to get real. I was a racist. This coming to consciousness allowed me to grow on from my roots in Africa that told me racism feels wrong, beyond my white savior do-gooder kindness to fix other races, and into a place of humble awareness of how little I know about BIPOC and how much I have endowed to me (good and bad) as a white person.

Political Relationships

The implications of my positionality on my academic and professional pursuits have caused me to deliberate if it is right for me to engage in the cause of equity. As Goodall Jr. states, "'Who has the right to speak for a culture?' is very much a question about who is entitled to represent it."[64] Whiteness and coloniality brought me to a crisis of representation.[65] As a member of the dominant community I have to negotiate a relationship of contribution devoid of hubris, for "when pride comes, then comes disgrace, but with humility comes wisdom."[66] I am thus compelled to have a political outlook that embraces my identity in two ways. First, through self-reflexivity, confessional tales, and humility to bring to the fore the voice of the majority I represent. As the marginalized are given voice as a means to challenge hegemonic forces that maintain oppression, so too must the dialogue include those in power to be true to the tenants of inclusion and "enlarged conversation."[67] Second, by using methodologies and theories in my practice such as relational (e)pistemologies,[68] constructive thinking,[69] critical theory, postcolonialism, and theories of difference I hope to continue a research and teaching agenda that engages issues of inequity in education that aspires to equality. It is my hope that difficult issues of representation and credibility will not be negatively impacted by my positionality but rather enhanced through thoughtful and reflective practices. My positionality on many levels compels me to action and so my academic and professional pursuits will continue to reflect a commitment to addressing issues of race and the dismantling of colonizer/colonized dichotomies, in whatever form they may present themselves.[70]

Implications

On my journey of conscious-raising I was informed by, among other things, the work of multiculturalism, a field that has directed me toward issues of equity and diversity in education. However, the concept of multiculturalism—particularly in regards to issues of racial inclusion—itself means different things to different people and here is possible locus of struggles between BIPOC and white students and the consequent impact on SET scores. It has been my trajectory to move through various stages of multiculturalism in terms of racial awareness and acceptance. Other whites are also on various journeys to (or running from) critical consciousness.

Conservative multiculturalists/monoculturalists see multiculturalism as a means to explore the problems caused by diversity. From their Eurocentric neocolonial patriarchal perspective difference is divisive and they seek to promote a "common culture."[71] This sort of discourse sounds like a binary *us* and *them*. This is the kind of rhetoric that is against those who question Manifest Destiny, imperialism, and fundamentalist Christianity and promote anti-racist thinking.[72] In this vein white students will likely judge their BIPOC educators as incompetent, divisive, and even anti-American.

Liberal multiculturalists seek to address inequality by promoting equal social and economic opportunities through education, but adhere to color-blind equality and the belief that racism is individualized (perpetrated by a few bad apples or in the past) and can go both ways (reverse racism). However, within this approach Eurocentric culture is the normative touchstone. Sameness in the form of individualism and citizenship is pursued by liberal multiculturalists.[73] This discourse sounds like *us* but the "us" is the dominant cultural group. Here we see Jeffersonian meritocracy being broadened by well-meaning whites to allow BIPOC to be included without dismantling the unequitable power structures. Students with this mindset will likely rate their BIPOC teachers more highly if they exemplify white patterns of upward mobility and don't challenge the status quo by soothing cognitive dissonance.

Pluralistic multiculturalists "celebrate human diversity and equal opportunity"[74] but this often manifests in a separate-but-equal focus on "heritage and cultural differences"[75] and a "cultural tourism."[76] This approach creates *us* knowing about *them* dichotomy. Think Black History Month and smashing piñatas on Cinco de Mayo. With this outlook white students will be supportive of being told about the culture of BIPOC, but will likely be unaware of "white" culture. If the voyeurism and let's-just-get-along ideal is disrupted, SET scores might reflect student discomfort.

Left-essentialist multiculturalism has an *us*, but "us" is the marginalized group, and has "concerned itself more with self-assertion than with the effort to build strategic democratic alliances for social justice."[77] Thus, a student with this mindset might positively rate their BIPOC educator because he/she/they is an Other (you do you) and the student wishes to bestow affirmation on the Other. However, this appreciation of the cultural enrichment a BIPOC offers becomes a safe diversity. If this student is challenged by the educator who seeks political and economic empowerment not only affirmation for BIPOC, the student might grade the BIPOC judgmental or the classroom environment as unsafe and unwelcoming.

Critical multiculturalism is concerned with how domination occurs and issues of power. Critical multiculturalism promotes self-reflection, individual conscious-raising, solidarity with marginalized groups, exposing and challenging privilege, and teasing out the intersections of race, class, and gender and their relation to domination, power, and inequalities.[78] Dr. Harvey exemplified this approach. However, critical multiculturalism can at times foster an understandable *us* and *them* binary. Consequently, white students might embrace an anti-racist outlook and being transformed, seek solidarity with BIPOC, and have gratitude toward their teacher such as the appreciation I felt toward Dr. Harvey, or it can cause students to feel persecuted and shamed, resulting in poor perceptions of the BIPOC educator who caused the discomfort.

Dr. Harvey also embodied Sonia Nieto's definition of multiculturalism. Nieto defines it as "embedded in a sociopolitical context and as antiracist and basic education for *all* students that permeates all areas of schooling, and that is characterized by a commitment to social justice and critical approaches to learning."[79] And here I suggest a potentially new paradigm emerges as Nieto describes multiculturalism: "My definition is an expansive one, comprising not only race, ethnicity, and language but also gender, social class, sexual orientation, ability, and other differences. Students from the majority culture certainly are included in this definition."[80] *Us* and *them* becomes *all of us*, diverse but inclusive. This is the ideal whereby a BIPOC instructor, such as Dr. Harvey, and white students/colleagues, like me, are able to explore difference critically while forging allegiances. However, I must qualify that the emergence of an anti-racist white person is (1) a process and occurs along a continuum and (2) BIPOC cannot be expected to nurture this growth. This the white community must do for itself. It is incumbent on people like me to educate myself and my racial community and urge them along their own conscious-raising journeys. Dr. Harvey didn't spoon-feed me—that wasn't her responsibility—but she did graciously invite me to the table.

Journeys of Conscious-Raising

The best way for me to explain what conscious-raising is for white folx is to talk about Thomas Jefferson. In the course of my career I have taught high schoolers, preservice teachers, and graduate students about Jefferson due to his obvious impact on the history of the Republic and his influence on education in this country. The journey white people in the United States have to take one that has to acknowledge that which is in plain sight and deal with it: our existence is different from BIPOC folx because of an unfair political and economic system that was designed to favor whites with freedom, opportunity, representation, and equality by enslaving, impoverishing, exploiting, raping, dehumanizing, miseducating, sterilizing, imprisoning, murdering, and marginalizing of BIPOC. By acknowledging one's racist privilege and racism and determining how to act going forward we can deal with this enormous cognitive dissonance. This uncomfortable step is vital because as Björn Freter points out: "There is a largely overlooked fundamental flaw in the Eurocentric epistemological foundation. Counter to the overwhelming ethos of the Enlightenment, this epistemological bedrock shockingly does not seem to be an epistemology of the human being, but only of the white human being."[81]

When I try to disrupt the teaching of superiorism[82] and foster critical engagement I ask students to compare the (1) preliminary version of the *Declaration of Independence* written down by John Adams with the text which was (2) Jefferson's rough draft and the final (3) engrossed copy of the *Declaration of Independence*[83] created in the summer of 1776. There is a fundamental omission: a section berating the King of England for supporting slavery. However, we see Jefferson's concern for the ending of slavery was not a moral concern, based on a belief in universal equality; it was predicated on a pragmatic superiorism based on the loathing of British rule and the needs of the new Republic and its white male leadership. Thus, the *Declaration's* initial philosophical paragraphs were arguing for a government that functioned to bring about the common good and this section sought to legitimize the colonial rebellion into a noble battle against a tyrannical ruler to gain moral approval for their actions.[84] It is thus vital to note that Jefferson—and the Congress—was using the Preamble to "establish the legitimacy of independence."[85] What they were *not* doing was "composing a universal human rights manifesto."[86] This was *not* a call for human equality. This would have been counter-productive for Congress' (half of which owned enslaved people at some point) second aim: to get the people of the American colonies to commit politically and militarily to independence with compelling reasons to rebel against the King.[87] Consequently, because of the divisive nature of the issue of slavery, the Congress deleted this section, opting to try garnering the support of all thirteen colonies. It is indeed a grave misrepresentation to see the *Declaration of Independence* as seeking equality; it was created to inspire patriotism and outrage in the colonists so they would support leaving the British Empire.[88]

However, when faced with the truth of the document that founded the nation, students struggle. They struggle when quotes from the Jefferson Memorial are shown in context and reveal his open racism.[89] They struggle when they learn he was a rapist who made an enslaved teenage girl his concubine until his death and then willed her to a relative.[90] They struggle when they learn he was waited on by his own brothers and sisters and in turn his biracial children served his white children.[91] They have been raised on a government-sanctioned mythology used to indoctrinate them.[92] Their cognitive dissonance has been soothed by ethnonationalism in the guise of patriotism, and thinly veiled racist meritocratic soothsaying hides economic and racial inequities. This journey from myth of democracy to reality of white supremacy requires a fundamental paradigm shift because the "good old days" are revealed to be the racist founding of a white nation. The problems of today must be acknowledged to be historic, systemic, and the logical outcome of an intentional plan that began 250 years ago and of which whites remain the primary beneficiaries.

The journey requires educating oneself, but ignorance of history is not all that has to be undone. Systemic racism from the conception of the nation must be uprooted, exposed, and destroyed. We must evaluate our books, music, movies, friends, traditions, jokes, contact lists to dig out the roots of supremacist thinking.[93] We must evaluate our textbooks, schools, check books, laws, hiring practices, minimum wages, our health care, our voting laws, our giving habits, and the way we value and devalue our teachers. What is needed is a *Jefferson Moment*: when we stop making excuses for Jefferson . . . and ourselves. We have to understand that he needed to breed enslaved

African workers, commit genocide against Native Americans, keep women in the home, and the poor whites in the fields and out of office to make the Republic happen, because he wanted the benefits of an aristocracy while providing democracy for himself. Blinded by our belief in our own liberal rhetoric we do not see that the United States is a country that was founded on a cognitive dissonance that continues to plague our government, education system, and economy to this very day. The United States still has not found a way to function without racism and classism.[94]

This *Jefferson Moment* can open the way to see racism as systemic and this is the hardest thing for white people. It means relinquishing unquestioned allegiance and blind nationalism. But through conscious-raising regarding our current system's impact on Black and white lives, personal agency can be made clear and whites can then make a clear choice to attend to the ideals of freedom, opportunity, representation, and equality *for all* and become anti-racist, or openly acknowledge their racist disinterest in the lives of BIPOC or their racist desire to continue in their white supremacy.

For me, anti-racism is constantly evolving. Multicultural education classes in graduate school, intersectionality with feminism, considering my relationships with Black people like Dr. Harvey, living life with my Black friends, being in class with my Black students, books, documentaries, seeking Black voices in social media, decolonizing my pedagogy and curriculum,[95] working to support Black lives in every way, considering how to relinquish privilege, accepting vilification from other whites, risking rejection by Blacks, seeking to ensure Black votes are counted are all part of a fallible ongoing journey toward "life, liberty, and the pursuit of happiness" for *all* Americans and beyond.

Cognitive Dissonance

Why whites should be compelled to act in one way or another toward BIPOC can be understood by considering Leon Festinger's theory of cognitive dissonance.[96] It is based on the hypothesis that people seek consistency within themselves. Thus, if they are inconsistent in their thinking or actions they seek a reduction in the dissonance and a return to consonance. If dissonance cannot be resolved, people will rather seek to avoid "situations and information which would likely increase the dissonance."[97] Let us take the example of the global response to the murder of George Floyd and the 2020 summer of large-scale protests against police brutality and the larger issues of systemic racism. The indisputable evidence of police violence toward BIPOC brought the perennial issues of racial discrimination and the inequalities faced by BIPOC to the forefront of white consciousness.

Evidence of economic, educational, legal inequalities, and in an election year, suppression of voting rights reported by mass media and BIPOC communities caused white people to experience discomfort. The inconsistency of their experiences of the United States and the principles of freedom, opportunity, representation, and equality and those of BIPOC caused them to seek to resolve this dissonance. Some whites have chosen to educate and ally themselves with the protest movements in favor of BIPOC while others have revealed their open support of white supremist counter-protest groups. The former moving to resolve their cognitive dissonance by aligning their principles of equality with actions to ensure equality for all. The latter have also found consonance as their supremacist beliefs are congruent with their racist actions. However, I suggest there is a dangerous neo-supremacist way. This is strikingly exemplified in a speech given by President Trump on September 17, 2020, at the self-proclaimed first White House Conference on American History.[98] The speech called for the sanitization of American History and demonstrates one way the ruling white class has chosen to respond to the inconsistencies they have been faced with, namely avoiding situations and information that cause cognitive dissonance and adopting other virtues, such as patriotism and national unity. Trump thus declared,

> Our mission is to defend the legacy of America's founding, the virtue of America's heroes, and the nobility of the American character. We must clear away the twisted web of lies in our schools and classrooms, and teach our children the magnificent truth about our country. We want our sons and daughters to know that they are the citizens of the most exceptional nation in the history of the world.[99]

We see that adherence to a xenophobic belief in American exceptionalism replaces the uncomfortable history recent events have re-centered. Trump declares instead that the

> left has warped, distorted, and defiled the American story with deceptions, falsehoods, and lies. There is no better example than the New York Times' totally discredited 1619 Project. This project rewrites American history to teach our children that we were founded on the principle of oppression, not freedom.[100]

Trump commits to preserve "our glorious inheritance: the *Declaration of Independence*" and foster the Jeffersonian narrative of meritocracy, where "[t]o grow up in America is to live in a land where anything is possible, where anyone can rise, and where any dream can come true—all because of the immortal principles our nation's founders inscribed nearly two and a half centuries ago."[101] The embarrassment of countless videos of police violence against BIPOC is countered with a narrative that the "left has launched a vicious and violent assault on law enforcement—the universal symbol of the rule of law in America."[102] In response to the uneasiness caused by evidence of racial inequalities and white privilege, Trump creates a more comfortable consonance by stating,

> Students in our universities are inundated with critical race theory. This is a Marxist doctrine holding that America is a wicked and racist nation, that even young children are complicit in oppression, and that our entire society must be radically transformed. Critical race theory is being forced into our children's schools, it's being imposed into workplace trainings, and it's being deployed to rip apart friends, neighbors, and families.[103]

Trump continues his reinforcement of meritocratic white privilege by cycling through conservative monoculturalism (calling for "national unity" through "shared identity"), multicultural pluralism (appropriating Marking Luther King Jr.'s words) and liberal multiculturalism (pretenses of racial appreciation). Trump closes his call to white-wash history by referring to King and Jefferson in the same breath and stating: "Our heroes will never be forgotten. Our youth will be taught to love America with all of their heart and all of their soul."[104] Uncomfortable coming to consciousness regarding issues of freedom, opportunity, representation, and equality are assuaged with the safety net of indoctrination and blind jingoism.

White Anti-Racist Allies

For so-called white allies like myself, I have sought to adapt Connie Titone's concept[105] of being aware of my positionality[106] and to continue to engage the subject of race no matter how clumsy or downright harmful my efforts might be. In light of my reinstating inequality by recentering whiteness within my relationship with Dr. Harvey and other BIPOC I have to continue to proactively work to combat inequity when it presents itself and educate myself to be anti-racist. My dominant community member power precludes me from being an insider within the marginalized community or claiming to understand the experience of BIPOC in academia. However, I have tried to position myself as willing to be involved when invited and to consciously acknowledge my privilege and attempt to deliberately uncouple myself from it through using culturally responsive pedagogy and anti-racist curriculum. I seek to critically leveraging my influence in my home, school, church, political activities, spending habits, and community service for the benefit of BIPOC.

Titone urges a commitment to "combat pathological whiteness and eradicate racism accompanied by all of its negative academic effects."[107] In this difficult journey of seeking to respect faculty of color for their merits and not because of white guilt, white people in academic spaces have to let go of white fragility[108] and move from exclusion, suppression, self-interest[109] and white privilege[110] through the swamp of over-compensation, to the bright day of a post-systemic racist future.

CONCLUSION

My attempt to better understand Dr. Harvey's life as a Black female working in academia is by no means claiming a comprehensive understanding of her, let alone all people of color, and it may seem unscholarly to have compared a human to an animal. However, my attempt at developing understanding through the vehicle of the elephant powerfully brings into focus the gap between us. This seemingly insurmountable difference between elephant and human (or Black and white) in fact creates a space for imagination and to find similarities were no similarities may seem apparent to the rational mind.[111] While the anti-speciesists among us might consider it a compliment to be compared to an animal, it is a powerful metaphor for the very reason that most of us intrinsically resist comparison between species—cognitive dissonance; it doesn't feel good and/or requires a paradigm shift in our own self-understanding. In the same way anti-speciesists see equality between the species, let us as anti-racists pursue equality between the so-called races, no matter how uncomfortable and imperfect.

The elephant is used in Swaziland as a metaphor for leadership; the male and female rulers are a combination of the man represented by a lion and the female being titled *Nolovukati*—She-Elephant.[112] This imagery is explained as necessary for the Swazi people; the lion and elephant are different but equal and complimentary, and at times assume characteristics of each other for certain rituals. This Swazi leadership metaphor takes a powerful social construct such as gender and creates a working relationship of governance. This offers hope that Black and white relationships too can negotiate through their Black/white subjectivities to bridge the gap that the social constructs of race, privilege, and marginalization have produced.

The reconciliation between humans and elephants has to traverse a bloody history of exploitation, incarceration, and threatened extinction. If my colonial body with the blood of my ancestors on my hands living in a usurped land can find my way to bring a small wooden token to the family of a woman of the formerly enslaved and continually lynched, there must be hope for bridging the gaps between species, between continents, between races, and between students and their teachers.

NOTES

1. Personal communication, 2020, Dr. Barbara Thayer-Bacon.
2. Personal communication, 2020, Dr. Clint Allison.
3. See Bonilla-Silva, 2014, 25.
4. See Taylor, 2020.
5. See Freter, 2020.
6. See Hill et al., 2020.
7. See Black Lives Matter, 2020.
8. See Bonilla-Silva, 2014, 25; Mills, 1997, 20; DiAngelo, 2018, 2.
9. See Alexander, 2020.
10. See Kendi, 2019.
11. See Bunyasi & Smith, 2019.
12. Ladson-Billings, 1995, 48.
13. Morrison, 1993, 10.
14. See Spanierman & Heppner, 2004.
15. Personal communication, September 2, 2020.
16. See Ross, 1992a, xx.
17. See Ross, 1992a, xx and Morrison, 1993, 7.
18. Ross, 1992a, xx.
19. Ross, 1992a, xx.
20. Ross, 1992a, xx.
21. See Taylor, 2020.
22. Although Dr. Harvey was not tenure track, she was still subject to SETs.
23. Ross, 1992b, 1.
24. Taylor, 2020.
25. Ross, 1992b, 1.
26. See Eastminster Prebyterian Church, 2014.
27. See Knoxville College, 2020.
28. See Eastminster Prebyterian Church, 2014.
29. Edwina Harvey, interview by author, Knoxville, September 15, 2020.
30. Edwina Harvey, interview by author, Knoxville, September 15, 2020.
31. Edwina Harvey, interview by author, Knoxville, September 15, 2020.
32. Edwina Harvey, interview by author, Knoxville, September 15, 2020.
33. Edwina Harvey, interview by author, Knoxville, September 15, 2020.
34. Edwina Harvey, interview by author, Knoxville, September 15, 2020.
35. See University of Tennessee Commission for Blacks 1984.
36. See University of Tennessee Commission for Women 1985.
37. See University of Tennessee Commission for Women 1984.
38. Harvey, 1999, 2.
39. Harvey, 1999, 2.
40. Teresa Harris, "Dr Denise Marie Harvey (1954–2011)—Find A Grave" Find a Grave, January 29, 2012, https://www.findagrave.com/memorial/84157792/denise-marie-harvey.

41. Moodley, 1972, 19.
42. Damon, 2019, 9.
43. Damon, 2019, 9–10.
44. Damon, 2019, 10.
45. Dr. Theresa Cooper [online obituary]. Legacy.com, June 20, 2011, https://www.legacy.com/amp/obituaries/dignitymemorial/152177571.
46. Ferlin McGaskey [online obituary]. Dignitymemorial.com, June 18, 2011, https://www.dignitymemorial.com/obituaries/alcoa-tn/denise-harvey-4718138.
47. Pamela Hindle [online obituary]. Legacy.com, June 21, 2011, https://www.legacy.com/amp/obituaries/dignitymemorial/152177571.
48. Janna Rudolph [online obituary]. Legacy.com, June 20, 2011, https://www.legacy.com/amp/obituaries/dignitymemorial/152177571.
49. Nissa D. Bra, online obituary, June 20, 2011, https://www.dignitymemorial.com/obituaries/alcoa-tn/denise-harvey-4718138.
50. LaDonna Braquet [online obituary]. Legacy.com, June 20, 2011, https://www.legacy.com/amp/obituaries/dignitymemorial/152177571.
51. Dr. Theresa Cooper [online obituary]. Legacy.com, June 20, 2011, https://www.legacy.com/amp/obituaries/dignitymemorial/152177571.
52. Craig Wrisberg [online obituary]. Dignitymemorial.com, June 20, 2011, https://www.dignitymemorial.com/obituaries/alcoa-tn/denise-harvey-4718138.
53. Raymond McDermott [online obituary]. Dignitymemorial.com, June 20, 2011, https://www.dignitymemorial.com/obituaries/alcoa-tn/denise-harvey-4718138.
54. Liz Capparelli [online obituary]. Dignitymemorial.com, June 19, 2011, https://www.dignitymemorial.com/obituaries/alcoa-tn/denise-harvey-4718138.
55. Barbara James [online obituary]. Dignitymemorial.com, July 3, 2011, https://www.dignitymemorial.com/obituaries/alcoa-tn/denise-harvey-4718138.
56. Jonathan Waller [online obituary]. Dignitymemorial.com, June 30, 2011, https://www.dignitymemorial.com/obituaries/alcoa-tn/denise-harvey-4718138.
57. Janna Rudolph [online obituary]. Legacy.com, June 20, 2011, https://www.legacy.com/amp/obituaries/dignitymemorial/152177571.
58. Dee Richard [online obituary]. Dignitymemorial.com, June 20, 2011, https://www.dignitymemorial.com/obituaries/alcoa-tn/denise-harvey-4718138.
59. See Ad-Hoc Committee, 1980.
60. See Parks, 1986.
61. South Africa was divided into three broad racial groups socially, geographically, and politically during *apartheid*: native (Black Africans), Colored (people of Malay, Indian, or biracial decent), and white.
62. Murillo, 2004, 156.
63. See DiAngelo, 2018.
64. Goodall Jr., 2000, 120.
65. See Goodall Jr., 2000, 120.
66. Proverbs 11:2.
67. Goodall Jr., 2000, 11.
68. See Thayer-Bacon, 2003.

69. Thayer-Bacon, 1998.
70. This exploration formed the basis of my dissertation. See Franklin, 2012.
71. Kincheloe and Steinberg, 2002, 3–4.
72. See Crowley, 2020.
73. See Kincheloe and Steinberg, 2002, 11–14.
74. Kincheloe and Steinberg, 2002, 15.
75. Kincheloe and Steinberg, 2002, 16.
76. Kincheloe and Steinberg, 2002, 18.
77. Kincheloe and Steinberg, 2002, 22.
78. See Kincheloe and Steinberg, 2002 23–25.
79. Nieto, 2010, 26 [emphasis added].
80. Nieto, 2010, 26.
81. Freter, 2018, 237.
82. See Freter, 2019, 2021.
83. See Independence Hall Association, 2020.
84. See Parkinson, 2012, 53.
85. Parkinson, 2012, 53.
86. Parkinson, 2012, 53.
87. See Parkinson, 2012, 53.
88. See Parkinson, 2012, 58.
89. See Washington, DC, 2018 and Thomas Jefferson Foundation, 2020.
90. Pybus, 2012, 277.
91. Pybus, 2012, 277.
92. See Mineo, 2020.
93. See Freter & Freter, 2021.
94. See Kendi, 2019 and Isenburg, 2016.
95. See Freter & Freter, 2021.
96. See Festinger, 1985.
97. Festinger, 1985, 3.
98. Trump, 2020.
99. Trump, 2020.
100. Trump, 2020.
101. Trump, 2020.
102. Trump, 2020.
103. Trump, 2020.
104. Trump, 2020.
105. See Titone, 1992, 159–160.
106. See Tetreault et al., 2010.
107. Titone, 1992, 159–160.
108. See DiAngelo, 2018.
109. See Brantlinger, 1996, 572.
110. See Rothenberg, 2015.
111. See Ross, 1992b, 2.
112. See Ross, 1992b, 2.

REFERENCES

Ad-Hoc Committee. 1980. "Conscientious Objection in South Africa." University of the Witwatersrand Johannesburg Historical Papers Research. http://www.historicalpapers.wits.ac.za/inventories/inv_pdfo/AG1977/AG1977-A5-58-001-jpeg.pdf.

Alcoff, Linda. 1988. "Cultural Feminism versus Post-Structuralism: The Identity Crisis in Feminist Theory." *Signs* 13: 405–436.

Alexander, M. (2020). *New Jim Crow: Mass Incarceration in the Age of Colorblindness*. New York: New Press.

Black Lives Matter. 2020. "About." Black Lives Matter. https://blacklivesmatter.com/about/.

Bonilla-Silva, Eduardo. 2014. *Racism Without Racist. Color-Blind Racism and the Persistence of Racial Inequality in America*, fourth edition. Lanham et al.: Rowman & Littlefield Publishers.

Brantlinger, Ellen, Massoumeh Majd-Jabbari, Samuel L. Guskin. 1996. "Self-Interest and Liberal Educational Discourse: How Ideology Works for Middle-Class Mothers." *American Educational Research Journal* 33: 571–597.

Crowley, Michael. 2020. "Trump Calls for 'Patriotic Education' to Defend American History from the Left." *New York Times*, May 31, 2020. Accessed October 12, 2020. https://www.nytimes.com/2020/09/17/us/politics/trump-patriotic-education.html.

DiAngelo, Robin. 2018. *White Fragility. Why It's So Hard for White People to Talk About Racism*. S.l.: Allen Lane.

Eastminster Prebyterian Church. 2014. "Robert Harvey – Member Profile." Eastminster Prebyterian Church. http://www.epcknox.org/02/robert-harvey-member-profile/.

Franklin, Yvette Prinsloo. 2012. "(Un)Packing Your Backpack: Educational Philosophy, Positionality, and Pedagogical Praxis. (PhD diss.) University of Tennessee. https://trace.tennessee.edu/utk_graddiss/1415.

Freter, Björn. 2018. "White Supremacy in Eurowestern Epistemologies. On the West's responsibility for its philosophical heritage." *Synthesis Philosophica. Journal of the Croatian Philosophical Society* 33: 237–249.

Freter, Björn. 2019. "Veganismus als Anti-Nihilismus. Ein Beitrag zum kaumtierlichen Superiorismus." *Zeitschrift für Kritische Tierstudien* 2: 93–99.

Freter, Björn. 2020. "Decolonization of the West, Desuperiorisation of Thought, and Elative Ethics." In *Handbook of African Philosophy of Difference: The Othering of the Other*, edited by Elvis Imafidon, 105–127. Cham: Springer.

Freter, Björn. 2021. "Decolonial Philosophical Praxis Exemplified Through Superiorist and Adseredative Understandings of Development." In *Essays on contemporary Issues in African Philosophy*, edited by Jonathan Okeke Chimakonam, Edwin Etieyibo, Ike Dimegwu. Cham: Springer, to be published.

Freter, Björn, Yvette Freter. 2021. "Embracing an Ethical Epistemological Approach in African Higher Education" In *The South African Epistemic Decolonial Turn: A Global Perspective*, edited by Siseko H. Kumalo. UKZN, Pietermaritzburg, to be published.

Goodall, Jr., Harold Lloyd. 2000. *Writing the New Ethnography*. New York, NY: Alta Mira Press.

Harris, Teresa. "Dr Denise Marie Harvey (1954-2011) - Find A Grave" Find a Grave, January 29, 2012. https://www.findagrave.com/memorial/84157792/denise-marie-harvey.

Harvey, Denise. 1999. "Beyond the Glass Façade: Women Deans of Education." Dissertation, University of Tennessee.

Hill, Evan, Ainara Tiefenthäler, Christiaan Triebert, Drew Jordan, Haley Willis and Robin Stein. 2020. "How George Floyd Was Killed in Police Custody." *New York Times*, May 31, 2020. Accessed October 12, 2020. https://www.nytimes.com/2020/05/31/us/george-floyd-investigation.html.

Independence Hall Association. 2020. "The Declaration of Independence: Compare Versions." Ushistory.org. http://www.ushistory.org/declaration/document/compare.html.

Isenburg, Nancy. 2016. *White Trash. The 400-Year Untold History of Class in America*. New York, NY: Viking.

Kendi, Ibram X. 2019. *How to be an Antiracist*. New York: One World.

Kincheloe, Joe L., and Shirley R. Steinberg. 2002. *Changing Multiculturalism*. Buckingham, UK: Open University Press.

Knoxville College. 2020. "Home." Knoxville College. https://knoxvillecollege.edu/.

Ladson-Billings, Gloria. 1995. "Toward a Critical Race Theory of Education" *Teachers College Record* 97: 49–50.

Lopez Bunyasi, Thehama and Candis Watts Smith. 2019. *Stay Woke. A People's Guide to Making All Black Lives Matter*. New York: New York University Press.

Mayer, Frances, Mary Kay Thompson Tetreault. *The Feminist Classroom: Dynamics of Gender, Race, and Privilege*. Lanham, MD: Rowman and Littlefield.

Mills, Charles M. 1997. *The Racial Contract*. Ithaca, London: Cornell University Press.

Mineo, Lizzy. Interview with Donald Yacovone. "How textbooks taught white supremacy." The Harvard Gazette. https://news.harvard.edu/gazette/story/2020/09/harvard-historian-examines-how-textbooks-taught-white-supremacy/.

Moodley, Strinivasa R. 1972. "Black consciousness, the black artist and the emerging black culture." *South African Students' Organisation (SASO) Newsletter* 2/3: 18–20. http://www.disa.ukzn.ac.za/samay72.

Morrison, Toni. 1993. *Playing in the Dark. Whiteness and the Literary Imagination*. New York: Vintage Books.

Murillo, Enrique. 2004. "Mojado Crossing Along Neoliberal Borderlands." In *Postcritical Ethnography: Reinscribing Critique*, edited by George W. Noblit, Enrique G. Murillo, Susana Y. Flores, 155–179. Cresskill, NJ: Hampton Press.

Nieto, Sonia. 2010. *The Light in Their Eyes: Creating Multicultural Learning Communities*. New York: Teachers College Press.

Parks, Michael. 1986. "Thousands Homeless: S. Africa–Fratricide at Crossroads." *Los Angeles Times*, June 11, 1986. Accessed September 19, 2020. https://www.latimes.com/archives/la-xpm-1986-06-11-mn-10415-story.html.

Parkinson, Robert G. 2012. "The Declaration of Independence." In *A Companion to Thomas Jefferson*, edited by Francis D. Cogliano, 44–59. Malden, Oxford, Chichester: Wiley-Blackwell.

Pybus, Cassandra. 2012. "Thomas Jefferson and Slavery." In *A Companion to Thomas Jefferson*, edited by Francis D. Cogliano, 271–283. Malden, Oxford, Chichester: Wiley-Blackwell.

Rehm, Marsha, Barbara Allison. 2006. "Positionality in Teaching Culturally Diverse Students: Implications for Family and Consumer Sciences Teacher Education Programs." *Family and Consumer Sciences Research Journal* 34: 260–275.

Rothenberg, Paula S. 2005. *White Privilege. Essential Readings on the other Side of Racism*, second edition. New York: Worth Publishers.

Ross, Doran H. 1992a. "Preface." In *Elephant. The Animal and Its Ivory in African Culture*, edited by Doran H. Ross, XX–XXI, Los Angeles: Fowler Museum of Cultural History.

Ross, Doran H. 1992b. "Imagining Elephants. An Overview." In *Elephant. The Animal and Its Ivory in African Culture*, edited by Doran H. Ross, 1–42, Los Angeles: Fowler Museum of Cultural History.

Ryan, William. 1971. *Blaming the Victim*. New York: Pantheon Books.

Spaniermann, L. B., M. J. Heppner. 2004. "Psychosocial Costs of Racism to Whites Scale (PCRW): Construction and Initial Validation." *Journal of Counseling Psychology* 51: 249–262.

Taylor, L. (Ed.). 2020. *Implication of Race and Racism in Student's Evaluation of Teaching: The Hate u Give Students*. Lanham, Maryland: Lexington Books. Manuscript in preparation.

Thayer-Bacon, Barbara J. 2003. *Relational "(e)pistomologies."* New York: Peter Lang Publishing.

Thayer-Bacon, Barbara J. 1998. "Transforming and Redescribing Critical Thinking: Constructive Thinking." *Studies in Philosophy and Education* 17:123–148.

Thomas Jefferson Foundation. "Quotations on the Jefferson Memorial." Thomas Jefferson's Monticello. https://www.monticello.org/site/research-and-collections/quotations-jefferson-memorial#Inscription_under_the_Dome.

Thompson Tetreault, Mary Kay. 2010. "Classrooms for Diversity: Rethinking Curriculum and Pedagogy." In *Multicultural Education: Issues and Perspectives*, second edition, edited by James. A. Banks, Cherry A. McGee Banks, 159–181. Boston: Allyn and Bacon.

Titone, Connie. 1998. "Educating the White Teacher as Ally." In *White Reign: Deploying Whiteness in America*, edited by Joe Kincheloe, Shirley Steinberg, 159–175. New York: St. Martin's Press.

Trump, Donald J. 2020. "Remarks by President Trump at the White House Conference on American History." White House. Accessed October 12, 2020. https://www.whitehouse.gov/briefings-statements/remarks-president-trump-white-house-conference-american-history/.

University of Tennessee Commission for Blacks. 1984. "Memo: Black Students Receiving Aid Administered by the Financial Aid Office." University of Tennessee, Tennessee Research and Creative Exchange (TRACE). *Miscellaneous Memorandums and Reports*. https://trace.tennessee.edu/utk_blackmiscreports/9.

University of Tennessee Commission for Women. 1984. "Correspondence re Sexist Language in Daily Beacon Crime Log." University of Tennessee, Tennessee Research and Creative Exchange (TRACE). *Issues, Proposals, and Recommendations.* https://trace.tennessee.edu/utk_womiss/53/.

University of Tennessee Commission for Women. 1985. "Meeting Minutes January 1984–November 1986." University of Tennessee, Tennessee Research and Creative Exchange (TRACE). *Meeting Minutes.* https://trace.tennessee.edu/utk_wommin/3/.

Washington DC. 2018. "Visiting the Jefferson Memorial in Washington, DC." Washington.org. https://washington.org/dc-guide-to/jefferson-memorial.

Young, Damon. 2019. *What doesn't kill you makes you Blacker.* S.l.: ecco.

Chapter 6

Keeping It 100

Speaking Black Truth to White Power

Jonathan Lightfoot

One of my favorite aphorisms is ". . . and the truth shall set you free, but first it will make you angry." It neatly captures the essence of my contribution to this collection of meditations about how Black scholars learn to navigate the institutional towers of higher education. Once we learn the truth about the ways white supremacy informs academic structures and then get over the anger this realization can stoke, our determination to succeed despite such obstacles should kick in. One such hurdle that can challenge our success in the academy is the system of student evaluations of faculty, which can be particularly challenging for Black faculty who work at predominantly white institutions. To succeed, Black faculty often explore alternative ways to minimize the negative impact student evaluations of teaching can have on their prospects for tenure, promotion and other incentive-based rewards. Hornstein persuasively highlights the decades-long challenges to the validity of student evaluations of teachings (SETs) as legitimate measures of effective and competent instruction.[1] Institutional dependence on an instrument of questionable validity and value to make beneficial and punitive personnel decisions should be challenged. A number of empirical studies find Black faculty at the lowest rungs of the ratings ladder when compared to their white counterparts.[2] The increasingly neoliberal obsession with positivistic responses to market challenges often fail to factor implicit and explicit racial bias into their instrumentation measurement models. Inherent in this obsession is the goal to adapt education, teaching, and learning to a scientific, meritocratic business model that treats students as customers who pay (tuition) for a satisfying experience. Faculty who dare to introduce academic rigor into their course syllabi risk accusations of causing discomfort, which can occur when students are challenged to think critically or temporarily exist in spaces of ambiguity and step outside of their comfort zones. Ultimately, SETs prove nothing about teaching competence,[3] but do speak to the degree with which students are satisfied with the "service/teaching" they receive.[4]

Black faculty at all levels would do well to become more knowledgeable about the structural bias inherent in the performance evaluation process, which includes bias found in the SET instrument design, bias within the culture of the institution and the bias demonstrated by students as they rate their course experience with various faculty. Ignorance about any one or all of the factors involved in how teaching is assessed and used to either improve performance or determine tenure and promotion can handicap candidate success and should not be left to chance. Comprehensive teaching portfolios that are developed with the guidance of an experienced and competent mentor can be invaluable. Dr. Tillman's study of African American faculty at predominantly white institutions challenged the literature on traditional faculty-to-faculty mentoring, particularly where "race" is a factor, and compelled such universities to take more affirmative actions to address concerns about isolation and improve their professional growth and development.[5]

It is perhaps the best strategic path forward marginalized faculty can take to control the narrative about how their teaching is assessed, while simultaneously decentering SETs from their potentially dominant influence on personnel decisions. A well-balanced teaching portfolio should include items that have a better chance of favoring competent faculty who, possibly due to implicit bias, tend not to fare well with traditional student rating systems. These items include faculty peer observations, selective small student focus groups, technologically enhanced multimedia artifacts, and the use of curricular course assignments that require students to self-evaluate their own learning, all of which hold more promise as better indicators of competent teaching among marginalized faculty. Of the three primary components that make up the traditional academic tenure and promotion file, including research, teaching and service, candidates may think there is little they can do to overcome the sometimes arbitrary and capricious nature of the conventional instruments used to determine their competence in teaching. Given the empirical evidence of racial bias, Black faculty are encouraged to develop a comprehensive teaching portfolio that can better attest to their effectiveness and competence in teaching and learning. Faculty who plan to include teaching portfolios in their tenure and promotion files should first inquire as to whether the institution values and will accept teaching portfolios as valid indicators of teaching excellence for personnel decisions. Such inquiries should appropriately and preferably be raised during the interview process. Sole reliance on SETs, such as those drawn from the traditional thirty-six-item end-of-course evaluation form, can be detrimental to a successful outcome for marginalized faculty, particularly at dominant institutions.

Conventional wisdom holds that larger Research I institutions place more emphasis on the level and quality of scholarship and research, whereas smaller liberal arts institutions tend to emphasize teaching and service when making personnel decisions. A study of 122 American PhD-granting political science departments about how they prepare their doctoral students for academic careers in political science found an inverse relationship between research productivity and curricular attention to university-level teaching. Only a small percentage of the political science programs offered a course designed to prepare doctoral students to teach, and the ones that did offer such courses were optional or elective. They also found that public university departments were more likely to offer university-level teacher preparation courses than private ones.[6]

There is plenty of anecdotal evidence of Black and other faculty of color at all types of institutions being denied tenure and promotion for any number of reasons. The challenge, however, is finding substantial empirical evidence of racial bias and discrimination in the institutional reward system, particularly where teaching competence based on student evaluations is identified (at least in part) as the reason for denial of tenure and promotion. Intelligent real-life decision-making is often the result of the use of a combination of evidence types to inform decisions. One does not reject outright anecdotal evidence because it was not subjected to the scientific method, nor does one accept without question empirical evidence because of its claim to scientific objectivity. You should trust your own judgment and value good information, whether it was based on personal testimony, the result of rumor through the grapevine or whether it was found in a top-tier peer-reviewed journal. For what it is worth, I offer my nearly twenty years of teaching experience as a Black male professor at predominantly white institutions for your assessment and review.

I can hardly recall a semester over the last two decades when I have not had to address student complaints about my anti-racist critical pedagogy. The most common refrain I hear regarding the nature of the complaints is that I talk about "race" and racism too much and that I am too focused on expressing my personal political opinions instead of teaching the objective facts related to the course content. In what I interpreted to be a failed attempt at empathy, a Department Chairperson once told me she was "sure that our students would much rather hear about race and racism from me than you because I am a white woman and you're a Black man; and they probably find you threatening." She was being honest with me, keeping it 100, and reflective of current research that finds Black men to be particularly profiled as "dangerous, threatening and inferior."[7] Students had complained to her about their discomfort in my Social and Cultural Foundations of Education classes, particularly during discussions about racism and other social justice issues.

The burden of racism directed toward Black scholars who teach in white institutions cannot be overstated. A recent article in the *Chronicle of Higher Education* by Emory University Professor of Philosophy, George Yancy, titled "The Ugly Truth of Being a Black Professor in America," offered a raw indictment of how white supremacy and racism effectively disregards Black existence and disrespects Black academic achievement at all levels.[8]

I took the scenic route to the academy, choosing first to spend professional time in the "real world" of corporate business and higher education administration after receiving my bachelor's and master's degrees. Admittedly, my pursuit of a doctoral degree was initially done with the intent to secure a senior-level position in higher education administration. My doctoral journey afforded me an extended opportunity to self-reflect and contemplate a career path that could effectively balance my income requirements with my desire to advocate issues of social justice and equality. How naïve of me to think I could effectively feign the allegiance required for success in the world of corporate management with my propensity for speaking truth to power with little regard for the consequences. The district manager who hired me at my first executive management job after college would often tell me that I was one of the exceptional Blacks, not like the stereotypical Black folks who struggle with employment, literacy, and other challenging life issues. After nearly three years, I was dismissed when I told him I could no longer tolerate his racist satire and ill-informed commentary about Black people. I was still several years away from landing on the tenure track, a career path that I hoped would allow me to enjoy the academic freedom to always keep it 100, speak my Black truth to white power and not get fired for doing so.

I eventually earned tenure after many years of preparation, but the threat to my enjoyment of academic freedom has been a persistent and frustrating theme of my academic experience both pre- and post-tenure. As one of a few full-time tenured Black professors at a predominantly white institution, I continually reflect upon my experience. My area of expertise is Social and Cultural Foundations of Education, which is designed to help prepare future teachers and school leaders to solve teaching and learning problems by subjecting them to a critical multiperspective analysis and assessment. Students who are preparing to teach in classrooms or lead schools require an understanding of the policies and practices that operate at the contextual intersections of history, philosophy, sociology, and politics that undergirds the institutional structures of American democratic society. Part of the neoliberal educational reform agenda includes not only the movement to privatize public spaces and institutions but also a relentless effort to eliminate Social and Cultural Foundations of Education coursework in teacher and leadership preparation programs. The impact of this insidious reform agenda is that future educators will be at a deficit in their ability to make important interpretive, normative and critical connections between school and society. Educators who are denied an opportunity to interrogate their biases in the preservice classroom will often lack the requisite knowledge, skills and dispositions to understand education and schools as socializing institutions that require an ability to conceptually frame social justice issues in political contexts, among other important contexts.

About seven years ago, our school voted to eliminate several Social and Cultural Foundations of Education courses as core and elective requirements in many of its programs. The result was an immediate and precipitous drop in the number of students enrolled in our Social Foundations of Education (SFE) courses. The traditional curriculum and instruction (C&I) and methods courses continue to enjoy institutional support. Writing this chapter has helped me to better clarify my thinking about how my journey as a Black professor at a predominantly white institution (PWI) in my struggle to keep Social and Cultural Foundations of Education instruction as a part of the teacher and leadership preparation curriculum is really a social justice issue. Institutional resistance to face historical and contemporary injustices with no incentive to right the wrongs of schools and society frustrates social justice warriors like me. A major factor that contributes to the frustration is the extra work needed to demonstrate how a flawed student evaluation of teaching system can be a particularly challenging obstacle to overcome when aspects of the subject matter being taught are inherently controversial and potentially unsettling to students. The perfect storm is created and exacerbated when the faculty being evaluated by these students fails to secure the full support of fellow colleagues and administrators whose job is to protect the academic freedom rights of its faculty. Faculty who are fortunate enough to work at institutions with a strong faculty union have a better chance of having their academic freedom rights protected from administrators and students who fail to value the standards inherent in academic freedom.

We fail as Social and Cultural Foundations of Education faculty when we avoid classroom discussions of societal ills like racism, white supremacy, sexism, heterosexism, poverty, unregulated capitalism, and other manifestations of social inequality out of fear of poor performance evaluations. It is better for future teachers and school leaders from diverse backgrounds to learn about the critical connection between schools and the ills that plague society during preservice education and training than to be blindsided once they have assumed their professional positions. Using professional development training to teach subject matter that should have been covered during preservice training becomes an after-the-fact, too little too late substitute for effective instruction, particularly where social justice issues and culturally competent pedagogy are concerned. The knowledge, skills and dispositions of teachers and school leaders must be evaluated for their knowledge and understanding of controversial content, skill and competence in addressing conflict and moral rectitude to always try to choose right over wrong, particularly where decision-making involving teacher-student relationships are concerned.

A study about the effect professor ethnicity and gender has on student evaluations found evidence of students who stereotype and judge their prospective professors before ever meeting them.[9] There are a number of relevant theories we can use in our attempts to explain the potential barriers and degrees of marginalization created by students and endorsed by institutional evaluation systems. Three theories in particular are worthy of noting here: (1) Critical Race Theory, (2) Occupational Stereotype Theory, and (3) Social Role Theory.

Critical Race Theory (CRT) is a conceptual framework that was developed out of a movement among progressive legal scholars back in the mid- to late 1980s.[10] It builds on the shortcomings of critical legal studies and critical theory in that it centers "race" as a primary feature of academic inquiry. Similar to the mission of the Social Foundations of Education, CRT seeks to reflectively assess and critique society and culture in an effort to illuminate and challenge its power structures. Several tenets combine to form the CRT framework and inform the experience of Black academics in dominant institutions, such as the pervasiveness of "race" and racism in American society. Storytelling and counter-storytelling is a valued tenet in that it allows the marginalized and oppressed to tell their story and reclaim the narrative from the dominant perspective. Legal historians often note the 1954 *Brown* v. *Board Decision* as one of the few victorious instances when qualitative social scientific research told the story of how school segregation conferred a badge of inferiority on Black children causing them to experience low self-esteem and impaired cognitive functioning.[11] Another often misunderstood and thus overlooked CRT tenet is interest convergence, which explains, in my humble opinion, a lot of the frustration we experience in our quest for justice and equality. Practically speaking, those with the power and authority to improve the lives of the disfranchised often lack the motivation to do so unless there is some benefit (financial, image, etc.) in it for them. Such awareness requires advocacy and activist groups to develop their demands for justice to the powerful with a "what's in it for me" or "quid pro quo" type component. Other CRT tenets such as experiential knowledge, interdisciplinary study and commitment to social justice can all be practically applied to better understand white supremacy and challenge its manifestations in our lived experiences as BIPOC.

I submit to you that our educational and judicial institutions are perhaps the most powerful and greatest socializing forces in society. Our individual and group experiences with the "rule of law" and "equal protection" are largely determined by our individual and group experiences with our educational system. Schools heavily influence our sense of self, teach us our hierarchical place in society, and with statistical accuracy determine what we can reasonably expect as to personal and professional fulfillment of our human potential. The implicit and explicit message sent by both these institutions is that one's racial assignment tends to be a most pernicious determinant of life's trajectory. Black professors who have beaten the odds thus far to achieve academic success discover that they cannot let their guards down and are advised to remain vigilant in order to achieve continued success. Dominant students who refuse to or find it difficult to appreciate their underrepresented professor's culturally or racially influenced pedagogy have been known to harness their privilege with a negative student evaluation that can then cause institutional power authorities to question their professor's teaching competence. CRT, in ubiquitous fashion, offers us both theoretical understanding and practical applications to deal with what can seem like a Sisyphean task, challenging both racial discrimination and bias in dominant spaces.

Occupational Stereotyping is one theory that professors seeking success in the "ivory tower" should seek to understand in order to better explain their experiences and recognize how it operates in the academy. Occupational stereotyping describes the preconceived attitudes one demonstrates toward a particular occupation and the people employed in those jobs, which also extends to one's attitude about the suitability of a person for that occupation or job.[12] Occupational stereotyping can negatively impact hiring prospects, employment satisfaction, advancement, and recognition. Kindergarten and primary school teachers are expected to be women. U.S. Senators and CEOs are expected to be white men. Artistic creators of dance, music, fashion, and entertainment are often stereotyped to be members or allies of the LGBTQ community. Pernicious stereotypes about Black people as incompetent, difficult, aggressive, illegitimate, and not deserving of their positions inform the implicit and explicit biases of those who are authorized and empowered to evaluate them.[13] As social scientists, we have been taught to reject stereotypes as bad and view them with righteous skepticism, but a study of their origin can reveal nuggets of truth that no longer serve our contemporary progressive reality. The hope, however, is that we gain the knowledge and will to overcome such thinking when perpetuation of negative stereotypes continues to serve the status quo, one that is rooted in racial oppression and other forms of abuse.

Social Role Theory helps us to understand why female professors receive more negative evaluations than male professors in the academy.[14] Women are expected to conform to their roles as nurturers, sensitive care-givers and selfless comforters, whereas men are expected to be ambitious, assertive, independent, and emotionally detached. To step outside of those gender norms could create cognitive dissonance among students who are charged to evaluate professors' effectiveness and competence as instructors. Bavishi, Medera, and Hebl further hypothesized about the interaction between professor ethnicity and gender.[15] Black women were thought to suffer the "double stigma" or "double jeopardy" of being stigmatized for being both Black and women.[16] Therefore, the expectation for the Black female professor to end up with the lowest rating on all rating dimensions compared to Black men and both female and male Asian and white professors is not unrealistic. A number of factors can be explored to better understand and address the inherent and applied bias in the student evaluation of teaching process. The movement to give voice to and empower students during the broader accountability movement of the 1980s is a good place to start, followed by the positivists' propensity to synthesize complex and nuanced phenomenon into simplified quantifiable metrics. American society has never embraced diversity awareness and racial truth and reconciliation as curriculum standards within our K-12 school system. Students therefore arrive at our college campuses fully immersed in the milieu of white supremacy, racial hierarchy, and negative stereotyping. It is thus beneficial to recognize being a Black academic in white American higher educational institutions as an occupational hazard and something we must learn to navigate. When we actively challenge the manifestations of such occupational hazards, we can mitigate the potential damage it can wreak upon our career success and mental health.

Before celebrating her promotion to full professor, one Black female professor in the College of Arts and Sciences at the Flagship University of Virginia decided she needed to do something cathartic first, so she decided to identify and reflect on all the people who had tried to destroy her career on her academic journey. Petty, no? Therapeutic, yes? Dr. Marlene Daut[17] may epitomize Ferdmans[18] and Thomas' & Miles'[19] depiction of the "double jeopardy" of being stigmatized for being a Black person and a woman in the academy. Her personal testimony of beating the odds did not come easy. She is a well-published, multilingual, award-winning scholar whose research is global and multicultural. I was impressed that she was able to complete her doctoral degree, have two children, write two books, publish numerous articles, experience the tenure track at three different institutions and achieve full professor, all by the age of thirty-nine. Dr. Daut clearly is driven and ambitious with a clear vision and tenacity to do what it takes to accomplish her career goals. Yet, she describes her time as an untenured Black female assistant professor as emotionally traumatic and filled with tales of both macro- and microaggressions at the hands of students, colleagues, and administrators. She discovered that the department had labeled her and the only other woman of color in her graduate program as bad teachers based on inappropriate personal comments made on their student course evaluations.

They were naïve to the fact that students had great power to influence their faculty colleagues and administrators via the teaching evaluation system. They also discovered that their white male and female peers enjoyed a level of "qualified" immunity and did not have to endure or challenge defamatory attacks based on stereotypically racialized perceptions of them as unintelligent, "mean," and underserving of their respect.

Dr. Daut demonstrated a level of resilience when constant challenges to her teaching as being too exclusive and her scholarship as being too narrow forced her into an exhausting and incongruent mental space. It is exhausting to keep it moving forward when you get the distinct feeling of being targeted because of your "race" but the evidence to corroborate your feelings remain elusive, particularly when the suspected perpetrators claim to be colorblind and believers in equity and equality. Interestingly enough, the damage done by colorblind racists is no less destructive than the damage done by the blatant tactics of Jim Crow racists. Dr. Daut noted that she often felt erased and attributed her articulate understanding of that feeling to feminist scholar, Tracy Sharpley-Whiting, who called the feeling "seen invisibility," or the condition of "being seen and not seen." Dr. Daut was awarded a $40,000 Ford Foundation postdoctoral fellowship with no accolades until another woman of color brought it to the attention of the department. I was incredulous upon reading that one of her colleagues begrudgingly congratulated her and then followed her kudos with the claim of having never heard of the Ford Foundation. Another noteworthy aggression occurred when a colleague shot down Dr. Daut's proposal to teach a new course on the Harlem Renaissance with the assertion that a *whole* class on this important era in Black literary life was too much, when it was no secret that she had a penchant to teach Langston Hughes' poetry in her classes. Dr. Daut's advice to up and coming women of color who seek success in the academy is to develop a targeted network of research support and to fight against the teaching obstacles that impede their progress. Institutions cannot afford to be neutral about racist behavior and expect to combat racism. Dr. Daut believes that students, faculty administrators and staff who engage in racist behavior should be purposefully reprimanded. I say good luck to getting any of them to admit to having exhibited racist behavior, let alone admit to being racist. Daut ends her celebratory reflection[20] with a reference to the research of Jerimiah L. Young and Dorothy E. Hines,[21] which shows how "toxic" classrooms, "personal attacks," and "hate emails" are really killing the souls of Black women on campus.

Even ethnic whites are not immune from the wrath of student evaluations of teaching when universities put too much weight on them. Bob Uttl,[22] originally from the former Czechoslovakia, was an assistant professor of psychology who taught courses in research methods and psychometrics at the

University of Oregon. He was denied tenure when a student who had been dismissed from his course for academic dishonesty wrote a letter to complain about his accent. Another complaint from a colleague's peer review claimed that the font he used on a handout showed disdain for students. He later discovered that this colleague had voted against his hiring years earlier. His tenure and promotions committee identified his SET scores as grounds for denying him tenure and later dismissal from the university. Fortunately, he sought relief in the federal court and prevailed. A federal court[23] cited the fact that the dean and other decision-makers failed to explain why his SETs were not sufficient to grant him tenure, even though his scores were similar to the department averages. The court ordered the university to retroactively grant Dr. Uttl tenure and promotion, but his reputation had already been damaged and his career derailed. He was unable to find comparable employment, and his U.S. work visa was subsequently canceled. Dr. Uttl eventually landed on his feet in neighboring Canada with a position as a professor of psychology at Mount Royal University.

We are the beneficiaries of his unfortunate experience he shared while at the University of Oregon as he has maintained an ongoing research interest in studying SETs. More recent research shows evidence of institutions that take the narrow approach of correlating SET scores with teaching competence may be coming to an end, at least at Canadian universities. The Ryerson Faculty Association recently won an arbitration decision in their dispute against the university, which determined that promotion and tenure committees could no longer consider faculty course surveys in their attempts to measure teaching effectiveness. The ruling has had a rippling effect across Canadian universities, as many are now revisiting their SET usage practices and its relationship to human resource policies.

In my search for stories of Black and other faculty of color who have been denied tenure, promotion or other personnel rewards, I did not find any instances of denial due to lack or quality of service. Conventional wisdom around the BIPOC and female experience in the academy is that they serve the institution and the profession above and beyond that of their dominant peers. They tend to be a draw for BIPOC students who seek advisement from faculty with whom they share an affinity and are often in high demand to offer the diversity perspective on programming and other committees on- and off-campus. In addition to the campaign to remove or diminish the emphasis on student evaluation of teaching in tenure and promotion decisions, it may be time to strengthen the emphasis BIPOC and women's service component have on the tenure and promotion file. Still, the primary reasons given for the vast majority of denial cases were for scholarship, research and student evaluations of teaching. A number of these professors had to decide whether to appeal their decisions, litigate or accept their fate and find other employment. Noticeably, a large number of the institutions that denied tenure and promotions to BIPOC and women candidates appear to have made a number of procedural and process errors. It is difficult to explain a negative decision when all of the evaluations and re-appointment letters for five to six years prior indicate that the tenure-track candidate is making adequate progress toward achievement of tenure and promotion. In the absence of sudden dramatic financial exigency, such as with the current COVID-19 pandemic, these institutions cannot move the goalpost and must be held accountable.

All things (racism, bias, discrimination, whim, etc.) considered, BIPOC tenure-track candidates are advised to simultaneously work the system while working to change the system. The myths of objectivity, neutrality, meritocracy, and colorblindness must all be understood and challenged for the subtle ways they work to undermine our scholarship, teaching and service. It is disconcerting to know that you were hired to bring much-needed diversity of perspective to an institution only to later find out that your emic qualitative research will never be truly respected in a department that only values etic quantitative research. How does a tenure-track candidate effectively manage their time to conduct research and properly prepare for classroom instruction when service obligations become burdensome and time-consuming? How do pre-tenured faculty enjoy the benefits of academic freedom and stay true to an academic agenda that is rooted in social justice and anti-racist critical feminist pedagogy? I look to the merits of comprehensive and holistic portfolio development as possible ways to address these questions and concerns.

The era of school reform that called for increased educational standards and teacher accountability is largely attributed to the 1983 report, *A Nation at Risk*,[24] which was commissioned by the Reagan presidential administration. It held that America's educational system was failing to educate students to proficiency and recommended that schools adopt a more rigorous curriculum, increase measurable standards, and hold teachers more accountable for student learning with quantifiable evaluation systems. As is often the case, K-12 schools are the bellwether for change in postsecondary and higher education institutions and if the history of America's post–World War II era teaches us anything, it is the fact that schools, collectively speaking, are the drivers of social change. The 1954 Supreme Court *Brown* v. *Board Decision* effectively ended the de jure segregation ushered in by the 1896 *Plessy* v. *Ferguson* decision. What followed was a gradual toppling of racial segregation in a number of other areas social and political life, including transportation, commerce, and media. So, when schools call for higher standards, more rigor, and measurable educator accountability, other areas of society tend to follow suit and adopt similarly punitive systems of accountability with their employees in attempts to improve the experience and level of customer satisfaction. However, when the federal government punishes school districts by restricting funding from schools that fail to meet student test score benchmarks and blame teachers for their student's standardized test performance, the result is a circular blame game where the student always loses.

If used properly, teaching portfolios have the potential to elevate the art and science of teaching to the level of research and scholarship, particularly at less research-intensive institutions that value good teaching and where SETs are still given more priority than they deserve when making faculty personnel decisions. Seldin et al. equate teaching portfolios to dossiers of research publications, grants, and other scholarship honors.[25] They advise that portfolios not be exhaustive, but selective, of its contents and clear as to whether its intention is to improve teaching performance or provide sound evidence for a personnel committee to make better decisions about a candidate's worthiness for tenure, promotion, or other reward.

The increased recognition and support for the teaching portfolio has been documented in the United States and Canada, such that in a matter of twenty years from 1990 to 2010, the number of colleges and universities that honor the value of portfolios grew exponentially from about 10 to an estimated 2,500.[26] Movement from reliance on the simplified metrics of student ratings and the faulty math of departmental comparisons to portfolios gives marginalized faculty a great opportunity to challenge the discrimination and bias inherent in these faculty evaluation systems with triangulated documentation of their teaching competence and impact on student learning.

Notwithstanding the progress being made in valuing alternative forms of student-teacher evaluation, racism, bias, and discrimination still has a way of disrupting the process to maintain the status quo of Eurocentric dominance. Over time, blatant Jim Crow racism has been largely replaced by the more subtle form of colorblind racism. The public explanation for denying tenure and promotion to marginalized faculty may stand in stark contrast to the less public more private explanation. A noted Black female anthropologist recalls her battle to gain tenure and promotion at a predominantly white university in the Northeast back in 1987. Her white male department chair stunned her with a very public declaration by saying, "We all know that women and blacks are mentally inferior."[27] Remember, this was 1987, not 1937 or 1887. "I was bewildered, stupefied, made senseless as if by a (physical) blow."[28] Thinking she must have misheard him, she asked him to repeat what he had just said, a request to which he willingly complied with no trace of irony or smile and in seeming defiance of any backlash that may have come from anyone in the meeting who would take offense, other than the only Black female in the room. Dr. Mwaria ultimately earned tenure and is the longest serving Black professor at the same institution that once employed a department chair who used IQ research data to support his claim of Black and female inferiority. More than three decades later, she still feels the isolation and pain of humiliation she felt at the time, which she says was exacerbated by the absence of any objection to the chair's statement by the other white male colleagues in the room. The story of Dr. Daut's road to tenure and promotion in 2019, that I recounted earlier, did not include such blatant and public racism and sexism that was directed at Dr. Mwaria, but there was apparently enough subtle and not so subtle colorblind racism and sexism to cause pain and humiliation similar to what Dr. Mwaria felt several decades prior in 1987.

Marginalized faculty are also advised to secure a mentor to assist them as they develop their teaching portfolios. College and university teaching are very different from K-12 teaching. Teaching preparation programs have evolved to become highly professionalized operations that are regionally accredited and regulated by state authorities. Practically no full-time permanent K-12 teacher is hired without going through a process that involves taking specific content and methods courses; passing certain licensure, certification and praxis tests; observing and being observed in different classrooms; practicing student teaching; getting health screenings and undergoing finger printing and full background checks. College and university professors need only earn a terminal degree or present other qualifying credentials that allow them to teach students at the postsecondary level of coursework. College and university teaching end up being a trial and error, and learn on the job as you go endeavor. When you have a PhD in chemistry, a faulty assumption is made that you not only know chemistry well but are also qualified to teach chemistry at the university level. Therein lies the challenge. For adjunct, clinical, and tenure-track faculty to be successful at teaching, they must be motivated to put forth the effort to learn as they teach and teach as they learn. This can be a difficult thing to do for faculty who entered the academy to primarily focus on research and scholarship or for faculty who discover their passion for advocacy and activism via service work. These faculty can probably benefit most from the assistance of a knowledgeable and professionally trained mentor. Institutions that value the importance of effective teaching, particularly those that use student-derived teaching evaluation data to make personnel decisions, should direct enough resources to encourage senior faculty to become mentors and offer professional mentorship development training programs for them to become effective mentors. The benefits of mentoring can serve the institution in many ways, including recruiting the best faculty candidates and retaining them to tenure and promotion. Just as mentors can assist pre-tenured faculty to publish and secure research grants, they can use the teaching portfolio as a collaborative tool for developing and promoting excellence in teaching. Seldin et al. note that the process of collaboration need not be discipline-specific.[29] While a mentor from the same discipline may share special knowledge and insights, a mentor from a different discipline can provide the broad view of the institution, which can be helpful when tenure and promotion committees are made up of faculty across several disciplines. Again, marginalized faculty stand to benefit from mentors who present a combination of expertise in the right discipline and the practical wisdom they have gained from reflective and engaged institutional memory.

Peer observations are another part of the teaching portfolio that deserves close attention. Again, distinctions are made between Research I universities and teaching-centered universities. Larkin examined and evaluated relevant literature covering faculty portfolios and found them to be effective presentations of their work and more suited for teaching-centered institutions. She concluded that the four primary components of faculty portfolios are: (1) thoughtful student evaluations, (2) critical peer evaluations, (3) teaching material samples, and (4) evidence of collegial behavior.[30] Many institutions have established clear guidelines and protocols around peer observations. For example, a junior faculty's observation of a senior faculty member may not carry much weight as would a senior faculty member's observation of a junior faculty's would. There may be stipulations as to the number and frequency of peer evaluations seeking personnel advancement. There also may be policy about whether random unannounced observations are allowed or whether all observations recognized for personnel decisions be planned and coordinated with the observed faculty in advance.

In the age of Covid-19, additional consideration must be given to protocols around remote teaching and learning observations. A lot of questions and concerns can arise as to the fairness of an observation whereby the observer is remotely observing a fully face-to-face socially distanced class or a hybrid class whereby part of the class is face-to-face and the other part is virtual. My suggestion is to make sure every aspect of the observation process is planned and documented from beginning to end to minimize any miscommunication or lack of clarification. Do not let any questionable statements or rating be placed in your tenure and promotion file without a thoughtfully written rebuttal. Should the observer share the observation with the observed prior to submission to the Department Personnel Committee (DPC)? Should students be notified as to the reason another faculty member is observing the class? Answers to these questions and more are important and deserve consideration and planned for accordingly. Departments usually require course syllabi to be up to date and accessible to anyone with a vested interest in the content.

The goal of peer observations should always be to help the observed improve their teaching via constructive critique and not to render judgment or other punitive commentary. Trust among members of a department is essential to its function and to the growth and development of faculty at all levels of the academic career path. Everyone can enjoy the protections and benefits of academic freedom when the guidelines and protocols governing peer observations are clearly articulated and publicized in easy to reference formats.

A number of institutions find value in conducting small student focus groups as a way to corroborate the traditional student evaluation of teaching form data. When a tenure-track candidate is ready to stand for tenure and promotion the first time at some institutions, a call goes out to all students who have ever been enrolled in a course taught by the candidate to invite them to participate in a committee meeting to share their experience with the professor. Others are invited to write letters of support or challenges to the professor's suitability for tenure as it relates to their teaching. This can be tricky for the professor who may not have the best student evaluation of teacher ratings. Will students who felt you were a terrible teacher five years prior still be motivated enough to sabotage your chances for tenure by writing a letter or show up at a tenure committee meeting or focus group session to express their continued disdain for you or your teaching? My recommendation for addressing issues and concerns with students who I suspect to be a present or future problem is to document all encounters verbally to the department chair or other administrator and put it in writing as a matter of record. The saying, it is better to have it and not need it than to need it and not have it is especially relevant when it comes to using timely documentation as a means of resolving conflict.

Personnel committees should understand the difference between student evaluation of teaching survey data and the data that is produced from small student focus groups that were specifically organized to help determine a candidate's competence and effectiveness in teaching. Several points regarding the distinction between these two sources of data are worth consideration. Survey data, as those generated from SETs are often less costly to organize, staff, and assess. Information can be gathered from a large number of students in a short period of time and allow for easy aggregation of the answers. Students may feel more comfortable completing anonymous surveys, particularly if do not require a lot of their time. However, many surveys are not structured or designed to elicit in-depth probing for subtlety and nuance, which could help detect dishonesty or hyperbole from the survey participants.

The intimacy of small student focus groups stands in contrast to mass-produced student surveys in that they are designed to allow for additional probing and better capture subtlety and nuance, from both individual participants and the group collectively. Focus groups, however, require more resources to organize staff and qualitatively code and analyze the data. They require well-trained, experienced, and competent leaders who have a good rapport and trust with students, which helps to engender honesty and open dialogue. Notetakers and recorders are worth the additional expense because they allow the group leader to devote their attention to the participants without distraction. Small student focus groups of no more than ten participants should be organized to be demographically representative of faculty candidate's formerly student population. Racial or ethnic diversity, gender, and level are all important areas to consider. For marginalized faculty who teach at PWIs, achieving student focus group diversity can be challenging. I taught social foundations of education courses to graduate students enrolled in a masters Speech, Language Pathology program for thirteen years. Over 95 percent of the students were white females. I recall having only two male students, both white and approximately ten Black and other females of color during the entire time. Needless to say, forming a gender and racially diverse student focus group from that program would be difficult. For what it's worth, there was some class and political diversity in the program. Discussions of "race" and racism sometimes created a degree of tension that drew students to polarized ends of the political spectrum. One particular discussion related to the school to prison pipeline has stuck with me over the years. I recall noting the hugely disproportionate rates of Black and Brown male incarceration, which inspired one young white female to interject with, "well aren't they the ones who are committing all the crimes?" Without digressing too much, suffice it to say that I believe I effectively and diplomatically seized the teachable moment such that the young lady probably left class regretting having made such an ill-informed and insensitive comment.

Prior to landing on the tenure track, I spent a year teaching as a visiting assistant professor at a small predominantly white rural liberal arts college. Another professor there introduced me to an assignment whereby students are given an opportunity to reflect on their learning throughout the course, which I quickly adopted and still use to this day. It is called the *Self-Evaluation of Learning Letter*. At the conclusion of every course I teach, I ask students to write me a formal letter, "Dear Professor Lightfoot . . . Sincerely, 'A' Student" and describe their learning in the course according to a guideline rubric that allows for a uniquely personal and reflective accounting of their learning experience in the course. I save all of my letters from each course and include the best ones in my teaching portfolio. I credit these letters, the good, the bad, and the ugly ones, with helping me to have improved my teaching and gain tenure by providing a qualitatively convincing counter-narrative against the questionable student evaluation of teaching ratings formally recognized by the institution. During our review of the syllabus on the first day of class we discuss the entire course requirements needed for successful completion of the course. They discover my philosophy of teaching and learning, which includes my one-third rule whereby I inform them that if they do not learn anything in this course, I would only accept one-third of the blame. They quickly discover where they can assign the remaining two-thirds of the blame if they fail to learn anything in the course in thirds. They must agree to accept personal responsibility for their own learning and thus assume one-third of the blame. The final one-third of the blame can be assigned to their peers, who must all agree to accept responsibility for the peer to peer and peer to teacher learning and teaching that happens during the course. From the very beginning my goal is establish trust and transparency. The same professor who introduced me to the Self-Evaluation of Learning Letter also introduced me to what has become my favorite quote which I use to engage my students to reflect on their role and responsibility in the classroom teaching and learning dynamic:

> There is, in fact, no teaching without learning. One requires the other. And the subject of each, despite their obvious differences, cannot be educated to the status of object. Whoever teaches learns in the act of teaching, and whoever learns teaches in the act of learning.[31]

We spend about a half-hour deconstructing the Paulo Freire quote and teasing out its wisdom. The quote captures the nexus of teaching and learning around the notion of power dynamics. Teaching and learning, as with all relationships, must be negotiated around power. In authoritarian, teacher-centered classrooms, teachers hold all of the power. In nonauthoritarian, student-centered classrooms, teachers are more willing to share the power. The power to teach and the power to learn can become a contested ideological terrain. Teachers as subjects cannot assume all the power and believe their role is to always "act upon" their students. By the same token, students as objects should not feel powerless and compelled to accept roles where they are always "acted upon" with no sense of agency in their learning.

The challenge for Black and other marginalized faculty at dominant institutions remains one that requires steadfast vigilance, forward thinking and mastering the art of double-consciousness and yet still remain sane and joyful. The inherent bias in traditional student evaluation of teaching instruments operates to maintain the status quo of a predominantly white male academy. It is up to marginalized faculty who have been hurt by the practice of over-reliance on a fraudulent system of simplistic metrics to challenge this system of how competence and effectiveness in teaching and learning are determined. In the meantime, we must continue to find creative alternative solutions to the problem of institutional bias and discrimination perpetrated by students, peer faculty, and administration. Thoughtfully prepared teaching portfolios developed with the assistance of competent mentors are great ways to showcase the talent of effective teachers with the added benefit of helping to facilitate growth, improvement, tenure, promotion, and other personnel recognition.

NOTES

1. See Hornstein 2017.
2. See Merritt 2008, Reid 2010, Smith & Hawkins 2011 and Basow, Codos & Martin 2013.
3. See Braga, Paccagnella & Pellizzari 2014.
4. See Beecham 2009.
5. See Tillman 2001.
6. See Ishiyama, Miles & Belarezo 2010.
7. Assari & Curry 2020, s.p.
8. See Yancy 2018.
9. See Bavishi, Medera & Hebl 2010.
10. See Crenshaw et.al. 1995; Delgado & Stefancic 2017, Ladson-Billings & Tate 1995.
11. See Clark & Clark 1947.
12. See Lipton et al. 1991.
13. See Reyna, Henry, Korfmacher & Tucker 2005.
14. See Eagly, Wood & Diekman 2000.
15. See Bavishi, Medera & Hebl 2010.
16. See Ferdman 1999 and Thomas & Miles 1995.
17. See Daut 2019.
18. See Ferdman 1999 in Bavishi, Madera & Hebl 2010.
19. See Thomas & Miles 1995 in Bavishi, Madera & Hebl 2010.
20. See Sharpley-Whiting in Daut 2019.
21. See JL Young & DE Hines 2018 in Daut 2019.
22. See Uttl in Peters 2019.
23. See Uttl v. Oregon State University 2005.
24. See National Commission on Excellence in Education 1983.
25. See Seldin et al. 2010.
26. See Seldin et al. 2010.
27. See Mwaria 2012, 129.
28. See Mwaria 2012, 129.
29. See Seldin et al. 2010.
30. See Larkin 2016.
31. See Freire 1998, 31.

REFERENCES

Assari, Shervin, Tommy J. Curry. 2020. "Black men face high discrimination and depression, even as their education and incomes rise." The Conversation, July 21, 2020. https://theconversation.com/black-men-face-high-discrimination-and-depression-even-as-their-education-and-incomes-rise-141027.

Basow, Susan A., Stephanie Codos, Julie L. Martin. 2013. "The Effects of Professors' Race and Gender on Student Evaluations and Performance." *College Student Journal* 47: 52–363.

Bavishi, Anish, Juan M. Madera, Michelle R. Hebl. 2010. "The effect of professor ethnicity and gender on student evaluations: Judged before met." *Journal of Diversity in Higher Education* 3: 245–256. doi: 10.1037/a0020763.

Beecham, Rod. 2009. "Teaching quality and student satisfaction: Nexus or simulacrum?" *London Review of Education* 7: 135–146.

Braga, Michaela, Marco Paccagnella, Michelle Pellizzari. 2014. "Evaluating students' evaluations of professors." *Economics of Education Review* 41: 71–88. doi: 10.1016/j.econedurev.2014.04.002.

Clark, Kenneth B., Mamie P. Clark, M. 1947. "Racial identification and preference in Negro children." In *Readings in Social Psychology*, 167–178, edited by Theodore M. Newcomb and Eugene L. Hartley. New York: Henry Holt.

Crenshaw Kimberle, Neil Gotanda, Gary Peller and Kendall Thomas (eds). 1995. *Critical Race Theory: The Key Writings That Formed the Movement*. New York: The New Press.

Daut, Marlene L. 2019. "Becoming Full Professor While Black." *The Chronicle of Higher Education* 66, September 6, 2019. https://www.chronicle.com/article/becoming-full-professor-while-black/.

Delgado, Ronaldo, Jean Stefancic. 2017. *Critical Race Theory: An Introduction*. Third edition. New York: New York University Press.

Eagly, Alice H., Wendy Wood, Amanda B. Diekman. 2002. "Social role theory of sex differences and similarities: A current appraisal." In *The Developmental Social Psychology of Gender*, edited by Thomas Eckes and Hanns M. Trautner, 123–174. Mahwah, NJ: Erlbaum.

Freire, Paulo. 1998. *Pedagogy of Freedom: Ethics, Democracy, and Civic Courage*. Lanham, MD: Rowman & Littlefield Publishers.

Gillborn, David, Gloria Ladson-Billings. 2010. "Critical race theory." In *International encyclopedia of education. Volume 6*, edited by Eva L. Baker, Barry McGaw, Penelope Peterson, 341–347. Oxford: Elsevier.

Hornstein, Henry. 2017. "Student evaluations of teaching are an inadequate assessment tool for evaluating faculty performance." *Cogent Education* 4: 1–8. doi: 10.1080/2331186X.2017.1304016.

Ishiyama, John, Tom Miles, and Christine Balarezo. 2010. "Training the next generation of teaching professors: A comparative study of Ph.D. programs in political science." *PS: Political Science & Politics* 43: 515–22. doi: 10.1017/S1049096510000752.

Ladson-Billings, Gloria and William F. Tate. 1995. "Toward a critical race theory of education." *Teachers College Record* 97: 47–68.

Ladson-Billings, Gloria. 1996. "Silences as weapons: Challenges of a black professor teaching white students." *Theory Into Practice* 35: 79–85. doi: 10.1080/00405849609543706.

Larkin, Amy L. 2016. "Effective faculty evaluation at the teaching-centered university: Building a fair and authentic portfolio of faculty work." *International Journal of Educational Management* 30: 976–988.

Merritt, Deborah J. 2008. "*Bias, the Brain, and Student Evaluations of Teaching*." St. Johns Law Review 82, 235–287.

Mwaria, C. 2012. Sexism and Racism in academe: Why the Struggle Must Continue. Commission on Race and Racism in Anthropology (CRRA) and the American

Anthropological Association (AAA) February 2012. http://s3.amazonaws.com/rdcms-aaa/files/production/public/FileDownloads/pdfs/cmtes/commissions/upload/10_Mwaria.pdf.

National Commission on Excellence in Education. (1983). A Nation at risk: The Imperative for educational reform.

Peters, Diane. 2019. "Do universities put too much weight on student evaluations of teaching?" Evaluations, March 06, 2019. https://www.universityaffairs.ca/features/feature-article/do-universities-put-too-much-weight-on-student-evaluations-of-teaching/.

Reid, Landon D. 2010. "The role of perceived race and gender in the evaluation of college teaching on RateMyProfessors.Com." *Journal of Diversity in Higher Education* 3: 137–152. doi: 10.1037/a00119865.

Reyna, Christine, P. J. Henry, William Korfmacher, Amanda Tucker. 2006. "Examining the principles in principled conservatism: The role of responsibility stereotypes as cues for deservingness in racial policy decisions." *Journal of Personality and Social Psychology* 90: 109–128. doi: 10.1037/0022-3514.90.1.109.

Seldin, P., Miller, and C. Seldin. 2010. *The Teaching Portfolio: A Practical Guide to Improved Performance and Promotion/Tenure Decisions*, fourth edition, Jossey-Bass.

Sherri L. Wallace, Angela K. Lewis, Marcus D. Allen. 2019. "The State of the Literature on Student Evaluations of Teaching and an Exploratory Analysis of Written Comments: Who Benefits Most?" *College Teaching* 67: 1–14. doi: 10.1080/87567555.2018.1483317.

Smith, Bettye P. 2007. "Student ratings of teaching effectiveness for faculty groups based on race and gender." *College Student Journal* 41: 788–800.

Smith, Bettye P. and Billy Hawkins. 2011. "Examining student evaluations of black faculty: Does Race Matter?" *The Journal of Negro Education* 80: 149–162. http://www.jstor.org/stable/41341117.

Tate IV, William F. 1997. "Critical race theory and education: History, theory, and implications." *Review of Research in Education* 22: 195–247.

Tillman, Linda C. 2001. "Mentoring African American Faculty in Predominantly White Institutions." *Research in Higher Education* 42: 295–325. doi: 10.1023/A:1018822006485.

Uttl v. Oregon State University 2005. https://www.courtlistener.com/docket/12041047/uttl-v-oregon-state-university/.

Wang, Guannan, Aimee Williamson. 2020. "Course evaluation scores: Valid measures for teaching effectiveness or rewards for lenient grading?" *Teaching in Higher Education*. doi: 10.1080/13562517.2020.1722992.

Yancy, George. 2018. "The Ugly Truth of Being a Black Professor in America." *The Chronicle of Higher Education* 64, April 29, 2018. https://www.chronicle.com/article/the-ugly-truth-of-being-a-black-professor-in-america/.

Zabaleta, Francisco. 2007. "The use and misuse of student evaluations of teaching." *Teaching in Higher Education* 12: 55–76. doi: 10.1080/13562510601102131.

Chapter 7

Desuperhumanizing Whiteness

Björn Freter

INTRODUCTION

When I recently attended a "Black Lives Matter" rally in a small town in the southeastern corner of Tennessee, the peaceful protest was now and then disturbed by someone shouting "All Lives Matter!"[1] Every time I heard this, it deeply angered me. Claiming "All Lives Matter" seeks to claim that: Black *and* white lives matter. But the assertion of the value of white lives hardly needs to be proclaimed.[2] There is scarcely a black person living in the United States who would doubt that white lives matter; there is hardly a black person living in the United States who has not personally experienced that white lives matter. Killer Mike (Michael Santiago Render) of Run the Jewels powerfully expresses this experience in the song "Walking in the Snow" in these bitter words:

The way I see it you're probably freest from the ages 1 to 4
Around the age of 5 you're shipped away for your body to be stored

You are, Killer Mike goes on, promised education, but you only are given tests and scores and predict the prison population

by who scoring the lowest
And usually the lowest scores the
poorest and they look like me.[3]

White supremacy is omnipresent, even though is it consistently and firmly denied again and again.[4]

The reason for the invisibility is simple: White supremacy is invisible to—most—white lives;[5] it might not be perceived by white lives, neither as oppression executed nor as privileged experienced, or it is simply forcefully ignored.[6] In any way, white people keep, intentionally or not,[7] the "dirty secret"[8] of white privilege well hidden. "Whiteness," as Robin DiAngelo points out, "is not acknowledged by white people, and the white reference point is assumed to be universal and is imposed on everyone."[9] Black inferiorization, in contrast, is glaringly visible, "people of color are not seen as racially innocent."[10] To black lives, white supremacist racism, that is, the black inferiorization, is an inevitable component of every experience—"bein' Black hurts"[11] said 2Pac (Tupac Amaru Shakur) in his "Letter 2 my Unborn." In fact, racism is primarily an experience, "it consists of experiences through systems and institutional practices used to elevate and/or advantage one race while depressing and/or subordinating others. Racism is lived experiences of poverty, unequal distribution of resources, and de facto segregation."[12] As Public Enemy observed in their song "Fight the Power,"

What we need is awareness, we can't get careless.[13]

Black lives have to be constantly aware that it is still up for debate whether their lives matter. Chuck D (Carlton Douglas Ridenhour) continues:

My beloved lets [sic] get down to business, Mental self-defensive fitness
[. . .]
Make everybody see, in order to fight the powers that be.[14]

Black lives in the United States are well aware that white lives matter, politically, socially, and economically. "Living while black"[15] means experiencing existential trepidation. In 1789, Olaudah Equiano described this vividly in his autobiography. Afraid to be flogged, Equiano hid in the woods, hoping he might "escape all those animals" while knowing he could not ultimately escape "those of human kind," and "thus I was like the hunted deer"—

Ev'ry leaf, and ev'ry whisp'ring breath
Convey'd a foe, and ev'ry foe a death.[16]

The voicing of "Black Lives Matter" is not a banal statement of the obvious. "Black Lives Matter" is, unlike "White Lives Matter," not a truism. "Black Lives Matter" suggests—not for the first time, but yet again[17]—that it is finally time to realize that black lives matter *too*. "Black Lives Matter" is precisely not pointing to the fact that "lives" matter, which "all lives matter." By adding the signifier "'black" to "lives" it is making obvious that certain lives are still not included among those lives that matter—a well-tended tradition since the Western Enlightenment in both Europe[18] and America.[19] It is necessary to say "Black Lives Matter," because many, too many, white lives continue to *not* agree that black lives matter—be it tacitly or more openly and aggressively again during and after the election of Donald J. Trump as president in 2016/2017.[20] Instead of addressing white supremacy, Trump's White House issued on June 16, 2020[21]—twenty-two days after George Floyd was murdered by Derek Chauvin[22]—a fact sheet that takes no action to secure black bodies. In fact, it does not even primarily aim to protect white bodies, wanting instead to "combat violence" [23]—a rather strange combination of words—and, more importantly, to protect *stone replicas* of *white bodies*, namely: the *statues of white bodies*. "Donald J. Trump," it can be read in this fact sheet, "is taking action to defend our Nation's historical monuments, statues, and memorials."[24] The document exudes white America's fear of unwhitening, it is a document of white "extinction anxiety."[25] The document goes on to state "left-wing extremists are rioting, looting, and calling for the destruction of the United States system of government,"[26] through "mob intimidation, these violent extremists are attempting to impose their ideology on the law-abiding citizens of this country."[27] Finally, some examples of "senseless destruction"[28] are decried, for instance that "mobs tore down statues of our Founding Fathers—George Washington and Thomas Jefferson."[29] Trump's White House is not interested in the least in that which continues to happen to all the black lives under the shadow of the statues of slave owner George Washington[30] or of slave owner and slave rapist Thomas Jefferson,[31] in whom we find "the most intense, extensive, and extreme formulation of anti-Negro 'thought' offered by any American in the thirty years after the Revolution."[32] The adoration, even deification[33] of these vicious anti-black Founding Fathers will continue to catch up with the black lives and hold them hostage whatever they do. Run the Jewels conclude in their 2020 song "Ju$t":

Mastered economics 'cause you took yourself from squalor (slave)
Mastered academics 'cause your grades say you a scholar (slave)
Mastered Instagram 'cause you can instigate a follow (shiiiit)

But then, after all . . .

Look at all these slave masters posin' on yo' dollar (get it).[34]

Each black person using a 1-, 2-, 20-, 50- or a 100-dollar bill is forced to look at the slave masters George Washington, Thomas Jefferson, Andrew Jackson, Ulysses S. Grant or Benjamin Franklin.[35] These slave masters remind every black person each time who they *first of all* are. Jay-Z (Shawn Corey Carter) rhymed in his "The Story of O.J.":

Light nigga, dark nigga, faux nigga, real nigga
Rich nigga, poor nigga, house nigga, field nigga
Still nigga, still nigga.[36]

And Mos Def (Dante Terrell Smith) rapped in his "Mr Nigga":

Got my mom the fat water-front crib yo I'm a get her them pretty bay windows
. . .
A fresh whip for my whole family to ride in And if I'm still Mr. Nigga,
I won't find it surprisin'.[37]

EPISTEMOLOGY OF IGNORANCE

In a paradoxical sleight-of-hand, most contemporary American white lives do not present themselves as avid racists; they live within a framework of an epistemology of ignorance[38] *producing the ironic outcome that whites will in general be unable to understand the world they themselves have made.*[39] It is a vital part of white privilege to foster "the ability to ignore the ways white racial identity has benefited [white people]."[40] The epistemology of ignorance enables white lives to practice a specific form of pseudo-non-racism: color-blind racism.[41] And this "colorblind racial ideology creates a façade of racial inclusion by suggesting that in a post–civil rights era, everyone has an equal opportunity to succeed."[42] Thus, if a black life fails to "succeed," it obviously must be personal failure and not the consequence of suppression. "If there is a consistent theme in American racist thinking," as Wellman pointed out more than forty years ago, it is to attribute "the responsibility for inequality . . . to the victim."[43] There is, as bell hooks puts it, "a deep emotional investment in the myth of 'sameness' [by white lives], even as their actions reflect the primacy of whiteness."[44] The color-blind racists support racism by claiming not to be racist *while*, and that is most important, not being anti-racist. This, as a consequence, invalidates the experiences of all those lives suffering from this racist pseudo-non-racism. Not only are *black bodies killed*, this racism targets the *black experience and minds* in general. What we see in the United States today is not only a gruesome unceasing repetition of anti-black-homicides but an ongoing centuries-old anti-black epistemicide.[45] *This* is why Latitra Wideman, sister of Jacob Blake, who was shot by the police in his back seven times in front of three of his children, remarked on August 25, 2020:

So many people have reached out to me telling me they're sorry that this happened to my family. Well, don't be sorry because this has been happening to my family for a long time, longer than I can account for. It happened to Emmett Till. Emmett Till is my family. Philando, Mike Brown, Sandra. This has been happening to my family and I've shed tears for every single one of these people that it's happened to. This is nothing new. I'm not sad. I'm not sorry. I'm angry. And I'm tired. I haven't cried one time. I stopped crying years ago. I am numb. I have been watching police murder people that look like me for years. [. . .] I'm also a black history minor. So not only have I been watching it in the 30 years that I've been on this planet, but I've been watching it for years before we were even alive. I'm not sad. I don't want your pity. I want change.[46]

"I WANT CHANGE"

The forty-fifth president of the United States does not want change. Everything is already fine. There seems no need to critically reflect and to do what Martin Luther King Jr. suggested sixty years ago, stating that "a primary goal of a well-meaning administration should be a thorough examination of its own operations and the development of a rigorous program to wipe out immediately every vestige of federal support and sponsorship of discrimination."[47] This is nowhere to be found in the current administration. Let us remember when Trump stated he was "the least racist person there is anywhere in the world."[48] The "hater-in-chief"[49] proclaimed his meritocratical nonracism—and thus he remains, *because* he is not anti-racist, a colorblind *racist* par excellence. However, as Ibram X. Kendi explains, "the claim of 'not-racist' neutrality is a mask for racism."[50] Trump is a prime example of that. And for someone like that, after all the "least racist person there is," there is no need for change. On September 17, 2020, Trump lamented that

> students in our universities are inundated with critical race theory. This is a Marxist doctrine holding that America is a wicked and racist nation, that even young children are complicit in oppression, and that our entire society must be radically transformed. Critical race theory is being forced into our children's schools, it's being imposed into workplace trainings, and it's being deployed to rip apart friends, neighbors, and families.[51]

This is not what Trump wants and, as he goes on, "that is why I recently banned trainings in this prejudiced ideology from the federal government and banned it in the strongest manner possible."[52] Ms. Wideman asked for change, twenty-three days later Mr. Trump's answer is: "We can't let that happen."[53] His vision of education in the United States in 2020 is: "Our youth will be taught to love America with all of their heart and all of their soul,"[54] that is, Trump's—white—youth will be taught to continue to proudly live with unearned privileges protected by systemic white supremacy. And Trump's black youth will be taught to continue to silently live with an undeserved lack of equality oppressed by systemic white supremacy while being taught that there is no such thing as white supremacy. "We do not show the Negro," mourned Carter Woodson in 1933, "how to overcome segregation, but we teach him how to accept it as final and just."[55] How is it possible that this is still true?

RACE

Race is understood as just an unfortunate matter of fact that cannot be changed. This has been denounced by Karen E. Fields and Barbara J. Fields as the "race-instead-of-racism ideological maneuver"[56] pioneered by Jefferson in his *Notes on the State of Virginia*. "Disguised as race, racism becomes something Afro-Americans are, rather than something racists do."[57] The problem is no longer that somebody is a racist; the problem is now that someone who happens to be of a particular race does something problematically. This is, as William Ryan has so accurately called it, the "cunning Art of Savage Discovery."[58] "Americans believe in the reality of 'race,'" writes Ta-Nehisi Coates, as a defined, indubitable feature of the natural world. Racism—the need to ascribe bone-deep features to people and then humiliate, reduce, and destroy them—inevitably follows from this inalterable condition."[59] But we should not be fooled—this is racism and does not follow an alleged natural fact. This is indeed a fact, but a social phenomenon. Should we allow to "naturalize the social phenomena which express . . . oppression," as Monique Wittig pointed out from a feminist perspective, we are "making change impossible."[60] "Race," as Coates goes on to say, "is the child of racism, not the father."[61]

The pseudo-natural factualness of race is a fiction. And this fiction is precisely what Trump expresses that he wants children to be taught. This will keep the white minds pleased and the black minds can be controlled and stay, as Jordan Peele has called in his movie "Get Out," in the "Sunken Place."[62] Carter Woodson again offers an explanation:

> When you control a man's thinking you do not have to worry about his actions. You do not have to tell him not to stand here and go yonder. He will find his "proper place" and will stay in it. You do not need to send him to the back door. He will go without being told. In fact, if there is no back door, he will cut one for his special benefit. His education makes it necessary.[63]

For the white supremacist Trump, education *in sensu strictu* is not needed. There is no need to learn to critically embrace the world; the world has already been sufficiently understood. All relevant questions have been answered. To put it more polemically: The youth of tomorrow can be handed the definitive *Dogmatic Encyclopedia of What Ought To Be and What Ought Not To Be*. All the answers are contained in there; they just need to be taught as an indisputable narrative and emotionally conflated with familial duty and faith—and one of the prime dogmas is: love thy country. This is frighteningly similar to a speech that was given on December 4, 1938, in Reichenberg, modern-day Liberec in the Czech Republic, wherein it says:

> This youth does not learn anything but to think German and act German. The boy and the girl enter our organization at the age of ten, . . . then four years later they move on from the Jungvolk to the Hitler Youth, where we keep them for another four years. And then we definitely do not give them back into the hands of those who created our old class and status barriers; instead, we immediately take them into the Party, into the Labour Front, the SA or the SS, the NSKK, and so on. . . . And so they will never be free again as long as they live. (Applause) And they are happy with it.[64]

For Trump's vision of America's future, we can indeed adopt the dreadful words of Hitler himself. Mr. Trump's educational agenda is: *This youth learns nothing but to think American and to act American*—and to be "happy with it."[65] We need to remember that just three years after Hitler presented this educational agenda for the German people, at the end of 1941, the first inmates were gassed in Block 11 of Auschwitz[66] and an entire country was complicit.

THERE IS ONLY RACISM AND ANTI-RACISM

The simple combination of being white and not white supremacist in a society like the United States is not possible. You can be either explicitly anti-racist or not anti-racist, namely: racist. "The subordination of people of color," remarked David T. Wellman, "is functional to the operation of American society as we know it and the color of one's skin is a primary determinant of people's position in the social structure."[67] It is impossible to be not racist without being anti-racist while being white because the United States's society is so entrenched in racism that, whether you want it or not, as a white person you will have privileges that exist solely because of white supremacy.[68] White lives "think of racism as voluntary, intentional conduct, done by horrible others," they seem to forget that white lives continue to be racist insofar as they "benefit from systemic white privilege."[69] As a country founded, and for the most time governed, by white supremacists, this country not only suffers from systemic racism, but its system itself is racism.[70]

WE, THE WHITE PEOPLE

Jefferson's "We, the people" is one of the many foundational fallacies of the United States. The message seems beautiful, concerned, unifying—a common tactic of racist thought visible until today.[71] Enshrouded racism can be seen in Jefferson as it can be observed in the European Enlightenment in Hume, Voltaire, Kant, Hegel, Fichte, and so many more. This message is only meant to sound beautiful to the masses, while in actuality, only white lives are blessed with being part of the "We." "We, the people" means, "We, the relevant people" and that means first and foremost: "We, the white people."[72] This is by no means a modern, anachronistic understanding of the Declaration of Independence. It was in 1783 when the abolitionist Quaker David Cooper wrote his "Serious Address to the Rulers of America, on the Inconsistency of Their Conduct Respecting Slavery," wherein he comments on the self-evident truths of the Declaration:

> IF these solemn *truths*, uttered at such an awful crisis, are *self-evident*: unless we can shew that the African race are not *men*, words can hardly express the amazement which naturally arises on reflecting, that the very people who make these pompous declarations are slave-holders, and, by their legislative, tell us, that these blessings were only meant to be the *rights* of *white men*, not of *all men*.[73]

Jefferson owned a copy of this text,[74] but it appears not to have positively influenced his thinking or actions. On the contrary: The "removal of property requirements of white males and the full disenfranchisement of blacks," as Paul Finkelman noted, "was the essence of Jeffersonian 'democracy.'"[75] The Declaration of Independence is a Declaration of white—male—Independence. Understood in this more realistic way, it is no longer a document of a radical new approach of human beings living together,[76] but just another iteration of white (and male) supremacy, presented in utterly meaningless pseudo-enlightened expressions of all-inclusivity. It is not a document for the inclusion of nonwhite people, but for white people to feel better about themselves. Black people, said Malcolm X (Malcolm Little) in 1964, "are ready, willing and justified to do the same thing today to bring about independence for our people. . . . And I say our people because I certainly couldn't include myself among those for whom independence was fought in 1776."[77] It is profoundly disturbing that President Obama in his Second Inaugural Address identified the allegiance to the "self-evident truths"[78] of the Declaration "that all men are created equal; that they are endowed by their Creator with certain unalienable Rights"[79] as what "makes us exceptional—what makes us American."[80] What a troubling historical ignorance, even exacerbated by the strange idea of emphasizing the allegiance to equality as exceptional—America is better than anyone else in believing in equality? Obama's ignorance—or, if we want to be more generous, his idealism—did not help: Black lives still do not matter; equality is only self-evident when white life is compared to white life. Black lives are still so irrelevant that they do not need to be excluded explicitly; no human is missing when black human beings are excluded. These lives are considered so deeply irrelevant that there is nothing missing if a black life is lost. This "is the most profound message of racial segregation," that "the absence of people of color from our lives is no real loss."[81] This is a most brutal form of Othering. "This is," remarked Teju Cole, "what it is to be a stranger: when you leave there is no void."[82] This message is what we still find everywhere in this country, in fact, in many places within the so-called Western world.[83] "White supremacy," wrote Damon Young, "is so gargantuan and mundane that sometimes its existence and its proficiency can't be measured, addressed, or even seen without a stark change in perspective. It isn't like gravity. It *is* gravity. It *is* a ceaseless pressure intended to keep blackness ground-bound and sick."[84]

There seems to be no part of life, from schools to elections,[85] that is not influenced by white supremacy. White supremacy was used to being in charge for so long that it became a quasi-natural phenomenon. Saying "Black Lives Matter" disrupts the pseudo-naturalness of white supremacy, "when you're accustomed to privilege, equality feels like oppression."[86] Brazilian philosopher Paulo Freire noticed:

> Conditioned by the experience of oppressing others, any situation other than their former seems to [the former oppressors] like oppression. . . . Any restriction on this way of life, in the name of the rights of the community, appears to the former oppressors as a profound violation of their individual rights.[87]

When you're accustomed to some people not being privileged, their desire to be equal feels like childish greed. In 1860, Mrs. Sarah Logue of Tennessee wrote to her fugitive slave, Rev. J. W. Loguen, complaining bitterly of what her slave did to her when he fled:

> I am a cripple, but I am still able to get about. . . . I write you these lines to let you know the situation we are in,—, partly in consequence of your running away and stealing Old Rock, our fine mare. Though we got the mare back, she never was worth as much after you took her;—and, as I now stand in need of

some funds, I have determined to sell you, and I have had an offer you, but did not see fit to take it. If you will send me one thousand dollars, and pay for the old mare, I will give up all claim I have to you. . . . I understand that you are a preacher. . . . I would like to know if you read your Bible. If so, can you tell what will become of the thief if he does not repent? . . . You know that we reared you as we reared our own children; that you was never abused, and that shortly before you ran away, when your master asked if you would like to be sold, you said you would not leave him to go with anybody.[88]

This appalling self-understanding seems to have survived until today. The call "Black Lives Matter" produces a problem for the white supremacist who understands white supremacy as the natural order of things, just as Rev. Loguen must have deeply confused Mrs. Logue when he answered her request, relentlessly pointing out her white supremacist incoherencies:

You say you have offers to buy me, and that you shall sell me if I do not send you $1000, and in the same breath and almost in the same sentence, you say, "You know we raised you as we did our own children." Woman, did you raise your *own children* for the market? Did you raise them for the whipping-post? . . . Where are my poor bleeding brothers and sisters? Can you tell? Who was it that sent them into the sugar and cotton fields, to be kicked and cuffed, and whipped, and to groan and die. . . . Wretched woman! Do you say *you* did not do it? Then I reply, your husband did, and *you* approved the deed—and the very letter you sent me shows that your heart approves it all. Shame on you![89]

If black lives also matter, how can the superiority of white lives still matter in the way that it is perceived as natural? This is what "All Lives Matter" aims at. It asks to not change things, to not take away from white lives what they need, since they *matter* . . .

ANTI-RACISM

Being silent about white supremacy means to be complicit with white supremacy, means to be a practical white supremacist regardless of what your moral theory might be. There is no comfortable middle way. The only way out of racism, as suggested for instance by Ibram X. Kendi[90] or by Eduardo Bonilla-Silva,[91] is anti-racism: active, practical anti-racism. This step from the careless or apathetic white non-racist to an active anti-racist has not been taken by the white United States, or, in fact, by many Western white people.

Just think back: slavery was certainly not abandoned because of a nation-wide moral revolution that acknowledged that black bodies were equal to white bodies. While Lincoln was certainly opposed to slavery, he "was a pragmatic white supremacist in his concept of domestic race relations but indulged a principled egalitarianism in his world outlook."[92] Slavery was *not* abandoned because it was finally and widely understood and acknowledged as moral failure.[93] There was no deep society-wide practical or philosophical revolution in the West[94] as a result of the Enlightenment, as foundational as it was for Europe and the United States. In fact, the Enlightenment thinkers, from Voltaire to Hume to Kant to Jefferson,[95] did not bring light to the prevailing racism. On the contrary, these thinkers helped to continue the anti-non-white, that is, racist, course of things. They helped to create the illusion of the West as the moral authority while consuming coffee and sugar harvested by slaves[96] and committing genocide of the Native People of North America and Africa at the same time. The Enlightenment thinkers speak, "with the attitude of addressing all human beings. However, this is not the case. Taking a look at the humans whom they do talk to, only so-called white humans can be found (and to make it worse, not even all of them, for they are certainly not talking to women, to homosexual persons, etc.). In other words: these philosophers are talking only to *actual* humans, to humans *that matter*, to humans of *value*"[97]—found only in white bodies. "By their failure," as Charles W. Mills emphasized, "to denounce the great crimes inseparable from the European conquest, or by the half-heartedness of their condemnation, or by their actual endorsement of it in some cases, most leading European ethical theorists reveal their complicity in the Racial Contract."[98] Thus, those that appear to be not racist are in fact deeply racist and only abandon racist practices when convenient, leaving racism intact and ready to reemerge in new iterations such as mass incarceration, disenfranchisement, and even the evaluations of educators of color.

DESUPERHUMANIZATION

Looking at white history is uncomfortable. Looking at *my* white past is uncomfortable. That is just the way it is. And it is the way it has to be. My white past is miserable. Should it be too much to ask of me and of my fellow white people to endure this simple matter of fact? For the sake of the world, I truly hope it is not.

We, the white lives, have to overcome our nonracism, our acceptance of injustice because we make ourselves believe that that is the way it is, we have to have a moral revolution—in the literal sense, we need to turn around—and become anti-racist, we need to desuperiorize ourselves. White lives need to learn that they are *part* of humanity and not its perfection.[99] If there is anything in the world that can be called *the* white task, it is to unlearn, to unwant the implicit or explicit superiority of whiteness.[100] This is, by the way, not primarily a matter of knowledge. Indeed, "it is not knowledge that is lacking. The educated general public has always largely known what outrages have been committed and are being committed in the name of Progress, Civilization, Socialism, Democracy, and the Market. [...] What is missing is the courage to understand what we know and to draw conclusions."[101] People of color who have been dehumanized by white lives have been able to rehumanize themselves, to adseredate (from Latin: *ad se redire*: to come back to oneself). The world is waiting on white lives to finally desuperiorize ourselves and overcome our adroitness in removing ourselves "as the complicitor in the problem [or racism] and at the same time plac[e] the responsibility for alleviating oppression with the oppressed."[102] White people need to rehumanize too, although not from having been dehumanized, but rather from the self-induced obsession of their superhumanization. White lives need to understand that they are human, just human, just plain boring humans. We white people tried to live in the sky, but we belong on earth; we are not superhumans. "White" "designates a political category, a sort of political fraternity"; however, "membership in it is not in the same sense 'fated' or 'natural.' It can be resisted."[103] The white dominion in the West is not because of our superhumanity, but because of our inhumanity. There is only one way out: white people need to *desuperhumanize*. We need to find our endless privileges and unwant them, deny them, reject them. We need to learn that we are not superhumans, not *the* authoritative form of humans, which we are simply not representative for the human being per se. And we white lives should be thankful that black lives will give us the chance to do so. We need to be thankful, deeply thankful. We should take to the deepest corner of our heart what Kimberly Latrice Jones put it in the most impressive and heartbreaking words:

> You broke the contract when you killed us in the streets and didn't give a f[uck]. You broke the contract when for 400 years, we played your game and built your wealth. You broke the contract when we built our wealth again on our own by our bootstraps in Tulsa and you dropped bombs on us, when we built it in Rosewood and you came in and you slaughtered us. You broke the contract. So f[uck] your Target. F[uck] your Hall of Fame. Far as I'm concerned, they could burn this bitch to the ground, and it still wouldn't be enough. And they are lucky that what black people are looking for is equality and not revenge.[104]

TEACHER EVALUATIONS

With this theoretical grounding from a philosophical perspective it is—sadly—therefore self-evident that the practical outcome would be negative evaluations of faculty of color, as the studies in this volume have shown in various ways.[105] Teacher evaluations are another iteration in which white supremacy can come to the surface. Therefore, to maintain and improve this important, democratic instrument of teacher evaluations—"one of the few places within school settings where students can use their voices to articulate their experiences of a course and, hopefully, to offer constructive criticism to improve a course"[106]—we have to continue to critically analyze white supremacy to enable students' teacher evaluations to represent the practices of the educator and not the color of their skin.

NOTES

1. My heartfelt thanks go to the editor of this volume for all her encouragement, insights and patience, thank you LaVada! This paper is dedicated to YF.
2. See Anderson 2016, Eddo-Lodge 2017, Di Angelo 2018 and Lopez Bunyasi & Watts Smith 2019, 7–46.
3. Run The Jewels 2020a.
4. See Bonilla-Silva 2014, di Angelo 2018.
5. "Nonwhites have always [. . .] been bemused or astonished by the invisibility of the Racial Contract to whites" (Mills 1997, 110), see also DiAngelo 2018, X, 8, 25; Dyer 2005, 11; Dalton 2005, 17; Morrison 1993, 9; McIntosh 2005, 109–110; Wildman & Davis 1995; Wellman 1977, 42.
6. Leonardo 2009, 107–125.
7. Lopez Bunyasi & Watts Smith 2019, 15.
8. Jensen 2015, 115.
9. DiAngelo 2018, 25.
10. DiAngelo 2018, 62.
11. 2Pac 2001.
12. Taylor, Implications of Race and Racism in Student Evaluations of Teaching: The Hate U Give, [5].
13. Public Enemy 1990.
14. Public Enemy 1990.
15. Young 2019, 235.
16. Equiano 1789, 51.
17. See Luther King Jr. 1963.
18. See Park 2013.
19. See Ferguson 1997, Jordan 1974, 189.
20. See the documents collected in Singh Sethi 2018.
21. White House 2020, s.p.
22. Hill et al. 2020.
23. White House 2020, s.p.
24. White House 2020, s.p.
25. Singer 2017, 286.
26. White House 2020, s.p.

27. White House 2020, s.p.
28. White House 2020, s.p.
29. White House 2020, s.p.
30. See Morgan 2000.
31. See Finkelman 2001 and Stanton 2012.
32. Jordan 1974, 193.
33. See Finkelman 2001, 163.
34. Run The Jewels 2020b.
35. White House s.a.
36. Jay-Z 2017.
37. Mos Def 1999.
38. See Mills 1997, 97; Mills 2007; Lopez Bunyasi & Watts Smith 2019, 74–75.
39. Mills 1997, 18, see also Tatum 1999, 24.
40. Alcoff 2000, 264.
41. See Bonilla-Silva 2014.
42. Watts Smith & Mayorga-Gallo 2018, 891.
43. Wellman 1977, 39, see also West 1993.
44. hooks 1992, 167.
45. See Lebakeng, Phalane & Nase 2006.
46. Wideman 2020, s.p.
47. Luther King Jr. 1961, 153.
48. Bump 2019, s.p.
49. Singh-Seti 2018, 3.
50. Kendi 2019, 9.
51. Trump 2020, s.p.
52. Trump 2020, s.p.
53. Trump 2020, s.p.
54. Trump 2020, s.p.
55. Woodson 1933, 65.
56. Fields & Fields 2014, 97, see Kendi 2019, 8.
57. Fields & Fields 2014, 96–97.
58. Ryan 1971, 29, see also Butler 1993.
59. Coates 2015, 7.
60. Wittig 1992, 220.
61. Coates 2015, 7, see also DiAngelo 2018, 16; Hund 1999, 10.
62. Peele 2017a; see also Peele 2019, 85. On Twitter Peele explained: "The Sunken Place means we're marginalized. No matter how hard we scream, the system silences us" (Peele 2017) and in his annotations to the movie's screenplay he writes: "The Sunken Place is not a magic spell. It's a manipulation of someone's own psyche" (Peele 2019, 172).
63. Woodson 1933, ix.
64. Quoted from Patel 2018, 181.
65. The parallels between Hitler and Trump are not only superficial. Just read this summary of Hitler's educational approach by Kiran Klaus Patel in which I have simply omitted the immediate references to Nazi-Germany: "Contempt for

intellectualism went hand in hand with a fascination with physical prowess; formal education, in contrast, was associated obsolete bourgeois culture. . . . Instead, . . . praised [was] bold leadership and unconditional obedience, even if these concepts tended to contradict each other. Other ideological tensions remained unresolved, too" (Patel 2018, 182).

66. See Wachsmann & Caplan 2010, 10.
67. Wellman 1977, 35.
68. See DiAngelo 2018.
69. Wildman & Davis 2005, 101.
70. Jensen 2005, 115.
71. See Wellman, 1977, 8; Bonilla-Silva 2014, 111–114.
72. See Mills 1997, 3.
73. Cooper 1783, 14.
74. Furstenberg 2011, 264.
75. Finkelman 2001, 120.
76. See Freehling 1994, 33 and Greene 1988.
77. Malcolm X 1964, 388.
78. Obama 2013, 202, see Rakove 2009, 77.
79. Obama 2013, 202, see Rakove 2009, 77.
80. Obama 2013, 202.
81. DiAngelo 2018, 68.
82. Cole 2014, 120.
83. See Lopez Bunyasi & Watts Smith 2019.
84. Young 2019, 81, see also DiAngelo 128.
85. See from the vast literature on this for instance Kendi 2016 and Kendi 2019.
86. Lopez Bunyasi & Watts Smith 2019, 149.
87. Freire 1970, 31sq.
88. Aptheker 1990, 449–450, see for many modern-day examples Bonilla-Silva 2014, 101–121.
89. Aptheker 1990, 450.
90. See Kendi 2019.
91. See Bonilla-Silva 2014.
92. Fredrickson 1975, 52.
93. Freter 2020, 113.
94. Mills 1997, see also Freter 2020, 114.
95. See for instance Eze 1997, Bernasconi, Park 2013 and Stanton 2012.
96. Dhawan 2016, 78.
97. Freter 2018, 242, see also Mills 1997, 27.
98. Mills 1997, 94.
99. See Fryre 1983, 117.
100. See Freter, Journey to Critical Whiteness in Higher Education, [15].
101. Lindqvist 1992, 171–172.
102. Wellman 1977, 42.
103. Fryre 1983, 126.
104. Jones 2020a, s.p., see also Jones 2020b.

105. See also the important—up to now unpublished—study Loonat 2020.
106. Kelly, Branch, Coleman, Be (Rate) My Professors Dot Com, [25].

REFERENCES

2Pac. 2001. "Letter 2 My Unborn." Track 6 on *Until the End of Time*. Amaru, Death Row, Interscope, compact disc.

Alcoff, Linda Martín. 2000. "What Should White People Do?" in *Decentering the Center. Philosophy for a Multicultural, Postcolonial, and Feminist World*, edited by Uma Narayan, Sandra Harding, 262–282. Bloomington, Indianapolis: Indiana University Press.

Anderson, Carol. 2016. *White Rage. The Unspoken Truth of Our Racial Divide*. New York, London, Oxford, New Delhi, Sydney: Bloomsbury.

Aptheker, Herbert. 1990. *A Documentary of The Negro People in the United States. I. From Colonial Times Through the Civil War*. New York: Carol Publishing Group.

Bernasconi, Robert. 2002. "Kant as an Unfamiliar Source of Racism." In *Philosophers on Race. Critical Essays*, edited by J. K. Ward, T. L Lott, 145–166. Oxford: Blackwell

Bonilla-Silva, Eduardo. 2014. *Racism without Racist. Color-Blind Racism and the Persistence of Racial Inequality in America*, fourth edition. Lanham et al.: Rowman & Littlefield Publishers.

Bump, Philip. 2019. "As Trump tells reporters how not-racist he is, a poll comes out showing that most Americans disagree" *Washington Post*, July 30, 2019. https://www.washingtonpost.com/politics/2019/07/30/trump-tells-reporters-how-not-racist-he-is-poll-comes-out-showing-that-most-americans-disagree/.

Butler, Judith. 1993. "Endangered/Endangering: Schematic Racism and White Paranoia." In *Reading Rodney King—Reading Urban Uprising*, edited by Robert Gooding-Williams, 15–22. London, New York: Routledge.

Caplan, Jane and Nikolaus Wachsmann. 2017. "Introduction." In *Concentration Camps in Nazi Germany. The New Histories*, edited by Jane Caplan and Nikolaus Wachsmann, 1–17. London, New York: Routledge.

Coates, Ta-Nehisi. 2015. *Between the World and Me*. New York: Spiegel & Grau.

Cole, Teju. 2015. Everyday if for the Thief. London: Faber & Faber.

Cooper, David. 1783. *A Serious Address to the Rulers of America, On the Inconsistency of Their Conduct Respecting Slavery: Forming a Contrast Between the Encroachments of England on American Liberty, and American Injustice in tolerating Slavery*. London: Trenton.

Dalton, Harlon. 2005. "Failing to See." In *White Privilege. Essential Readings on the other Side of Racism*, edited by Paula S. Rothenberg, second edition, 15–18. New York: Worth Publishers.

Dhawan, Nikita. 2016. "Doch wieder! Die Selbst-Barbarisierung Europas." In *Die Dämonisierung der Anderen. Rassismuskritik der Gegenwart*, edited by María do Mar Castro Varela, Paul Mecheril, 73–83. Bielefeld: transcript.

DiAngelo, Robin. 2018. *White Fragility. Why It's So Hard for White People to Talk About Racism*. S.l.: Allen Lane.

Dyer, Richard. 2005. "The Matter of Whiteness," In *White Privilege. Essential Readings on the other Side of Racism*, edited by Paula S. Rothenberg, second edition, 9–13. New York: Worth Publishers.

Eddo-Lodge, Reni. 2017. *Why I'm No Longer Talking to White People About Race*. London: Bloomsburg Publishing.

Equiano, Olaudah. 2002 [1789]. "The Interesting Narrative of the Life of Oladauh Equiano, or Gustavus Vassa, the African." In *The Classic Slave Narratives*, edited by Henry Louis Gates Jr., 15–247. London: Signet Classic.

Eze, Emmanuel C. 1997. "The Color of Reason: The Idea of 'Race' in Kant's Anthropology." In *Postcolonial African Philosophy. A Critical Reader*, edited by Emmanuel C. Eze, 103–140. Cambridge: Blackwell.

Fields, Karen E. and Barbara J. Fields. 2014. *Racecraft. The Soul of Inequality in American Life*. London: Verso.

Finkelman, Paul. 2001. *Slavery and the Founders. Race and Liberty in the Age of Jefferson*, second edition. New York: M. E. Sharpe.

Fredrickson, George M. 1975. "A Man but Not a Brother: Abraham Lincoln and Racial Equality." *The Journal of Southern History* 41: 39–58.

Freehling, William W. 1994. "The Founding Fathers, Conditional Antislavery, and the Nonradicalism of the American Revolution." In *The Reintegration of American History. Slavery and the Civil War*, 12–33. New York, Oxford: Oxford University Press.

Freire, Paulo. [1970], 2017. *Pedagogy of the Oppressed*. S.l. Penguin Random House.

Freter, Björn. 2018. "White Supremacy in Eurowestern Epistemologies. On the West's responsibility for its philosophical heritage." *Synthesis Philosophica. Journal of the Croatian Philosophical Society* 33: 237–249.

Freter, Björn. 2020. "Decolonization of the West, Desuperiorisation of Thought, and Elative Ethics." In *Handbook of African Philosophy of Difference: The Othering of the Other*, edited by Elvis Imafidon, 105–127. Cham: Springer.

Freter, Yvette. 2021. Journey to Critical Whiteness in Higher Education. In *Implications of Race and Racism in Student Evaluations of Teaching: The Hate u Give*, edited by LaVada Taylor, 113–138. Lanham, Maryland: Lexington Books.

Frye, Marilyn. 1983. "On Being White: Toward A Feminist Understanding Of Race And Race Supremacy." In *The Politics of Reality: Essays in Feminist Theory*, 110–127. Freedom: The Crossing Press.

Furstenberg, François. 2011. "Atlantic Slavery, Atlantic Freedom: George Washington, Slavery, and Transatlantic Abolitionist Networks." In *The William and Mary Quarterly* 68: 247–286.

Greene, Jack P. 1988. *Pursuits of Happiness. The Social Development of the Early Modern British Colonies and the Formation of American Culture*. Chapel Hill, London: University of North Carolina Press.

Hill, Evan, Ainara Tiefenthäler, Christiaan Triebert, Drew Jordan, Haley Willis and Robin Stein. 2020. "How George Floyd Was Killed in Police Custody." *New York Times*, May 31, 2020. Accessed October 12, 2020. https://www.nytimes.com/2020/05/31/us/george-floyd-investigation.html.
hooks, bell. 1992. *Black Looks. Race and Representation*. Boston: South End Press.
Hund, Wulf D. 1999. *Rassismus. Die soziale Konstruktion natürlicher Ungleichheit*. Westfälisches Dampfboot.
Jay-Z. 2017. "The Story of O. J." Track 2 on *4:44*. Roc Nation, compact disc.
Jensen, Robert. 2005. "White Privilege Shapes the U.S." In *White Privilege. Essential Readings on the Other Side of Racism*, edited by Paula S. Rothenberg, second edition, 115–118. New York: Worth Publishers.
Jones, Kimberly Latrice. 2020a. "Kimberly Latrice Jones BLM Video Speech Transcript." Accessed October 12, 2020. https://www.rev.com/blog/transcripts/kimberly-latrice-jones-blm-video-speech-transcript.
Jones, Kimberly Latrice. 2020b. "How Can We Win." YouTube Video, 6:46. June 1, 2020, https://www.youtube.com/watch?v=sb9_qGOa9Go.
Jordan, Winthrop D. 1974. *The White Man's Burden. Historical Origins of Racism in the United States*. London, Oxford, New York: Oxford University Press.
Kelly, Hilton, Eleanor Branch and Stacey Coleman. 2021. [(Be)Rate My Professors Dot Com: Cautionary Tales from the Curious World of Student Evaluations]. In *Implications of Race and Racism in Student Evaluations of Teaching: The Hate U Give*, edited by LaVada U.Taylor, 67–88. Lanham, Maryland: Lexington Books.
Kendi, Ibram X. 2016. *Stamped from the Beginning. The definitive History of racist Ideas in America*. London: Bodley Head.
Kendi, Ibram X. 2019. *How to be an Antiracist*. New York: One World.
Lebakeng, J. Teboho, M. Manthiba Phalanea and Dalindjebo Nase. 2006. "Epistemicide, institutional cultures and the imperative for the Africanisation of universities in South Africa." *Alternation* 13: 70–87.
Leonardo, Zeus. 2009. *Race, Whiteness, and Education*. New York, London: Routledge.
Lindqvist, Sven. [1992] 1996. *Exterminate All the Brutes*, translated by Joan Tate, New York: The New Press.
Loonat, Farhana. 2020. "Dissecting The "Diversity, Equity, and Inclusion" Illusion for Women Faculty of Color." Unpublished manuscript.
Lopez Bunyasi, Thehama and Candis Watts Smith. 2019. *Stay Woke. A People's Guide to Making All Black Lives Matter*. New York: New York University Press.
Luther King Jr, Martin. 1991 [1963]. "In a Word: Now." In *A Testament of Hope. The Essential Writings and Speeches*, edited by James M. Washington, 167–168. New York: HarperOne.
Luther King Jr, Martin. 1991 [1961]. "Equality Now: The President Has the Power." In *A Testament of Hope. The Essential Writings and Speeches*, edited by James M. Washington, 152–159. New York: HarperOne.
Malcolm X [Malcolm Little], 1988 [1964]. "Liberation by Any Means Necessary. Address to a Meeting in New York, 1964." In *Afro-American History. Primary Sources*, edited by Thomas R. Frazier, 383–396. Chicago: Dorsey Press.

McIntosh, Peggy. 2005. "White Privilege: Unpacking the Invisible Knapsack." In *White Privilege. Essential Readings on the other Side of Racism*, edited by Paula S. Rothenberg, second edition, 109–113. New York: Worth Publishers.

Mills, Charles M. 1997. *The Racial Contract*. Ithaca, London: Cornell University Press.

Mills, Charles M. 2007. "White Ignorance." In *Race and Epistemologies of Ignorance*, edited by Shannon Sullivan, Nancy Tuana, 13–38. New York: State University of New York Press.

Mos Def. "Mr. Nigga." Track 15 on Black on Both Sides. Rawkus, Priority, compact disc.

Morgan, Kenneth. 2000. "George Washington and the Problem of Slavery." *Journal of American Studies* 34: 279–301.

Morrison, Toni. 1993. *Playing in the Dark. Whiteness and the Literary Imagination*. New York: Vintage Books.

Obama, Barack. 2013 [2017]. "'We, the People . . .' Second Inaugural Address." In *We are the Change we seek. The Speeches of Barack Obama*, edited by Eugene J. Dionne Jr, Joy-Ann Reid, 201–208. London, Oxford, New York, New Delhi, Sydney: Bloomsbury.

Park, Peter K. J. 2013. *Africa, Asia, and History of Philosophy: Racism in the Formation of the Philosophical Canon, 1780-1830*. Albany: State University of New York Press.

Patel, Kiran Klaus. 2018. "Education, Schooling, and Camps." In *A Companion to Nazi Germany*, edited by Shelley Baranowski, Armin Nolzen, Claus-Christian W. Szejnmann, 181–197. Medford: Wiley Blackwell.

Peele, Jordan (director). 2017a. *Get Out*. Universal Pictures.

Peele, Jordan (@JordanPeele). 2017b. "The Sunken Place means we're marginalized. No matter how hard we scream, the system silences us." Twitter, March 17, 2017, 12;12 AM. https://twitter.com/JordanPeele/status/842589407521595393.

Peele, Jordan. 2019. *Get Out*. Los Angeles: Inventory Press.

Public Enemy. 1990. "Fight the Power." Track 20 on *Fear of a Black Planet*. Def Jam, Columbia, compact disc.

Rakove, Jack N. (ed.). 2009. *The Annotated U.S. Constitution and Declaration of Independence*, Cambridge, London: Belknap Press.

Run The Jewels. 2020a. "Walking in the Snow." Track 6 on *RTJ4*. Jewel Runners, BMG, compact disc.

Run The Jewels. 2020b. "Ju$t." Track 7 on *RTJ4*. Jewel Runners, BMG, compact disc.

Ryan, William. 1971. *Blaming the Victim*. New York: Pantheon Books.

Singh Sethi, Arjun (ed.). 2018. *American Hate. Survivors speak out*. New York, London: The New Press.

Singer, Thomas. 2017. "Trump and the American Collective Psyche." In *The Dangerous Case of Donald Trump. 27 Psychiatrists and Mental Health Experts assess a President*, edited by Bandy X. Lee, 281–297. New York: St. Martin's Press.

Stanton, Lucia C. 2012. *'Those Who Labor for My Happiness.' Slavery at Thomas Jefferson's Monticello*. Charlottesville, London: University of Virginia Press.

Tatum, Beverly Daniel. 1999. *'Why Are All the Black Kids Sitting Together in the Cafeteria?' And Other Conversations About Race*, revised with a new Introduction by the author. S.l;: Basic Books.
Taylor, LaVada. 2021. [Introduction, Their Voices Must Be Heard. The Influence of of Race and Racism in Student Evaluations: The Hate U Give]. In *Implications of Race and Racism in Student Evaluations of Teaching: The Hate u Give*, edited by LaVada U. Taylor, 1–16. Lanham, Maryland: Lexington Books.
Trump, Donald J. 2020. "Remarks by President Trump at the White House Conference on American History," White House. Accessed October 12, 2020. https://www.whitehouse.gov/briefings-statements/remarks-president-trump-white-house-conference-american-history/.
Wellman, David. 1977. *Portraits of White Racism*. London, New York, Melbourne: Cambridge University Press.
West, Cornel. 1993. "Learning to talk of Race." In *Reading Rodney King—Reading Urban Uprising*, edited by Robert Gooding-Williams, 254–260. London, New York: Routledge.
White House. S.a. "Slavery in the President's Neighborhood FAQ." White House. Accessed October 12, 2020. https://www.whitehousehistory.org/slavery-in-the-presidents-neighborhood-faq.
White House. 2020. "President Donald J. Trump Is Combating Violence and Protecting America's Monuments, Memorials, and Statues." White House June 26, 2020. Accessed October 12, 2020. https://www.whitehouse.gov/briefings-statements/president-donald-j-trump-combating-violence-protecting-americas-monuments-memorials-statues/.
Wideman, Latitra. 2020. "Jacob Blake Family Press Conference Transcript August 25." Accessed October 12, 2020. https://www.rev.com/blog/transcripts/jacob-blake-family-press-conference-transcript-august-25.
Wildman, Stephanie M. and Adrienne D. Davis. 2005. "Making Systems of Privilege visible." In *White Privilege. Essential Readings on the other Side of Racism*, edited by Paula S. Rothenberg, second edition, 95–101. New York: Worth Publishers.
Wittig, Monique. 1997 [1992]. "One is not Born a Woman." In *Feminisms*, edited by Sandra Kemp, Judith Squires. Oxford, New York: Oxford University Press.
Woodson, Carter G. 2005 [1933]. *The Mis-Education of the Negro*. Mineola: Dover Publications.
Young, Damon. 2019. *What Doesn't Kill You Makes you Blacker*. S.l.: ecco.

Index

Note: Page numbers followed by "n" refer to notes.

ability, 47–48
academia: Black scholars in United States, 44–45; history of Black faculty, 44–46
academy structures student evaluations, 68
achievement gaps, in United States, 122
African Americans: faculty, 44, 45; gay professor, 83; scholars, 76; woman, 82, 84n1
African elephants, 115–16
"All Lives Matter," 159, 168
American exceptionalism, 128
American Sociological Association, 27
Anderson, Claud, 19
anti-*apartheid* Progressive Party, 121
anti-black epistemicide, 9
anti-black-homicides, 162
anti-Negro 'thought,' 161
anti-racism, 113, 114, 127, 165–66, 168–69; team, 71
anti-racist critical pedagogy, 141
anti-racist teaching, 100; opportunities for, 92, 96; pedagogical challenges to, 97; risks for, 92; teacher education in, 99

Aruguete, Mara S., 43–44
Aubrey, Ahmad, 2
autoethnographic accounts: interpretations of, 75–83; students have power, 81–83; students not disinterested observers, 78–81; students' reading of teacher's body, 75–78

Baiocco, Sharon A., 80; *Successful College Teaching*, 80
Banks, James, 19
Barr, William, 1
Bavishi, Anish: *The Effect of Professor Ethnicity and Gender on Student Evaluations: Judged before Met*, 5, 29
Baxter-Magolda, Marcia, 30, 31
Behari-Leak, Kasturi, 54
Beyond the Glass Façade (Harvey), 118
Bhabha, Homi, 54
Black faculty, 43, 139; academia for, 51; in academia, history of, 44–46; anecdotal evidence of, 141; enter white universities, 52; ideological assumption, 56; of promotion and tenure criteria, 55; in research,

179

teaching, service, and unofficial diversity, 53; structural bias inherent, 140
Black, Indigenous and People of Color (BIPOC), 2, 22, 31, 32, 89, 90, 113; anti-racist teaching opportunities and risks for, 92; and dominant epistemologies, 100–102; experience of, 115; in HWUs, 94, 96; killability of, 100; marginalization of, 105; opportunity for, 100; perspectives of, 27; protest movements in favor of, 128; risk of teaching to, 98; social justice, 91; student course evaluations of, 18; in TEPs, 104; in United States, 20; violence against, 99; violence holds implications for, 96; and whites in higher education, 114; and women's service component, 148
"Black Lives Matter," 159–61, 167, 168
Black racial identity, 8
Black subject(ivity): historical events, 116–17; implications, 119–20; political relationships, 118–19; social responsibilities, 117–18
Black teacher, 51, 77; educator, 44; in higher education, life of, 119; identities in colonizing spaces, construction of, 47–48; intelligence, ability, and eugenics, 47–48
Blake, Jacob, 162
#BLM, 113
Bohmer, Susanne, 82
Bonilla-Silva, Eduardo, 168
Braithwaite, E. R., *To Sir, with Love*, 75–76, 78, 85n2
Branch, Eleanor, 8, 71–73, 76–78, 80, 82
Briggs, Joyce L., 82
Brown v. *Board Decision*, 144, 149
Brown v. *Board of Education*, 48
Bryant, William, 53
"bubble," 92

Canada, teaching portfolio documented in, 150
Canton, David, 45
capitalism, 93, 143
Casad, Bettina, 53
Chauvin, Derek, 161
Chronicle of Higher Education (Yancy), 142
coercive power, 81
cognitive dissonance, 127–29
Cole, Teju, 167
Coleman, Stacey, 8, 73–75, 78–80, 82
"combat violence," 161
"common good," 89, 91–93, 96, 99, 104
"commonsense" idea, 97
"commonsense teaching," 93
composite stories, 23
comprehensive teaching portfolios, 140
conscious-raising, 123; journeys of, 125–27
"constructive criticism," 96
constructive thinking, 123
conventional wisdom, 141, 148
"cookbook" class, 97
Cooper, Anna Julia, 45, 46, 51, 58n9
Cooper, David, 166
counter-storytelling, 22–23; "Until the Lion Tells the Story," 23–24
Covid-19, 152
"crazy stuff," 93, 94, 97
critical consciousness, 113, 123
critical discourse analysis, research in, 56
critical multiculturalism, 124
critical race theory (CRT), 8, 18, 113, 144; centrality of race, 21; challenge to dominant ideology, 22; commitment to social justice, 21; components of, 21–22; experiential knowledge, 21–22; principle of Whiteness, 98; transdisciplinary perspective, 22
"critical thinking," 101

dangerous teaching, 97–98
Daut, Marlene, 146, 147, 151
Davis, William Boyd Allison, 45, 46
Declaration of Independence, 125, 126, 128, 166, 167
decolonial knowledge, 93
decolonial thinking, 100
Deep South: A Social Anthropological Study of Caste and Class, 45
de jure segregation, 1, 2
Denzin, Norman K., 68
Department Personnel Committee (DPC), 152
de-segregation, of schools, 50
desuperhumanization, 169–70
DeWaters, Jamie N., 80; *Successful College Teaching*, 80
DiAngelo, Robin, 160
dissemble, 69, 70, 77, 84n1
diversity, 2–5; and inclusion, 90, 92, 97, 104, 105
"double stigma"/"double jeopardy," 146
DuBois, W. E. B., 45
Dyke, Eva Beatrice, 45, 58n9

The Effect of Professor Ethnicity and Gender on Student Evaluations: Judged before Met (Bavishi), 5, 29
elephant considerations, 115–16
Elephant: The Animal and Its Ivory in African Culture (Ross), 115–16
English language, 56
epistemic disobedience, 99, 101; of Whiteness, 104
equality: equity and, 147; social justice and, 142
Equiano, Olaudah, 160
eugenics, 1, 2, 47–48
Euro-centered epistemologies, 89, 90, 93, 95, 97, 103–5
European American teachers, 5
European colonization, 19
European Enlightenment, 166, 169
European Imperialism, 19–20
experiential knowledge, 21–22

expert power, 81
explicit bias, 78–81; racial, 139

faculty of color: attribute to students, 29; course evaluations, 18; presence in college and university spaces, 32
Fanon, Frantz, 20, 47
feminist movement, development of, 74
Festinger, Leon, 127
Fields, Barbara J., 164
Fields, Karen E., 164
"Fight the Power," 160
Finkelman, Paul, 166
Floyd, George, 2, 113, 127, 161
forced racial segregation, 121
formal power, 82
Founding Fathers, 161
Franklin, Benjamin, 161
Freire, Paulo, 18, 27, 155, 167
French, Jr., John R. P., 81
Freshman Composition course, 71
Freter, Björn, 9, 125
Freter, Yvette, 8–9

gender: ethnicity and, 144, 146; and students' evaluation of teaching, 10n24; unconscious gender discourses, 79; working relationship of governance, 130
glass ceiling, 118
Goffman, Erving, 50
Goodall, Jr., Harold Lloyd, 122
"good teacher," 51–52
Grant, Ulysses S., 161
Great Chain of Being, 20
Green, Lydia, 24–29

Hall, Stuart, 19, 21
Harris, Kamala, 118
Harvey, Denise, 113–17, 120, 124, 125, 127, 129, 130; *Beyond the Glass Façade*, 118; political relationships, 118–19; social responsibilities, 117–18
Harvey, Edwina, 114, 116, 117

Harvey, Robert, 116
The Hate U Give, 1
Hine, Darlene Clark, 84–85n1
Hines, Dorothy E., 147
Hitler, Adolf, 165, 172n65
hooks, bell, 54
Hornstein, Henry, 139
Hughes, Langston, 147

ignorance, epistemology of, 162–63
implicit bias, 78–81; racial, 139
implicit social cognition. *See* implicit bias
"individual thoughts," 95
inequity: in education, 123; in United States, 113
informal power, 82
institutional dependence, 139
instructors, professional development for, 52
insurgent pedagogy, 93–94
insurgent teaching, 99
intellectual inferiority, 43
intelligence, 47–48
interpretive autoethnography, 68
Ivy League Institution, 46

Jackson, Andrew, 161
Jacob, Skylar, 24–25, 27, 28, 30, 31
Jeffersonian meritocracy, 124, 128
Jefferson Moment, 126–27
Jefferson, Thomas, 125, 126, 161; "We, the people," 166–68
Jim Crow, 45, 48, 76, 147; racism, 150
Jones, Kimberly Latrice, 170
Journal of Blacks in Higher Education, 44

Kelly, Hilton, 8, 69–71, 77, 78, 81, 82
Kendi, Ibram X., 163, 168
King, Jr., Martin Luther, 163
K-12 school system, 92, 102, 146, 149

Ladson-Billings, Gloria, 113
language, 56
Larkin, Amy L., 152

left-essentialist multiculturalism, 124
legitimate power, 81
liberal multiculturalists, 123–24
Lightfoot, Jonathan, 9
Lincoln, Abraham, 169
Littleford, Linh N.: "Perceptions of European American and African American Instructors Teaching Race Focused Courses," 4
Logue, Sarah, 167, 168
Loguen, J. W., 167, 168

Madyun, Na'im, 31
Malcolm X, 166
Marable, Manning, 19
marginalized faculty, 140, 150–52, 154, 155
Martinez-Saenz, Miguel, 80
Mid-Western University, Strategic Resource Allocation, 17
Mills, Charles W., 169
"mis-education of the Negro," 48
The Miseducation of the Negro (Woodson), 21
Mohr, Eric S., 3
Mohr, Kathleen A. J., 3
Moodley, Strinivasa (Strini), 118
Morrison, Toni, 79, 114
Mossell Alexander, Sadie Tanner, 45, 58n9
multicultural education classes, 127
multiculturalism, 2–5, 123; critical, 124; definition of, 124–25; left-essentialist, 124
multiplier effect, 48–49; school identity, 49–51; stigmatized identities, stereotype threat, and oppositional gaze, 51–55
Mwaikindaekella, Joshua S. R., 43–44
Mwaria, C., 150, 151

Nast, Heidi J., 80
A Nation at Risk, 149
neutral teaching, 93
Ng, Roxana, 82

Nieto, Sonia, 124
non-Western epistemologies, 99

Obama, Barack, 113, 166, 167
occupational stereotyping, 145
Omi, Michael, 19
oppositional gaze, multiplier effect, 51–55
Othering, 97, 104, 105, 167
other people's stories, 23

Patel, Kiran Klaus, 172n65
Peele, Jordan, 164
peer observations, 140, 152–53
"Perceptions of European American and African American Instructors Teaching Race Focused Courses" (Littleford), 4
pernicious stereotypes, 145
Perry, Armon, 5
"personal offense," 95
personal stories, 23
personnel committees, 150, 153
Plessy v. *Ferguson*, 45, 48, 149
pluralistic multiculturalists, 124
political relationships: Black subject(ivity), 118–19; White subject(ivity), 122–23
positionality, 123
positive criticism, 94
predominantly white institutions (PWIs), 8, 54, 143
prison industrial complex, 1, 2
problematizing learning, 102–3
"properly teaching," 94

quantitative course, 68

"race-instead-of-racism ideological maneuver," 164
race/racism, 1, 19–21, 75, 140, 141, 147, 164–66; in American society, 144; centrality of, 21–22; Jim Crow, 150; as negative and dominant academic discourse, 72; pseudo-natural factualness of, 164; research on, 3; sexuality and hostility, 69; as source effects, 28; in students' evaluative feedback, 7; toward Black scholars, burden of, 142; in United States, 48–49; White authors to talk about, 77; white supremacy and, 142
Racial Contract, 169
racial inequalities, 129
racialized oppression, 93
RateMyProfessors.com, 68–70, 82, 83; negative evaluation on, 72; public and anonymous review on, 73
Raven, Bertram, 81
referent power, 81
reward power, 81
risky teaching, 96–97
Roseboro, Donyell L., 8
Ross, Doran, *Elephant: The Animal and Its Ivory in African Culture*, 115–16
le Roux, Nataliele, 54
Ryan, William, 164
Ryerson Faculty Association, 148

Sanchez, Angelina, 26–27, 29–32
Schmid, Jeanette, 69
school identity, 49–51
school reform era, 149
Schoonover, Steven, 80
Seldin, P., 151
self-authorship, 30–31
Self-Evaluation of Learning Letter, 154, 155
SETs. *See* student evaluations of teachings (SETs)
sexism, 1, 151
sexuality, 69–70
Shakur, Tupac A., 9
Sharpley-Whiting, Tracy, 147
Simpson, Georgiana, 45, 58n9
Slater, J., 43–44
slavery, 76, 168–69
small student focus groups, 140, 153, 154
Social and Cultural Foundations of Education, 141–44
social class exploitation, 1, 2

social justice, 90, 91, 102, 119, 122, 124, 141; commitment to, 21; and equality, 142; issues in political contexts, 143
social power, 81
social responsibilities: Black subject(ivity), 117–18; White subject(ivity), 122
social role theory, 145–46
Solórzano, Daniel G., 19, 21, 22
"source effects," 5
South Africa: *apartheid*, 114; race-bound barriers in, 121; racial groups, 132n61
South African Defense Force, 121
SRA. *See* Strategic Resource Allocation (SRA)
stereotype threat, multiplier effect, 51–55
stigmatized identities, multiplier effect, 51–55
storytelling, 22–23
Strategic Resource Allocation (SRA), 17, 32; support of SETs, 23
student course evaluations, validity and integrity of, 43
student-desired knowledge, 98
student evaluations of teachings (SETs), 2, 17, 89, 90; advocating for, 32; faculty of color on, 9; gender and, 10n24; literature on, 3; as punishment, 95; in research findings, 6–7; rethinking, 104–5; sole reliance on, 140; SRA support of, 23; statement of problem, 3–9; validity of, 139; violence of, 91, 95–96, 104
students: have power, 81–83; not disinterested observers, 78–81; reading of teacher's body, 75–78
Successful College Teaching (Baiocco and DeWaters), 80
Sullivan, Amy, 24, 28
Swazi leadership metaphor, 130
Syphilis, Tuskegee, 47

systemic racism, 4, 11n39, 99, 113, 122, 127; eradication of, 44; permeance of, 93; in teacher education, 100

Talk, Titian, 11n39
Taylor, Breonna, 2
Taylor, LaVada U., 8
teacher education, quantifying learning in, 96
teacher education programs (TEPs), 8, 122; BIPOC faculty in, 104; "commonsense" idea, 97; non-Western epistemologies in, 99
teacher evaluations, 170–71
teacher's body, students' reading of, 75–78
teacher-student relationships, 144
teaching: benefits of, 70; dangerous, 97–98; definition of, 52; insurgent, 99; opportunities and risks, 100; risk in, 96–97; in social sciences, 68; of superiorism and foster critical engagement, 125
teaching portfolio, 150–52, 154
teaching preparation programs, 151
tenure-track candidates, 149, 153
TEPs. *See* teacher education programs (TEPs)
testimonio, 89, 91, 96
theory of cognitive dissonance, 127
Thug Life Volume 1, 1
Tillman, Derrick, 11n39
Tillman, Linda C., 140
Titone, Connie, 129
To Sir, with Love (Braithwaite), 75–76, 78, 85n2
traditional curriculum and instruction (C&I), 143
Trump, Donald J., 128, 129, 161, 163–65, 172n65
2Pac, 1–3, 160

"unbiased approach," 93
United States, 146; achievement gaps in, 122; BIPOC in, 20; Black

lives in, 160; Black people in, 45; Black scholars academia in, 44–45; colonial occupation of, 48; destruction of, 161; development of feminist movement in, 74; impact on teaching, research, and policy in, 48; inequity in, 113; operation of, 165; race relations and racism in, 48–49; teaching portfolio documented in, 150; white supremacist in, 165
"Until the Lion Tells the Story," 23–24
urban teaching, 92
U.S. educational system, 50
Uttl, Bob, 147, 148

Vasquez, Ramon, 8, 89
violence: against BIPOC faculty, 99; combat, 161; holds implications BIPOC, 96; of SETs, 91, 95–96, 104
Visual, Aural, Reading/Writing, and Kinesthetic (VARK) learning modalities, 25

Warren, Earl, 48
Washington, George, 161
well-balanced teaching portfolio, 140
Wellman, David T., 162, 165
Wesley, Charles H., 45
Western epistemologies, 90, 99, 101
What Doesn't Kill You Makes You Blacker (Young), 118–19
white anti-racist allies, 129–30
White counter-resistance, 98–99
white faculty, 52, 71
White knowledge, 90, 93, 98, 105
"White Lives Matter," 160

Whiteness, 93, 100, 101, 160, 170; and coloniality, 122; course evaluations as reproductions of, 55–57; critical race theory principle of, 98; dimension of, 98; epistemic disobedience of, 104; hegemony of, 95; as property, 90, 98, 99; recentering of, 93–94
White racism, 101, 105
White subject(ivity): cognitive dissonance, 127–29; historical events, 120–22; implications, 123–25; journeys of conscious-raising, 125–27; political relationships, 122–23; social responsibilities, 122; white anti-racist allies, 129–30
white supremacy, 89, 91, 103, 105, 113, 160, 167; perpetration of, 105; and racism, 142
White university (HWU), 92; BIPOC faculty in, 94, 96
Wideman, Latitra, 162, 163
Winant, Howard, 19
Wittig, Monique, 164
Woodson, Carter G., 20, 45, 48, 164; *The Miseducation of the Negro*, 21

Xers, 3

Yancy, George, *Chronicle of Higher Education*, 142
Yosso, Tara J., 19, 21, 22
Young, Damon, 167; *What Doesn't Kill You Makes You Blacker*, 118–19
Young, Jerimiah L., 147

About the Editor and Contributors

EDITOR

LaVada U. Taylor is an associate professor of Education in the School of Education and Counseling at Purdue University Northwest. She received her BA in Political Science/Public Administration from Fisk University, MEd in Education Administration Supervision of Instruction from Tennessee State University and PhD in Curriculum and Instruction with concentrated emphasis in Curriculum Theory from Louisiana State University. An urban educator with nearly thirty years of classroom experience at the secondary and post secondary level, Taylor's research and teaching interest includes critical race theory, black studies, post-structuralism, post-colonialism, urban education, critical race feminism, abolitionist teaching, critical multiculturalism, culturally sustaining pedagogy, assessment, and oral history as pedagogy.

CONTRIBUTORS

Eleanor Branch is associate professor and chair of the English/Foreign Language Department at Livingstone College. She has a PhD in English from the University of California at Berkeley. Her research focus, while originally African American Literature, has grown to include anti-racist pedagogy and practice. A contentious tenure battle and subsequent lawsuit has given Branch a deeper perspective on the evaluation process for faculty of color at predominantly white institutions. She continues to advocate for a multi-layered evaluative process in both tenure and promotion given the problematics of student evaluations.

Stacey Coleman, chairs the Criminal Justice & Sociology Department and is assistant professor of Sociology at Livingstone College in North Carolina. Her research focuses on Marriage & Family, Race, and the Intersectional Approach. In her spare time, she enjoys reading, cycling, and hiking.

Björn Freter received his doctorate with his thesis "On Facticity and Existentiality" in 2014 from Free University, Berlin, Germany. He is now working as an independent scholar based in Knoxville, Tennessee. His research fields include political philosophy, African philosophy, post-colonial philosophy, animal ethics, phenomenology of normativity and literary studies.

Yvette Prinsloo Freter was raised and educated in Cape Town, South Africa. She is a white woman, descended from Dutch and British colonists. She matriculated from Wynberg Girls High School and proceeded to get her teaching qualification from Cape Town Teachers' Training College. After extensive traveling, she went to Maryville College, Tennessee, and graduated with a Bachelor of Arts in Elementary Education. Yvette has received her master's degree in Cultural Studies in Education and her doctorate in Learning Environments and Educational Studies from the University of Tennessee, Knoxville. She teaches philosophy of education and history of education courses at the University of Tennessee and Tennessee Technological University and is a full-time high school teacher while pursuing her work as an independent researcher. Her research focus is positionality, social justice, care theory, and postcolonial issues in relation to equitable educational outcomes for all students.

Hilton Kelly is professor and chair of Educational Studies at Davidson College. His research and teaching interests include the Age of Jim Crow, education in African American history and culture, the lives, work and careers of black educators, critical race theory, and social memory studies. He is the author of *Race, Remembering, and Jim Crow's Teachers* in the Routledge Studies in African-American History and Culture Series. His articles have appeared in *Urban Education*, *Educational Studies*, *The Urban Review*, *The Journal of Negro Education* and *The American Sociologist*.

Jonathan Lightfoot is an associate professor in the Teaching, Learning & Technology Department and Inaugural Director of the Center for "Race," Culture and Social Justice at Hofstra University. He received his PhD in Policy Studies from the University of Illinois at Chicago, Master's degree with a concentration in School Law and Segregation from Harvard University's Graduate School of Education and Bachelor's degree in Economics from Cornell University. Dr. Lightfoot represented Hofstra's School of Education on the University Senate as chair of the Graduate Academic Affairs Committee. He also served the faculty union as part of the AAUP Collective Bargaining Team that successfully negotiated a multi-million dollar five-year contract with senior administration. He enjoys advising various student groups, conducting professional development workshops for school districts, and delivering keynote addresses and panel presentations on critical "race" matters, identity construction and social justice issues.

H. Richard Milner, IV is a Cornelius Vanderbilt distinguished professor of Education in the Department of Teaching and Learning at Vanderbilt Peabody College of Education and Human Development. He has secondary appointments in Peabody's Department of Leadership, Policy and Organizations and the Department of Sociology in Vanderbilt's College of Arts and Science. Milner is a researcher, scholar and leader of urban education and teacher education. Centering on equity and diversity, he has spent hundreds of hours observing teachers' practices and interviewing educators and students in urban schools about micro-level policies that shape students' opportunities to learn. He examines the social context of classrooms and schools and and schools and looks at ways in teacher talk (particularly about race) influences student learning, identity, and development.

Donyell L. Roseboro is a professor at the University of North Carolina Wilmington, the daughter of working-class Black parents. She received her BA in Secondary Education from the University of North Carolina Chapel Hill, MA in History from Wake Forest University and PhD in Curriculum & Teaching/Cultural Studies from the University of North Carolina Greensboro. She has over thirty publications, including a guest-edited issue (with Sabrina Ross) of *Vitaé Scholasticae: The Journal of Educational Biography* on the pedagogies of Black educators, a book *entitled Jacques Lacan and Education: A Critical Introduction* and an edited volume with the late Dennis Carlson, *The Sexuality Curriculum and Youth Culture.* In 2016–2017 she was the Lead Principal Investigator on a Fulbright-Hays Group Study Abroad grant for just under $90,000 to take twelve teachers on a month-long study abroad experience to South Africa and just recently she was the co-PI on a $208,000 Fulbright grant that brought twenty-two international teachers to study the educational system in the United States for six weeks.

Ramon Vasquez is an assistant professor of Teacher Education at the State University of New York at New Paltz. His areas of specialization include Critical Race Theory, Decolonizing Pedagogies, Curriculum Studies, Indigenous Methodologies, and Abolitionist Education. Prior to working in higher education, he served as bilingual elementary teacher in Los Angeles. Dr. Vasquez received his PhD from the University of Wisconsin-Madison.

www.ingramcontent.com/pod-product-compliance
Lightning Source LLC
Chambersburg PA
CBHW020744020526
44115CB00030B/914